A SAILOR IN THE SAHARA

Hugh Clapperton, Commander RN

Portrait in oils by Gildon Manton, 1825
courtesy of Ministry of Defence Art Collection

A SAILOR IN THE SAHARA

The life and travels in Africa of
Hugh Clapperton, Commander RN

JAMIE BRUCE LOCKHART

I.B. TAURIS

LONDON · NEW YORK

Published in 2008 by I.B.Tauris & Co Ltd
6 Salem Road, London W2 4BU
175 Fifth Avenue, New York NY 10010
www.ibtauris.com

In the United States of America and Canada distributed by Palgrave Macmillan
a division of St. Martin's Press, 175 Fifth Avenue, New York NY 10010

ISBN: 978 1 84511 479 4

15568130)

A full CIP record for this book is available from the British Library
A full CIP record is available from the Library of Congress

Library of Congress Catalog Card Number: available

Printed and bound in Great Britain by TJ International Ltd, Padstow, Cornwall
From camera-ready copy edited and supplied by the author

The weariness, the fever and the fret

(John Keats, *Ode to a Nightingale*, 1820)

CONTENTS

ILLUSTRATIONS

MAPS

Travels in Africa in 1822–1827 by Hugh Clapperton

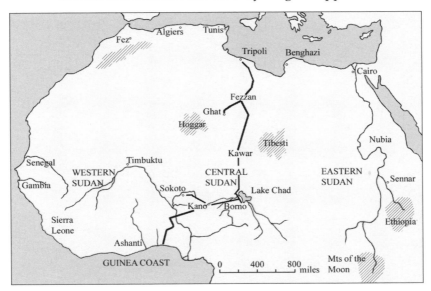

'who has measured every degree of latitude from the Mediterranean to the bight of Benin' [*Quarterly Review*, 1829, Vol. XXXIX, No. LXXVII, p. 177]

PREFACE

His career as an explorer began in 1821 when, as a thirty-three year-old half-pay naval lieutenant, Hugh Clapperton accepted a friend's invitation to accompany him on an official expedition across the Sahara in search of the termination of the River Niger. By the time of his death in the central Sudan some six years later he had become a seasoned and impassioned traveller, the first man to chart every degree of latitude of northern Africa from the Mediterranean Sea to the Bight of Benin. His was the first western account of states and civilizations (then unknown, since eclipsed) in a hinterland previously unpenetrated by Europeans, and his trail-blazing achievements were as remarkable in their time as is space travel today. For a while his name and exploits reverberated throughout Britain, celebrated alike by the general public and the geographers and natural scientists of the Enlightenment, but, outside academic circles, he is little known today and a biographical memoir is long overdue.

I first crossed Hugh Clapperton's path in Lagos in 1987, and in a series of sorties by Land Rover and local taxi I followed in his footsteps from the forests and swamps behind the Guinea Coast to Sokoto, Lake Chad and the desert's edge. Familiarity with the Scottish borders, where he was brought up, and with Lake Huron, where he had commanded schooners in 1814-17, in turn prompted me to look further into his background and life. My researches led to the discovery of manuscript diaries in The National Archives in Kew and in The Brenthurst Library in Johannesburg and I ended up transcribing and editing his journals of travels in Africa for eventual publication in three volumes. Having pored over several hundred pages of Hugh Clapperton's notebooks, sketches and maps I felt I had come to know the man and was ready to embark on this memoir.

With respect to the preparatory research for this book, I owe special thanks to Jack Wilson, historian of Lochmaben and former president of The Dumfriesshire and Galloway Natural History and Antiquarian Society, who has guided my research in Scotland for many years. My valued mentor in studying the War of 1812 on the Great Lakes in Canada was Rosemary Vyvyan, Curator of the Historic Naval and Military Establishments at Penetanguishene. And many are the archivists and curators to whom I am most grateful for their patient responses to my requests for assistance, in particular Charlotte Henwood at the Ministry of Defence, Diana Madden at The Brenthurst Library, Johannesburg, Neil Moffat at The Ewart Library, Dumfries, and Virginia Murray at the John Murray Collection, London. Illustrations have been reproduced with the kind permission of Aberdeen Art Gallery & Museums, The Brenthurst Library, The John Murray Archive at the National Library of Scotland, Ministry of Defence Art Collection, London, The National Archive, Kew, and The National Portrait Gallery, London.

In connection with the background to Clapperton's travels in Africa, my debts to numerous scholars have been recorded in the three edited volumes of his journals (see Bibliographic Notes). Here I should like to repeat my obligation to John Wright and to Harry Norris who told me what I needed to know about Tripoli, Fezzan and the Sahara; also to the late John Lavers, to Jean Boyd, Norbert Cyffer, Phil Jaggar and Robin Law, for guidance when I first embarked on my studies of pre-colonial Sudan. From Adam Jones I learned a lot about the transcription of manuscripts; and Paul Lovejoy has been a companion on the long road to whom I owe a special debt of gratitude. Others have generously shared with me their knowledge of the history of Nigeria, among them Ken Lupton and Howard Pedraza; and it has been my constant pleasure to receive elucidation on all manner of arcane subjects – from medical curiosities to poisonous forest plants and nineteenth-century Arabic script to military technology – from many scholars and enthusiasts in their particular subjects in Britain and abroad.

Footstep-following in Nigeria was facilitated by the kind assistance of many friends at different times, notably Tassos Leventis, Harold Blackburne in Kano, and Bukar Gana, Gisela Brikay and the late William Seidensticker in Maiduguri. At the later stages of preparation of the memoir, Crispin Jones provided helpful advice on methodology, Gilpatrick Devlin generously and expertly took on the preparation of the maps, the illustrations and the text for camera-ready copy and Lester Crook and his colleagues at I.B. Tauris provided appreciated support and guidance. I remain most grateful to them all. Last and in reality first, I would also like to thank my wife Flip for her help at every stage of the project, from painstaking research in the archives to skilled assistance with the drafting of this memoir and the checking of proofs.

The story of Hugh Clapperton's achievements was first told in the narratives of the mission to Borno and through the explorer's own posthumously published journal of his second expedition, and the detail has been further chronicled in the three volumes of edited original journals and remark-books already mentioned. The few biographical sketches by his contemporaries (the main sources are listed in the Bibliographic Notes) provide a picture of the boy and of his twelve years of service at sea. *A Sailor in the Sahara* draws the strands together; and I have purposely refrained from offering a personal analysis of this unsung Scottish hero and from inter-preting his travels in terms either of my own footstep-following or of modern philosophical approaches to early-nineteenth century journeys of discovery.

It is a straightforward tale. Hugh Clapperton signed up for the African adventure for fun and because he was at a loose end. But in the end the adventure took over his life: as he himself explained to Robert Hay, Under-Secretary at the Colonial Department, on the eve of departure on his second expedition, 'I have only this wish on earth – to complete what yet remains undone'.

Middleton, Suffolk
August 2007

Chapter 1: Annandale 1788–1805
a light heart and a thin pair of breeches

Family background – upbringing in Annan – a Scottish education traditions and influences on a growing boy – apprenticeship at sea

Hugh Clapperton's early years were spent in Annandale in south-west Scotland, a land of warm, wet winds and late harvests lying somewhat apart from the mainstream of economic development in the late eighteenth century.

Hugh's grandfather Robert was the first Clapperton to settle in Annandale.[1] After studying medicine in Edinburgh and Paris he lived, and married, in Elgin in the far north of Scotland. In his late thirties, accompanied by his wife Elizabeth and their two small children, he moved south to the Borders and set up in practice on his own in the hamlet of Crowdieknowe, before settling in the nearby town of Lochmaben. There his practice flourished and after ten years he was able to purchase and refurbish a substantial house (designed by William Adam, father of Robert Adam) on the edge of the town, where the gardens and orchard ran down to the loch and there were grand views over the wooded valley and bracken-tussocked hills beyond.

A highly respected doctor, family patriarch and prominent member of the local well-to-do gentry, Robert Clapperton was a man of parts – amateur expert in mineralogy, compulsive collector of objects of natural history and tireless investigator of Roman remains and early churches in the district, with a passion for local history and traditional ballads. A 'most ingenious man and an able antiquarian'[2], he collaborated closely with other antiquaries in south-west Scotland and maintained a regular correspondence with luminaries in the principal institutes of the day in Edinburgh.

In his home community, Robert was a leading figure in the church and an enthusiastic Freemason – he was Grand Master of the Lochmaben Lodge for an unprecedented twenty-year term. Energetic and sociable, the doctor was brilliant but disorganized. Dishevelled in appearance and chaotic in his ways, he was also phenomenally careless with money and charitable almost to a fault, frequently declining payment for his professional services. Hugh's grandfather was adjudged very good company indeed.

Robert's wife Elizabeth came from the Highlands; for her the Border country was akin to foreign territory, and any sense of herself as an outsider was no doubt heightened by the fact that she was a Campbell, a cousin to the Campbells of Glenlyon (such connections continued to evoke dark emotions even a century and a half after the massacre of the hapless Macdonalds at Glencoe). But Elizabeth was kept fully occupied tending to her eccentric husband and managing the affairs of her large and unruly family. In Lochmaben further children were born to the couple, of whom four sons grew to adulthood; they followed their father into the medical profession and all were affable, open-handed extroverts.

Hugh's father, George, had studied medicine at Edinburgh University, and then returned to assist Robert in the Lochmaben practice. When, in December 1772, George had married Margaret Johnstone, a child was already on the way and they were rebuked before the Sessions of the Kirk for the (not uncommon) irregularity and required to pay a guinea to the poor. In 1774, after the birth of a second child, George moved to Annan, a small town some two miles from the Solway coast and about twenty miles south of Lochmaben, to set up in medical practice on his own.

George Clapperton was a skilled doctor, his services sought by people living as far away as Carlisle and Dumfries, but he was temperamentally quite unsuited to a settled professional career. Over six foot tall, athletic and tremendously sociable, charming and easy-going, George took after his father – generous, chaotic and forgetful. Despite his standing in the community, his earnings were modest and not surprisingly they were soon whittled away. From neither side of the respectable, middle-class family had there been patrimony to pass on and times were hard. And in 1788, after sixteen years of marriage George, then aged thirty-three, and Margaret, a year older, were facing personal as well as financial difficulties.

Hugh was the last of their eleven children (of whom four did not survive childhood). He was born on 13 May 1788 at half past two in the morning in the Clapperton home at 22 Butts Street, a small, low-ceilinged building with a crowded parlour, a kitchen and a couple of back rooms, located on a lane on the north side of Annan's main thoroughfare, a modest quarter of the town.[3] The cramped conditions in Butts Street made the bearing and raising of her numerous children an exhausting task for the doctor's wife, a burden which took an escalating toll on her health – she herself had been raised in easier circumstances. Margaret hailed from an old-established family living comfortable lives on a three hundred and fifty-acre farm three miles outside Lochmaben; her father's kin, the Johnstones, had farmed the prosperous estate at Thorniethwaite for several generations. And the Hendersons, her mother's people, had owned castle lands in Lochmaben since the seventeenth century.

By the time of Hugh's birth, his father was increasingly given to the pleasures of talk, sport, the bottle and womanizing rather than concerning himself with his profession and his family. Respectable mid-nineteenth century chroniclers disparaged George's lack of financial motivation and 'improvident disposition'[4], somewhat harsh criticisms in view of the doctor's limited circumstances, and crack and hard drinking were linch-pins of provincial social commerce.

Hugh's arrival probably afforded his impecunious father mixed feelings of affection and exasperation. George had already seen four sons raised and educated and he was spending less and less time in Butts Street, and Margaret was thus the one stable element in the child's life. But her health was rapidly failing and, chronically exhausted, she died in August 1792 at the age of forty. Hugh was only four and a half; his mother's death and its aftermath turned his hitherto warm and secure world inside out.

At the time of Margaret's death, Hugh's four older brothers had already left home. John, at nineteen, was serving as a Royal Marine on board HMS *Elephant* in the West Indies, while young George, aged eighteen, lived in Edinburgh, studying to be a doctor with the intention of joining his father's practice in Annan. The same career was intended for Alexander, fifteen years old and already a medical student; and when Margaret died thirteen year-old William was sent away almost immediately to further his education.

Hugh never knew his paternal grandmother – like his mother's parents, Elizabeth Clapperton had died before the boy was born. His Johnstone uncle, John, a lieutenant of Marines, was abroad and the only close maternal relatives who could attend the child's nursery days were the two unmarried sisters who continued to live at Thorniethwaite.

Of the three children who remained at home, little Margaret Isabella at six years old was far too young to be of much help in looking after either the house or her two younger brothers. She went to Lochmaben, to be cared for by the Thorniethwaite aunts; and Charles, aged five, and Hugh remained in Annan with their father for their first steps at school. George and the two young boys rubbed along well enough together, no doubt with some out-side help, but it was hard for all of them.

The following year George Clapperton had a brief liaison with Mary Stewart, a girl from Lochmaben, who in November 1793 bore his illegitimate son. And then, in 1794, when Hugh was six, George remarried, taking as his second wife a twenty-one year-old woman, Jean Gass, who came from a lower social class and whose family lived on the outskirts of the town.[5] In 1795 the first child of the second marriage, Hugh's half-sister Elizabeth, was born and the births of more children followed in annual succession. The loss of his mother, the resultant dislocation of family life and the arrival on the scene of a step-mother despised and ostracized by many of his father's friends all had a profound effect on Hugh.

The doctor's new wife was soon busily preoccupied with her own children, and in later years Hugh was wont to describe his childhood days as miserable. While her regime was harsh and despotic, Jean was not a cruel step-mother (as some chroniclers would have it) but Hugh was unquestionably deprived of that early opportunity to learn to relate to others, inside and outside the family circle, traditionally afforded to young children playing about their mothers' skirts. Left more and more to his own devices and having to fend, perhaps instinctively choosing to fend, for himself he grew wilful and increasingly difficult to control.

If George Clapperton had no patrimony to pass on to his many children, he nevertheless followed contemporary Scottish middle-class tradition in ensuring that his sons received the best education available. Hugh was sent first to a dame school in a house two doors away (run by Peggy Paine, an elderly woman related to the liberal philosopher Tom Paine and much respected in Annan) and later to a schoolmaster in the town. There were several dominies in Annan who could be hired privately or collectively by those able to afford the fees, and when the time came for Hugh to leave the dame school George's choice fell upon Bryce Downie.

Aged in his forties, and already losing his sight, Downie was a considerable figure in the town, 'a man of general information... chiefly celebrated as a mathematician, who, in the opinion of persons resident on the spot, has done more towards the nurture of the youth of Annan than any other teacher who has resided in the place during the last half century'.[6] He had been a councillor of the Burgh for many years, and was the author of two known published works, a sentimental novel, *The Cottage Fireside*, and a rather more serious tome, *An Elector of Annan – A Catechism for*

Candidates – with Reasons Annexed.[7] If the subjects of his writings appear rather dull, his gifts as a teacher were not in doubt.

Young Hugh much respected the inspiring dominie, for whom he conceived a lifelong affection. In the schoolhouse in a lane off the High Street, Bryce Downie afforded his pupils a thorough grounding in reading (classical texts), writing (grammar) and arithmetic; Latin and French, albeit at a rudimentary level, also formed part of the curriculum. Lessons progressed to geography and trigonometry, and included navigation – Hugh could already draw quite well and all subjects with a practical content appealed. Downie also introduced his charges to current affairs, requiring them to read to him from the newspapers. Legend has it that Hugh would go round the neighbourhood borrowing newspapers for his teacher; on an elderly gentleman questioning his right to do this, the boy retorted, 'I'm sure we neither dirty nor keep them long, and your lads, I can tell ye', hang all their washings to dry on Mr. Downie's line'.[8]

Though wayward and stubborn at home, Hugh was said to have been an obliging boy at school, owing no doubt in large measure to the dominie's personal methods of instilling obedience. A disruptive unruliness, if not outright mayhem, was more the norm in a great many educational establishments; Thomas Carlyle, who was born and brought up in nearby Ecclefechan and attended the newly-opened Annan Academy in 1805, later teaching there for two years, had been appalled by the ungovernable wildness and the bullying he witnessed among 'those coarse, unguided, tyrannous cubs'.[9] But in Bryce Downie's schoolhouse the leather thong was not spared, and Hugh would have come in for his fair share of rough and ready justice.

Besides his brother Charles, for companionship there were the children of several of George Clapperton's associates, among them Robert and Thomas, the sons of local merchant John Dickson, and the Irving boys, John and Edward, who lived next door and also took their first lessons from Peggy Paine, later attending Bryce Downie's school. Hugh was very much at home in the Irvings' house. Gavin, from a local farming family, was a tanner and a bailie of the town, easy-going, matter-of-fact and very popular in the community; his wife Mary, 'tall with swift black eyes'[10], was an assiduous housewife. On summer evenings the boys played in the Irvings' barn or studied under the elm trees in the communal back yard, and in winter Hugh shared their meals and a fireside corner when learning his lessons. Their friends became his friends.

There was little to occupy Hugh and his brother Charles at home, and outside school hours the town itself was naturally the youngsters' playground. Annan's red stone buildings huddled around the ruins of an ancient fort. Its population numbered one thousand, three hundred and fifty souls and the parish counted another one hundred families from outlying hamlets. Central to Annan life was the market cross where the townsfolk came to buy goods, make deals, swap gossip and generally pass the time of day. Fishermen and local farmers gathered there to exchange news; and everyone joined in the Hallow-e'en Fair, when people stocked up on salt beef to last throughout the raw winter months. There too the boys played pitch-and-toss and hide-and-seek, shot marbles on the flagstones outside the gaol and noisily chased each other, younger siblings and animals around the square.

Annan Waterfoot, Dumfriesshire

The town's youth learnt at an early age to handle small boats, and an attraction which never palled was the River Annan, at the mouth of which the fishermen set their nets for salmon and sea-trout; and in the warmer months the deep pool above the town at Gallowbank was the favourite place for river bathing. A popular dare involved crossing the wooden toll-bridge along the outside of the parapet which projected one foot from the uprights some thirty feet above the river. Water held no terrors for Hugh and he never could resist a challenge; on one occasion, urged on by his friends, he clung to a stone at the bottom of the river to see how long he could remain submerged,

> He felt as if a calm and pleasing sleep was stealing over his senses, and thought that gay and beautifully painted streamers were attached to his legs and arms, and that thereby he was buoyed out into the sea; but he always declared that he experienced no pain until efforts were making to restore him to a state of animation. At this time he was an expert swimmer, having been previously taught that useful art by his brothers; but he had exhausted his strength by continuing too long in the water. When the alarm of his danger was given by someone to his father, he hastened to the spot, plunged in and found his son in a sitting posture in very deep water.[11]

The Solway Firth, a vast expanse of sand and salt-water rock pools, of shifting channels and mud-banks, wove a dangerous enchantment of its own; many were the tales of adventure, ill fortune and narrow escape associated with its rip tides and the treacherous sinking sands at low water. But at low tide it was also possible to cross the estuary on foot or by cart on a carefully charted track, and on summer days there were Sheltie ponies to ride on the beach. In the winter months, the children went tobogganing and skated on local ponds and lochs; and the young boys were introduced to curling, a major sport and social activity in south-west Scotland and a particular favourite in the Clapperton family. And in season there were brown trout in the river and streams and pike and bream in the ponds and lochs, rabbits and hares to snare on the town marches, pigeons in the woods and larger game in the dales and on the moors above.

Although the Clappertons were town dwellers, many of their acquaintances earned their living directly or indirectly from the land. Annandale's principal income derived from the raising of cattle, the small Galloway breed, and the rearing of hogs. Barley, oats and potatoes were cultivated on the small holdings; flax was also widely grown, and woven in the cottages. At the turn of the century, however, much of the valley floor remained common land; dank moor and bog offered scant pasturage and in an area of high rainfall and long wet summers the margins between success and failure were very fine. From holidays with his maternal aunts at Thorniethwaite and through venturing further afield with his friends to neighbouring settlements, cottages and farm houses,

Hugh acquired a deep respect for country folk; keenly aware of the commitment and stoicism required to bring off a successful season even in a good year, he was mindful of the destitution, dirt and despair which were the lot of the poor in leaner times.

Thomas Carlyle remarked upon the 'thrifty, cleanly poverty of those good people, their well saved coarse clothes with fashions twenty years out of date' who had moved into the town, become genteel and 'left their relatives to rustic solidities'. And, while he was dismissive of the 'long continued bouts of drinking' and the generally comatose nature of Annan society, he acknowledged the existence of a small minority, 'argumentative, clear headed, sound hearted and more given to intellectual pursuits than some of the neighbours'.[12] The Clappertons numbered among those few.

Classical eighteenth-century texts and poetry were familiar to every household (though novels were ill-regarded, being full of lies) but the Clappertons, through Hugh's grandfather Robert and his circle, had kept pace with literary trends. Robert himself was acquainted with James Hogg, the border poet and novelist, and with Robert Burns who had settled in Dumfries in 1791 to take up employment as an exciseman on the coast. Burns had become a familiar figure in Annan and his poems were much admired, none more so than his ballad *The De'il's awa' wi' the Exciseman*, said to have been composed in the town or on the nearby Solway shore while waiting to intercept a smuggler's brig.

Hugh imbibed a strong sense of the history, patriotic traditions and legends of border Scotland. Annan men were justly proud of the history of their town which had 'at divers times, been burnt and destroyed and the burgesses and inhabitants of the same, in times of peace as well as of war, been plundered and slain by our ancient enemies of England'.[13] The traditions, the loyalty and courage of their ancestors (who over four centuries, commanded by different war-lords, had fought each other as much as they did the old enemy) lived on in story and ballad and in the very stones of ancient ruins scattered throughout the countryside. In an age when there was little intercommunal visiting, the coach journey from Annan to Lochmaben was in itself a memorable experience. The road ran through seignorial estates in the lower valley and climbed over wild moorland, descending again to wind along dark, wooded river-banks; brooding Pele towers and the lonely sites of famous battles added substance to the tales told at every borderer's hearth. Hugh had heard them all, heady stuff for an impressionable nine-year-old, at Robert's house in Lochmaben.

But in December 1797 his grandfather died and a vital link to the outside world was lost to the boy.

George was Robert's principal executor and thus responsible for unravelling the numerous claims against his father's estate (it took him nearly five years). Andrew Brown, an emissary from Edinburgh University, attended the auction in Lockerbie in July 1801, hoping to acquire important papers or collectables,

> On the first day's sale, the Rubbish of the house, and a few bows and arrows were produced to the gaping crowd... but the Dr's Son and Heir had charged himself fully with the Spirit of Molasses, the present substitute for Whisky, and declared he would purchase every thing in the shape of papers cost what it would. This declaration and the state in which he and many of his Cronies had got into made it a painful task for any decent person to interfere. No arrangement had been made of books or writings. Every thing was confusion[14]

In 1801 George and Jean Clapperton moved to a larger house at 30 North Side, near the centre of Annan, where their neighbours were well-established, well-to-do folk. The new family home was no great distance from Butts Street, but the move doubtless served to heighten Hugh's feelings of loss following the death of his grandfather and the departure from home of the last of his older brothers and coinciding with his own progressive exposure, rising ten years of age, to strong formative influences outside the home.

In Annandale the old order was beginning to break down; the entrepreneurial classes were keenly aware of the reforms taking place the length and breadth of Britain and significant changes were in the wind. For generations local politics had seemed unalterable and social structures pre-ordained; the same established Annan families had managed the Burgh's affairs, and their private interests, with a firm hand and political influence remained in the grip of aristocratic landowners, the Marquis of Queensberry and his successors, whose powerful factors controlled the land, its produce and its trade. Bribery and corruption permeated everything from land tenancies to church livings, and strong-arm tactics were commonly employed during local elections. By the turn of the eighteenth century, however, a new social awareness and sense of responsibility prevailed. Politically the Burgh was Whig; the general mood was ardently reformist and politics were hotly debated. Dumfriesshire's merchants had begun the process of modernization, and their activities were already changing the framework of life in Annandale, both socially and economically.

Close friends of George's, James Scott and Jonathan Nelson were leading lights among Annan's entrepreneurs. Together they founded the town's first commercial bank, raised finance for new mercantile and industrial ventures and devised self-help and cooperative projects in business and housing. Their patron was soldier-scientist General Alexander Dirom, a former adjutant-general of the army in India, who 'more than any other man of his time was responsible for rousing Dumfriesshire out of the lethargy of the previous century'.[15] The foremost local landowner and a popular Whig parliamentary candidate, Dirom involved himself in everything new, from farming methods to forestry, mineralogy and quarrying enterprises; and his wife, Magdalene, was equally as energetic in promoting welfare projects.

In such liberal circles no subject was taboo, even the tenets and traditions of religion being called into question. The church had exerted a commanding influence in the town and religion played a significant part in each child's upbringing. In every Annan household, family prayers ('taking the book') claimed precedence over all other activities, the head of the family reading from a leather-bound, brass-clasped Bible inscribed from generation to generation. In 1790, a handsome new church of red stone had been built, large enough to accommodate a congregation of one thousand nine hundred people (the parish's population numbered just over two thousand). The word of the Elders and the decisions of the Kirk were absolute law. In the Calvinist tradition in which Hugh was brought up no grey areas were permitted.

But the authority of the established church, under the guidance of William Henry Moncrieff, Annan's quaint, melancholic minister, was already on the wane. A fair number of parishioners had been drawn to join the Burgher Scotch Seceders, one of the oldest of the dissenting congregations in the south of Scotland. The movement in the main attracted the poorer classes; but it also held a singular appeal for those of enquiring mind, among them Edward Irving and Thomas Carlyle. The country-folk of Annandale warmed to the fundamentalist revival; they were prepared to walk miles in all weathers, collecting together in small chapels, 'their streaming plaids hanging up to drip'[16], to hear the fiery preachers of the day. In later years, Hugh's profound Christian faith came to reflect that fundamentalism, and his beliefs were coloured by predestinarian influences, combining a strong sense of moral duty with a certain degree of liberal scepticism about the affairs and motivation of the traditional religious establishment.

Stimulated by the changes all around him, Hugh Clapperton began seriously to consider his own future. Towns were small, incomes from agriculture modest and opportunities for the young were limited. For decades it had been customary for junior sons from larger families to seek if not their fortunes at least a reasonable living away from kith and kin. Most of his older brothers, and his uncles before them, had in their turn left home for pastures new – to a man they had either entered the medical profession or joined the armed services, or indeed both. Hugh decided it was time to follow suit; but he himself felt no call to a medical vocation, and while general mobilization for the French wars had earlier offered opportunities to serve king and country, recruitment had fallen off following the peace treaty of 1801. In the end, resolution of his quandary lay closer to home.

He would have been hard put to it to recall a time when the sea had not loomed large in his life. The sight of sail coming and going over the bar at Waterfoot conjured up vistas of exotic and enticing lands. Nearer to home, smaller vessels transported raw materials, agricultural produce and light manufactured goods between the coastal ports of northwest Britain, and an active fleet of revenue cutters was deployed to counter a flourishing trade in contraband all along the coast. The townsfolk secretly admired the smugglers who ran in brandy from France through the nearby Isle of Man, brought back rum and tobacco from the West Indies and shipped whisky to England from Scotland's innumerable unregulated stills; colourful tales of adventure and derring-do, of skilful manoeuvres and hairbreadth escapes were two-a-penny and new anecdotes were eagerly passed around.

The Solway beckoned and, following in the path of so many Scottish younger sons who set off 'with little more than the sailor's inheritance of a light heart and a thin pair of breeches, to push their way in search of fortune over every quarter of the globe, and in every kind of employment'[17], Hugh Clapperton went to sea. In the spring of 1802, informing rather than consulting his father, he secured himself a berth as a ship's boy on an Annan coastal vessel, becoming a junior deck-hand in the merchant marine; and, as he had hoped and expected, the life suited him well. The following year he took steps to put his career on a more rewarding footing.

At a time of general economic growth and increasing prosperity, maritime merchantry was a secure and remunerative business that attracted the interest of many a go-ahead entrepreneur. Becoming a ship's master was a reasonable ambition for Hugh Clapperton, holding out the prospect of amassing income and capital either by trading for himself or investing in the owner's shares; or he might settle abroad and operate his own merchant fleet. But it would require patronage and so, some twelve months after first going to sea, Hugh turned to his father for help.

George Clapperton's merchant friends were eager to recruit reliable and enterprising young men into their businesses, and it was Jonathan Nelson of Port Annan who came to the family's aid. Through marriage to the daughter of a surgeon at Maryport, he had good personal connections on the Cumberland shore of the Solway, and early in 1803 Nelson arranged for Hugh to be bound over as an apprentice to a Maryport merchant captain, John Smith, commander of the Sailing Ship *Postlethwaite*.

Most of Maryport's fleet of fifty vessels had been designed for Cumberland's coastal trade and were of less than one hundred tons burden, the majority owned by three or fewer persons (those merchants who had raised capital from small investors, partners in trade or personal friends). SS *Postlethwaite* herself, however, was intended for a broader trade. Launched in 1797, she was one of some half-dozen larger vessels capable of ocean passage. At two hundred and fifty tons burden, *Postlethwaite* was sturdily built and registered A1 at Lloyds. She was ship-rigged, with square courses, had a single deck and was worked by a crew of fifteen. Unusually for a Maryport ship, she was also pierced for twenty guns.

Captain Smith had recently bought out his partner and begun to trade out of London and Liverpool as well as from his home port. He needed able and reliable crewmen for the wide-ranging and more lucrative ventures on which he intended to embark. Hugh Clapperton was a promising young lad, with sea-going experience, and Smith was happy to sign him on as cabin-boy and apprentice. Hugh was more than content with his lot. Maryport was home to a successful commercial sea-faring community. The town's merchants had caused a deep-water harbour to be built, turning what was once a fishing port (for herring) into a thriving base for shipbuilding and marine repairs. The port's shipwrights, dockworkers, chandlers, insurers and agents, together with the merchants, owners, captains and seamen, formed a close-knit and sociable community.

Over the next two years John Smith extended his operations to encompass Philadelphia, Halifax and other North American ports, with occasional voyages to the West Indies; he also developed a trade on the Baltic coast. Hugh's career at sea began in earnest, though some of his duties as cabin-boy irked him (indignant and stubborn, he had at first refused to black Captain Smith's boots). Menial duties aside, working a two hundred and fifty-ton ship on Atlantic passage called for quite some physical endurance and a cool head, and Hugh revelled in the challenges. As a full member of a crew of fifteen, he stood watches at sea and in dock. He necessarily learnt quickly and well, and accounts received in Annan of progress in the first years of his apprenticeship reflected the kind of glowing testimonials to be expected from supportive family friends. Captain Smith attested to a high degree of dexterity and intrepidity; Hugh had clearly come up to expectations. By the end of 1805 he was well settled in his chosen career, the comradely spirit on board, the adventure and the journeys of discovery to far-flung countries affording him personal pleasure and fulfilment.

But in February 1806 the course of his life was abruptly and radically altered. SS *Postlethwaite* was berthed in Liverpool, her crew billeted in a boarding house in the town; and on board was a cargo of rock salt, a commodity in very short supply. One day Hugh carried on shore, hidden in his handkerchief, a few pounds of salt which he intended to present to his landlady. He was caught red-handed by a revenue officer. Nineteenth-century biographers waxed either evasive or sentimental on the subject, the Reverend J. Dodds prefacing his remarks, 'Having committed some offence against the Revenue Laws'[18], while others maintained that the lad had acted out of the kindness of his heart. Robert Chambers was moved to propose that Hugh had been 'most improperly enticed in this action by his landlady'[19], while uncle Samuel Clapperton, clearly embarrassed by the whole affair, preferred simply to record, 'After making several voyages in that vessel [SS *Postlethwaite*] he either left her or was impressed into the Royal Navy'.[20]

Impressed Hugh most certainly was. He could hardly have been ignorant of the Revenue Laws, nor indeed would ignorance have afforded any protection against charge or sentence. Convicted of smuggling and given the option of imprisonment or impressment, he chose the latter and, on 8 February 1806, was duly bound over to serve in His Majesty's navy.

Chapter 2: The Mediterranean 1806–1809
the bonny muckle midshipman

Impressment – life before the mast
on the quarterdeck at Gibraltar – action in the Mediterranean
passage to the East Indies – a rescue at sea

Last-named on a list of two hundred men given into the charge of
Captain Samuel Colquitt on the guard ship HMS *Princess*, Hugh
Clapperton thus unwillingly entered into service with the Royal
Navy at Liverpool on 26 February 1806, 'Hugh Clatterton [*sic*],
Age not given – From Liverpool Rendezvous, Pressed, Ordinary
Seaman'. Two weeks later he was sent to Spithead on board a
crowded naval transport.

Nursing his injured pride and bitterly regretting the abrupt
loss of his chosen career, Hugh did not appreciate his new circumstances one whit. He could not accept that his actions had in any
way constituted a crime; he had simply been doing his landlady a
kindly favour and he considered the sentence handed down to
him to be not only unwarranted but manifestly inappropriate.

After three years in the merchant marine, Hugh was familiar
enough with the processes of the Impress Service, its searches for
able-bodied sea-faring men in the local public houses, brothels
and boarding-houses ashore where seamen and privateersmen
traditionally gathered, and its recourse to courts and gaols. He
was also aware that while impressment into the Royal Navy was
common, the number of desertions was also high. Once entered,
naval service was for life; there were only three ways out of the
Navy: death, discharge or desertion. Death usually supposed
sickness or accident (loss overboard or a fall from the rigging), the
number killed in action representing barely one per cent of total
deaths at sea. Overall, only one third were discharged, and about
one third deserted (and were listed as Ran). He also knew that in
the end, even if relentlessly flogged until they learned their duty,
the majority of pressed recruits were proud to be part of the world's
strongest naval force. But he had previously given the possibility
of his own impressment little if any thought, and the situation he
found himself in was extremely disagreeable.

In Portsmouth, Clapperton was one of seventy men (half of
them volunteers, the others pressed) put on board HMS *Royal*

William, a guard-ship serving as a holding point for the supply of seamen to new vessels entering commission, to tenders and to other vessels. He was issued with slop clothes and set to work below decks as a cook's mate before being sent to join his new ship, HMS *Gibraltar*. On *Gibraltar*, however, account was taken of his time at sea in the merchant marine and on 26 March 1806 he was entered on the muster list, 'Hugh Clapperton, Aged 18, From Annan, Able Seaman'. Compared with *Postlethwaite*, Clapperton's new home was of massive proportions. A Third Rate ship of the line of over two thousand tons burden, with an overall length of one hundred and seventy-eight feet and a beam of fifty-eight feet, HMS *Gibraltar* carried eighty guns and a crew of six hundred. When Clapperton sailed with her from Spithead, she had been assigned to patrol duty with the Channel Fleet and in May took up station at the Nore on the broad mouth of the Thames estuary.

The life of an ordinary seaman was hard. On deck, Clapperton could look forward to unremitting toil in all weathers, the discipline rough and only too ready; time off-watch was spent for the most part cooped up in the cramped, mephitic lower decks. Rations were meagre, the company was rowdy, brutal and often brutal-ising, and the pay a mere pittance. Nor was there any prospect of action to relieve the tedium of sluggish patrols in the grey-brown chops of the English Channel, where conditions varied in winter from dank mists and drizzling rain to icy gales.

On 16 May 1806, the British Cabinet ordered the blockading of all continental ports from Brest to the Low Countries. Following Nelson's victory at Trafalgar the Royal Navy held sway at sea, but France still controlled continental Europe. Britain's strategy was therefore one of containment, and her ships were charged with enforcing a comprehensive economic barricade. The French not offering to come out and fight, the Channel squadron could only patrol and wait. Morale on board slumped; the officers grew jaded, the men ill-tempered. And Hugh Clapperton morosely continued to nurse his wounded pride. The abrupt and humiliating change in his personal circumstances was not something Hugh could comfortably aver to family and friends. He had a very good notion of his own worth and suddenly to have become a mere nonentity among a vast and anomalous company of men, virtually confined to the din and squalor of the bowels of the ship, was not at all to his taste.

When HMS *Gibraltar* moved down Channel in late June, half a dozen men ran at Falmouth, one of them a fellow recruit from the

Royal William, and Clapperton resolved to escape when the next suitable occasion presented itself. His chance came a few weeks later when he was ordered to join a detachment sent to man a detained ship and take her into Plymouth. Once in port, he chose a moment when he was not observed, threw himself overboard and swam to a vessel moored nearby, a privateer. (*Gibraltar's* muster log recorded his flight, 'Hugh Clapperton AB ~ R[an] 13 August 1806 ~ Plymth ~ from a detained ship'.)

It was an impetuous, ill-judged action. Clapperton had formed no plan beyond immediate escape. He was too far from home, from any port where he had the necessary connections, to contemplate rejoining the merchant service. As a first step, therefore, he had to make do with what was on offer, and signed up for service on the privateer. She set sail for the Mediterranean, carrying her letters of marque from the British government under which she was licensed to attack French and Spanish shipping, a mercenary enterprise and effectively a form of authorised piracy; and before long she was engaged in violent action. Clapperton was wounded by grapeshot, seamed and scarred but fortunate to have been hit in the body rather than in the face or limbs which could have disfigured or deformed him for life.

The coarseness and gratuitous cruelty of the so-called rock scorpions sickened Clapperton, but neither the pain of his wounds nor the objectionable company touched him very deeply. Unable to conjure up the smallest degree of allegiance to the privateer, he remained a prisoner of circumstance and it was particularly galling to concede that he had no one to blame but himself; he would have to get away. His opportunity came three months later, when the privateer went alongside the Gibraltar Mole for reprovisioning. Clapperton jumped ship, headed straight for a nearby naval frigate, HMS *Renommee*, and volunteered his services.

Marched on deck before an officer, Hugh Clapperton described his sea-going experience. It was pointed out to him that he could be flogged as a deserter, and that he must swear to perform his duty faithfully before being accepted as a volunteer. Possibly relying on the premise that desertion by an impressed seaman would be considered a less serious offence than that of a sailor absconding from a volunteered engagement, Clapperton asked for time to reflect before making a final decision (he was still in two minds about a return to the merchant marine). Looking upon the fine, upstanding and apparently well-qualified seaman, the officer immediately ordered him into solitary confinement, whereupon

Clapperton lost no time in giving the necessary undertaking; and on 25th November 1806 he was taken onto *Renommee*'s books as an able seaman ('volunteered at Gibraltar, born Annan, Dumfries, aged 20' – he was in fact eighteen and a half, a modest enough exaggeration), after which he was released and allowed to go on shore on parole.[1]

HMS *Renommee* was Clapperton's home for the next twenty months. A Fifth Rate ship armed with forty guns, she carried a crew of two hundred and forty-six men and some forty-five marines. She had been captured from the French in the West Indies and was relatively old fashioned and lightly armed for the time, but her Scottish captain, Sir Thomas Livingstone, Bart, son of the Earl of Linlithgow, was an experienced officer and her record on the Mediterranean station was good. The Mediterranean fleet had a dual role, containment and harassment. Containment involved keeping the main French and Spanish fleets locked into Toulouse and Cadiz and preventing any enemy movement in the western Mediterranean; such tasks were carried out by ships-of-the-line from British bases at Gibraltar, Malta and Sicily. Harassment was principally concerned with the dislocation of French commerce, weakening France's ability to provision her population at home and her armies abroad, and British frigates, brigs and sloops were involved in a series of cutting-out actions to capture enemy ships and in raids on harbours and ports to deny the enemy operational shore bases. Clapperton's new shipmates had recently been in action off the coasts of Spain and Majorca; all operations had been carried out without loss of life and with few men wounded, prize money had been won and morale on board was high.

Following Christmas at Valetta, *Renommee* put to sea on a series of four-week patrols, broken only by returns to Gibraltar for re-provisioning. In May 1807, Clapperton finally got his chance to see action when the frigate participated in the capture of a Spanish brig; and a few days later she seized a number of Spanish fishing boats. Conditions aboard *Renommee* were a far cry from those endured during winter patrols in the Channel. The warm sea and fine early summer weather allowed the crew space and fresh air; and the British men-of-war had very much the upper hand in the ongoing game of cat and mouse. The dash and clash of cutting-out actions in company with other British ships, and the pride and satisfaction afforded by swift, well-executed manoeuvres in the relatively calm waters of the Mediterranean littoral were exhilarating experiences for the young Scottish able seaman.

In July, Captain Livingstone received orders to join the main fleet on blockade duties off Cadiz; there the crew's mettle was tested in very different ways. They spent seemingly endless hours holding position in the heaving Atlantic swell. Hugh Clapperton, AB, again proved himself well-qualified, competent and reliable on deck. *Renommee* continued on station off Cadiz until October, when the blockade was lifted. British naval squadrons had succeeded in preventing Napoleon's attempt to coerce the King of Portugal into the war on France's side. And *Renommee*'s participation in Atlantic fleet duties off Cadiz also delivered a sudden and very agreeable new direction to Clapperton's burgeoning naval career.

His uncle Samuel was Captain of Marines[2] on board one of Lord Collingwood's ships-of-the-line, HMS *Saturn*, and in mid-October 1807, during a return to Gibraltar for refitting, reprovisioning and watering, *Renommee* and *Saturn* lay alongside each other at the mole. Hugh was able to get a letter to his uncle and learnt that Samuel Clapperton and Sir Thomas Livingstone were former messmates, lieutenants together at the Cape of Good Hope. Samuel lost no time in calling on Livingstone to intercede on behalf of his nephew, and Livingstone, happy to oblige an old friend, agreed to take Hugh Clapperton onto his quarterdeck. Uncle and nephew went off to celebrate in the town, where Samuel provided Hugh with clothing and equipment suitable to his new status.

On 25 October 1807, Hugh Clapperton was officially promoted midshipman; the dilemmas of the past eighteen months and the grievous injuries to his personal pride could now be consigned to history. Secure in the necessary patronage with which to make a fresh start at sea, he could look forward to pursuing a rewarding career as an officer in the Royal Navy.

He saw action immediately in his new role as a junior officer. HMS *Renommee* returned to another tour of coastal watch in the Mediterranean. On the night of 6 November, boats from *Renommee* and the 18-gun sloop *Grasshopper* cut out a French and a Spanish merchantman lying under the Torre de Estacion near Cartagena, 'As soon as the vessels were carried, they were unhappily swept ashore by the current, just under the Tower, where the Spanish guns could bear on them. Two of the British and several of the prisoners were wounded before it was decided to abandon the prizes'.[3] One month later *Renommee* and *Grasshopper* drove a 12-gun Spanish brig-of-war, *San Josef*, on shore under Cape Negretta. Raiding parties from the frigates attacked and took the brig and, in spite of heavy fire from troops on the cliffs above, succeeded in floating off their prize. Clapperton received a head wound which though seemingly negligible at the time, apparently 'afterwards gave him much annoyance'.[4] Such operations brought him his first experience of leadership in close-quarter fighting – his physique and disposition particularly suited him for cutlass work.

Having won his first laurels in the new appointment and made a mark with *Renommee*'s captain, Clapperton was hungry for more action. But the ageing frigate was unable to stay the course, and Livingstone had to report that she was slow and leaking. In April 1808 the Admiralty Commissioners ordered *Renommee* back to England for repairs. She reached Spithead on 17 May and three weeks later was taken to Deptford, where the crew were put at their Lordships' disposal. On 11 June 1808 Hugh Clapperton was officially discharged to HMS *Venerable*, newly built that very year, a Third Rate ship-of-the-line and effectively twice the size of *Renommee*.

He used his brief shore leave constructively, getting word to family in Annan where a year previously his brother George had joined their father in the medical practice. The Clapperton family turned to old friends to help secure the patronage necessary for Hugh's continued advancement. The banker James Scott set the ball rolling by approaching General Dirom, who was attached part-time to the General Staff in Edinburgh and a very influential figure; however it was Magdalene Dirom and her family who produced the desired connection. Her brother, Sir Thomas Pasley, was Admiral of the White and her sister was married to Stephen Briggs, a former chief surgeon in Madras. Magdalene approached Stephen's son, her nephew Captain Thomas Briggs, who had recently been given command of the frigate HMS *Clorinde* and had just brought her home from the West Indies for refitting at the Nore, ready for service on the East Indies station. Briggs agreed to take on the Diroms' protégé; Hugh Clapperton was informed and immediately applied for a discharge from *Venerable* to join *Clorinde*.

HMS *Venerable*, however, had meanwhile put to sea, as flagship for Sir R.J. Strachan commanding the Channel fleet, and Clapperton continued aboard her. When by August there was still no word of his transfer, the family informed General Dirom, who first applied personally to Sir Home Popham, Commandant at the Nore, and then tried what he might achieve through his old friend and patron from India days, the Marquis of Hastings. Alas, the wheels of naval bureaucracy were slow to turn and Clapperton remained on board HMS *Venerable* on Channel stations throughout the winter, with little prospect of action; the work was monotonous, sailors ran, and his limited patience was sorely tried. And then, in mid-February 1809, he learnt to his dismay that HMS *Clorinde* had already sailed for the East Indies. Ten days later, however, the long-awaited orders arrived; and on 27 February he was discharged from *Venerable* for a passage to join *Clorinde*, a passage that took another fifteen months to complete.

In early March, Clapperton arrived on board the guard-ship HMS *Royal William* at Spithead, but how different were the circumstances from those surrounding his appearance three years earlier as an impressed ordinary seaman. Confusion over sailing orders for the convoys to the east, however, involved yet further delay and more transfers, but in May he was received as a supernumerary on board HMS *Hindustan* (Captain Pasco), a transport bound for the Cape of Good Hope, the headquarters of the East Indies station. Armée en flute, *Hindustan* was large and slow; in addition to her own complement, she carried three hundred and forty troops, sixty-eight women and forty-three children. Her next port of call was Rio de Janeiro, the route taking her through the mid-Atlantic trade-wind zones, and on the voyage there Clapperton's courage and seamanship were put to a severe test.

On 4 June, in strong westerly gales in mid-Atlantic, Latitude 42° 22′N and Longitude 11°12′W (some six hundred miles west of the Canary Islands), Captain Pasco responded to a distress signal from HMS *Magicienne*. One of *Hindustan*'s barges was made ready and Clapperton was put aboard. As they prepared to push off, he declared to his messmates that the small boat could not possibly live in the sea that was running but that it was not his place to question the orders of his superior officer; then, instructing them to share out his belongings equally among themselves, he bade them farewell. Almost immediately the barge was swamped in a heavy squall and capsized. The anxious crew of HMS *Magicienne* looked on as men were swept away and drowned. Clapperton struggled to save a warrant officer but was not able to maintain his grip on the man. At the last only the bowman and Clapperton remained. Encouraging each other as best they could, they clung to the upturned barge for a further two hours, until the gale had abated. *Magicienne* survived and Pasco was able to lower further boats to rescue his men. When they were hauled back on board *Hindustan*, Clapperton overheard the wives of the Scottish sailors exclaim, 'Thank heaven, it is na our ain kintryman, the bonny muckle midshipman that's drownded after a'!'[5]

Following reprovisioning in Rio, HMS *Hindustan* sailed for the Cape, where she arrived in late September. But there were no craft in harbour bound for the east. With ten others, Clapperton was put on board the cutter *Olympia* to await a passage; at least he was now on station and part of a large naval force. The squadrons of the East Indies station operated from major shore establishments in India and Ceylon, utilising provisioning depots dotted around the Indian Ocean, the Malay Straits and the South China Seas (where capture of Dutch territory had considerably expanded British dominion). In late 1809, the station's commander-in-chief, Admiral Albermarle Bertie, was principally engaged in countering French designs on India and the Far East. France still possessed garrisons and naval depots on Ile de France (Mauritius) and Ile de Bourbon (Réunion), and her fleet was being held in check by a British squadron based at nearby Rodriguez, reinforced as needed from India. Clapperton was eager to take part in the action, but transhipment problems conspired to delay his arrival by a further nine months.

He eventually secured a passage east in early November and four weeks later he was discharged to the garrison on Rodriguez for onward transfer. On account of the early onset of the hurricane season, however, there were fewer ships than usual sailing to India. Clapperton spent two and a half months at the depot on the barren mid-ocean island and when at last, on 14 March 1810, he arrived in Bombay on board HMS *Psyche* (Captain Edgecombe), it was to discover that HMS *Clorinde* was away, sailing on the east coast of India. He was re-entered on *Psyche*'s books, no longer as a supernumerary but in the capacity of midshipman – Edgecombe was glad to make use of the talents of the thrusting and energetic young petty officer on his quarterdeck. The following month *Psyche* left Bombay, bound for Madras. Three weeks later she was at anchor at Back Bay at Trincomalee in the Crown Colony of Ceylon (the principal staging post between the east and west coasts of India), safely sheltered under a wooded bank and in water so deep that even a 74-gun ship could anchor within a few yards of the beach. And on 9 June 1810, in a strong breeze which had already carried away some of her sails, HMS *Clorinde* arrived in the Trincomalee Roads.

Chapter 3: The East Indies 1810–1813
diligence, sobriety and obedience to command

*First through the breach at Mauritius – patrols in the eastern seas
return to England – cutlass training – from Portsmouth to Canada*

On 11 June 1810, two years to the day from his discharge from
Renommee, Hugh Clapperton reported aboard HMS *Clorinde* to pay
his duty and compliments to her captain. Captain Briggs' protégé
came well recommended; just turned twenty-two, he had been at
sea for eight years. He had been wounded in action in the Mediterranean, had seen service on patrols in the Channel and the
Atlantic and had performed his duty with acknowledged valour
in a dangerous mid-ocean rescue operation.

Thomas Briggs was doing very well in the Royal Navy. Aged
forty-two, and one of the most senior captains on the East Indies
station, he enjoyed the full confidence of his admiral and first-rate
personal connections in India, ashore and afloat, through his father
the former chief surgeon in Madras. HMS *Clorinde*, a Fifth Rate ship,
had an overall length of one hundred and sixty feet and a forty-
one foot beam. She was armed with thirty-eight guns and carried
her full complement of three hundred and thirty men, four officers
and three midshipmen, and seven marines under a sergeant. And
on going aboard, Clapperton was delighted to find that she had
been ordered to Madras to be refitted and reprovisioned in order
to take part in a major offensive. In company with *Psyche*, *Clorinde*
set sail for Madras on 12 June, and Clapperton began his new
duties in good heart and with renewed vigour.

The Governor General of India, Lord Minto, had 'conceived the
great design of clearing the Indian Ocean of all that was hostile to
Britain'[1] and by 1810 the strategists in London were finally ready
to take the initiative. Following the capture of the last remaining
French possessions in the West Indies by Admiral Cochrane earlier
that year, further reinforcements could be made available. Determined to complete operations before the start of the hurricane
season, Admiral Bertie had already put his fleet into action and on
6 July a British force invaded Réunion, in two days taking possession of the capital and two smaller towns and capturing valuable
quantities of ordnance and ammunition. The way was now open

for a move against Mauritius, France's main base in the east and a much tougher proposition altogether. Ashore, the French were well-garrisoned and well-armed, with two thousand regulars and some five thousand militia; their fleet included a considerable number of Royal Naval vessels and several East Indiamen captured in previous months, and had recently been reinforced by the arrival of two frigates and a corvette. Admiral Bertie was consequently assembling a considerable invasion force.

At Madras on 20 August, survey officers went on board *Clorinde* to assess her needs. Alongside her patrol duties she would be required to carry (and support) troops, extra boats and landing craft. As a senior and experienced midshipman, Clapperton was actively involved in the complex business of refitting the frigate; passages at sea were long and the necessary equipment was often unavailable in port. The frigate's sails were all much the worse for wear after a lengthy cruise, and the actual refit was more a matter of general improvisation and making do. There were also a number of changes among the crew. Briggs ran a tight ship and a lieutenant of Marines and a purser were brought before courts martial; the first was reprimanded, the second dismissed from the service.

A month later *Clorinde* sailed in convoy, reaching Rodriguez on 4 October. There she spent six weeks moving men and supplies between the garrison and the men-of-war standing off Port Louis holding the French squadron in check and, under cover of feigned attacks, reconnoitring the coastline, while attending the order to invade. On 24 November a fleet of seventy sail was gathered off Mauritius awaiting suitable weather conditions for a landing. The combined invasion force was divided into two wings, each carrying a battalion of infantry. Briggs had command of the right wing. Clapperton, however, was detached to the left wing to lead a party of *Clorinde*'s seamen supporting the artillery landing. The site chosen for the landing, the small beach at Mapou Bay three miles to the west of Grand Bay and well away from the French gun emplacements, required the negotiation of a narrow channel through the reef, and its entrance had already been surveyed and buoyed.

On the morning of 27 November, the breeze was favourable and the day fine as forty-seven boats transporting one thousand seven hundred and fifty men pulled towards the bay. The artillery, one hundred and sixty gunners and seamen on board twelve cutters and yawls, armed with 6-pounder and howitzer guns, were first on shore, tasked with setting up a battery near the beach to protect the infantry landing. Hugh Clapperton was in the front line on board HMS *Alexander*'s yawl, in command of twenty men from *Clorinde*. In company were *Alexander*'s cutter, carrying one 6-pounder gun and eight gunners, and the flagship *Africaine*'s cutter, carrying twelve Lascar gunners and a howitzer. In the midst of a great deal of excitement and some apprehension, the boats rowed ashore against the strong westerly-setting tide.

Behind the three boats, two brigs stood in close to the opening in the reef, ready to sweep the shore with grapeshot. Behind them, five frigates with landing craft were poised to deliver the main force. But conditions were not ideal. One boat was completely swamped, and the strength of the tide prevented the flats and heavy boats from maintaining their positions. No resistance was met with on shore, however, and the bridgehead was created without a shot being fired. As their enemy's reinforcements formed up on the beach, the French at Grand Bay began to retreat, first blowing up their magazine. By five in the afternoon a party of British troops had set off into the woods, heading for Port Louis over higher ground; and by the end of the evening the remainder of the force had landed and established secure positions with the requisite arms, ammunition and food (and spirits) for the men. That night there was a successful skirmish with the French, who had deployed three thousand five hundred troops above the capital to repel the invasion force, retaining their other units in the forts ready to counter an attack from the sea.

At dawn the advance guard attacked the enemy in a flanking movement; the main party, supported by naval offshore guns, moved along the coast and Clapperton and his men helped haul the heavy ordnance alongside them and over a rocky river-bed to the edge of the town's ramparts. It was exhausting and thirsty work. French troops on the heights were compelled to retire and the British contingent thrust forward for an assault on the town's fortifications; by mid-day the guns were in position, the infantry had formed up for the attack and reinforcements had been landed from the sea with orders to capture the main batteries. The French were out-positioned and outnumbered. Their commanding general came forward to agree terms of surrender, and the British troops entered the town; Clapperton was among those first through the breach in the walls to haul down the French colours at Port Louis.

It was an historic victory for British forces on the East Indies station. And, whether or not he personally hauled down France's colours (as his family always maintained), Clapperton was justly proud of his own part in the combined operation. There was little time for rest or celebration, however, since victory had to be consolidated before the monsoon season. Over forty French ships had been captured; and for the next four weeks *Clorinde*'s officers took charge of eight French prizes, six frigates and two sloops, all needing to be fitted-out and manned. Prisoners had to be secured and embarked, men and supplies moved into the newly-acquired garrison, and the sick and wounded cared for. And always there were sailors to command and control, both on board and ashore (a small number took the opportunity to desert).

In early January the naval withdrawal began, and *Clorinde* set sail again to help move supplies and troops between the island depots before making her way back to India, where good news awaited her on return to Bombay in mid-March 1811: prize money was paid to her company for one of the French frigates, and there was the enticing prospect of further action. Ships were being made ready for an expedition, on an even grander scale, to the islands of the East Indies where French forces had seized control of Dutch interests. A month later, HMS *Clorinde* sailed with the fleet, though under separate orders. She was bound for China on an extended patrol, her mission to assist and protect the East India Company's commercial convoys and to support British and allied establishments in the region, an enduring and high-priority assignment for the East Indies station. Briggs was also charged with diplomatic liaison both with the allied commands and with the influential committee of supercargoes in Canton.

For Clapperton, disappointed of action in the Java operation, there was consolation of a heady kind – further promotion. At Penang on 21 June 1811, he was made up to master's mate, the most senior petty officer on board, with overall responsibility for the sailing of the ship. Answerable to him were the captain of the foretop and a captain of the maintop, each with his own crew. Clapperton himself had sixteen general hands directly under him. He was also in charge of the artisans on board: the sail-maker and his mate and three men, a caulker and three men, a cooper and four men, a rope-maker and an armourer. The advancement was a crucial step towards his prime goals, an officer's commission and his own ship. Prolonged patrols in the South China seas would provide practical experience of command and serve to put on a solid, long-term footing the vital patronage first conferred through family endeavours and since earned in action with Thomas Briggs.

Though the patrol in the east in 1811 was uneventful in terms of armed action, Clapperton's new office on board *Clorinde* was no sinecure. Lying between the tropical storm-belt and the Doldrums, the South China seas suffered extremes of maritime conditions – as did the Bay of Bengal where the worst hurricane for a quarter of a century had just devastated the harbour and wrecked many ships in the Madras Roads. Navigation through the innumerable island narrows presented no small challenge; anchorages were commonly hazardous and ships' boats often had great difficulty getting on shore. Because of the distances involved and all the difficulties in obtaining supplies en route, it was standard practice to refit and reprovision for remaining at sea for months on end. The master's mate on board was accountable for all such tasks. And in an overwhelmingly inhospitable climate, commanding men on and below deck during lengthy unbroken periods at sea was not for the faint-hearted. Tropical fevers were rife, yellow fever amongst them, and internal disorders commonplace. Men were regularly discharged into hospitals on shore, and all too frequently died there; off Batavia that autumn, the squadron lost two hundred and twenty men from such sicknesses, seventy-one from the flagship *Illustrious* alone. The crews perforce bore those risks and other attendant miseries as stoically as they might.

In July *Clorinde* sailed for Manila, where several members of the crew were punished for drunkenness and a number deserted, and in late September she headed northwest to Canton, to re-provision and hold herself ready to escort the East India Company's autumn tea convoy. For two months, on constant alert for Ladrones (pirates from the eponymous islands), Briggs patrolled the coast and moved between Macao and the Canton river, to press and allocate men among naval ships and to assist the East Indiamen in their cooperation with powerful Company officials at Whampoa. In late November *Clorinde* set sail with a small convoy from the watering station at Chuenpu for the Straits of Malacca, returning to Bombay on 31 January 1812. Turn-around time was short and two weeks later Briggs was ordered to the Indian Ocean islands, on a three-month voyage to assist in the movement of ships, men and supplies between the island establishments, Trincomalee and Bombay. By the time *Clorinde* returned to Madras in April 1812, Hugh Clapperton had indeed amassed valuable experience of sea-faring and command; he had also formed an extensive acquaintance among the station's officers afloat and ashore. And in Madras itself another and more significant connection was established.

At the turn of the year, Admiral Sir Samuel Hood had arrived off the Cape to take over as commander-in-chief of the East Indies station, continuing directly to Madras to establish his own head-quarters on the spot, determined to rationalize British naval presence in the East as speedily as possible. He had come to stay; and his large personal retinue included his young wife, the eldest daughter of Francis Humberstone Mackenzie, Lord Seaforth[2], and her sixteen-year-old brother, Francis (Frank) Mackenzie who was newly entered in the Royal Navy, an enthusiastic young fellow fresh from Eton College. The Mackenzies enjoyed numerous personal acquaintances among civilian and military staff in India where Baron Seaforth had previously commanded a regiment. Admiral Hood, a flag officer since 1807, was also well connected there, and Thomas Briggs was a personal friend. On arrival in Madras in May 1812, Hood placed his brother-in-law on board HMS *Clorinde* as an able seaman, to allow the youngster to gain experience in Briggs' care. The move brought Frank Mackenzie under the immediate supervision of Hugh Clapperton, reinforcing the latter's own links to a veritable clan of Scottish senior officers on the station – all of whom were well pleased with their new commander-in-chief, held to be a very likeable man as well as an experienced leader, 'There was ever observable a boyish hilarity about this great officer which makes it delightful to serve officially under him and enjoy his friendly companionship'.[3] Briggs sailed later the same month for a further tour of duty as Hood's senior officer commanding His Majesty's vessels in the China seas; and Clapperton continued as master's mate on board *Clorinde*.

In Penang that June, fever was rife in the fleet and naval vessels returning to Madras required considerable assistance and renewed drafts of impressed seamen to enable them to complete the passage. And, to complicate matters further, at the end of the same month a huge conflagration destroyed more than a third of the town – Clapperton had charge of fire parties ashore when Briggs landed one hundred and fifty men to assist in fighting the blaze. In July, a stormy crossing to Manila necessitated repairs before *Clorinde* could continue her journey to Canton. Then, after a month on coastal patrol and another passage to Manila for stores, Briggs repaired to Chuenpu in October to organize the flotilla of naval and merchant vessels for the homeward voyage with the precious tea harvest.

Naval ships which Briggs considered superfluous to the convoy's requirements were ordered to return to India to join Hood's flag without further delay; wrecked vessels were moved, lost anchors fished in fine weather at the height of spring tides, and straggling Indiamen damaged in storms were brought safely to anchorage at

Whampoa. By this time total numbers aboard *Clorinde* had grown considerably, Briggs often victualling a hundred more men than there were able crew mustered – they included deserters, invalids, impressed men carried as supernumeraries as well as military and civilian personnel awaiting passages to India or home. *Clorinde*'s sick-list also grew apace; the incessant rains had increased the incidence of typhus fever on board.

In November *Clorinde* finally set sail for India; and at that same time, after six months before the mast, the Admiral's brother-in-law was taken onto Briggs' quarterdeck as a midshipman. Fellow countrymen and messmates, Hugh Clapperton and Frank Mackenzie quickly became firm friends. When Mackenzie went down with typhus, Clapperton looked after him, encouraging him when he was fevered and later helping him with his theoretical instruction as he recuperated. But Mackenzie, like so many invalids, turned fractious and moody and his other messmates shunned him; and they put it abroad that Clapperton had attached himself to the commander-in-chief's young relative in order to further his own prospects for promotion to lieutenant (for which important examination he had indeed been studying when his shipboard duties allowed). Sensitive to their many differences in upbringing and connections, Clapperton stopped keeping Mackenzie company. Frank, however, decidedly put out by his friend's distant manner, insisted upon an explanation; the air was eventually cleared and their old comradeship comfortably resumed.

On *Clorinde*'s return to Bombay in January 1813, Clapperton learnt that in his absence he had been appointed master's mate on board Hood's flagship, HMS *Illustrious*, and that *Illustrious* had been ordered back to England, for England was now at war with America. When, in the face of strong and repeated objections from Britain, the United States had persisted in trading with France and France's allies, the British had moved swiftly to take counter-measures. In June 1812, goaded beyond endurance by the Royal Navy's constant interference with her ships and impressment of her citizens, America had declared war. A series of naval engagements had already taken place on the eastern seaboard of the United States and on the Great Lakes in Canada, and Hood was required to release resources for the new front.

Meanwhile, the squadron's flagship was in port and, by order of Admiral Hood, Clapperton appeared before a naval examination board in pursuance of his lieutenant's commission,

We have examined Mr. Hugh Clapperton, who appears by Certificate to be more than nineteen years of age and has been to sea more than six years in the ships and qualities under-mentioned, viz:

He produceth logs kept by himself in His Majesty's Ships Renommee, Venerable, Clorinde, and certificates from Captains Livingstone, King, Pasco, Edgecombe and Briggs of his diligence, sobriety and obedience to command. He can splice, knot, reef a sail, work a ship in sailing, shift his tides, keep a reckoning of the ship's way by plain sailing and Mercator's, observe by the sun or star, find the variation of the compass, and is qualified to do his duty as an Able Seaman and Midshipman.

Given under our hands on board HMS Clorinde, Bombay Harbour, 7 February 1813.

Signed, Thos. Briggs, Captain HMS Clorinde, William H. Webley, Capt. HMS Illustrious, Geo. Elliott, Capt. HMS Hussar[4]

Six years after volunteering at the Gibraltar Mole, Clapperton had made the grade, thanks both to his own perseverance and to his enhanced personal connections. He was jubilant, even though there was no prospect of an early award of the coveted commission. Hostilities against the French were coming to a close, and the Royal Navy had begun to retrench.

In the eastern seas, the French had already retreated and the guns had fallen silent; only on the Atlantic station were armed operations actually in train. The competition for good postings was fierce and ambitious officers were eager to get home to lobby for appointments; and Hood and Briggs were keen to see the fit and most able officers redeployed to healthier climes. Bombay in February was an uncomfortable place to be. Temperatures soared and in the humid confines of the harbour the sick-lists lengthened daily, Frank Mackenzie's name once again figuring on them. The announcement of the new deployments came as a great relief.

On Illustrious, Captain Alexander Skene (another Scot, and the son of a flag officer) had readily agreed to take over patronage of the experienced senior midshipman. An able man, Skene had served for three years under Admiral Hood and he too looked for a new operational appointment. Before sailing for Trincomalee, the Admiral transferred his pennant to HMS Clorinde and petty officers were moved between the two ships. Taking grateful leave of Captain Briggs, Clapperton reported on board HMS Illustrious on 28 February. His new appointment constituted an important step upwards in authority and responsibility. *Illustrious* was a First Rate ship-of-the-line. Armed with seventy-four guns and carrying a crew of five hundred and ninety men, she was much larger and more powerful than the frigates on which Clapperton had hitherto seen service. She was familiar to him from her flagship role in the Indian Ocean, and her serving captain was already known to him through Thomas Briggs.

One month later *Illustrious* began her return home with a voyage to Madras, sailing in company with *Clorinde* as far as Trincomalee where they learnt that an epidemic had already killed a quarter of the town's population and one hundred members of the garrison. As Frank Mackenzie's health had singularly failed to improve, Hood ordered his young brother-in-law's release from the Royal Navy and put him aboard *Illustrious* for the passage to Madras to be cared for by relatives and family friends on shore. Clapperton had looked after Frank on board but, having seen him safely ashore in Madras, never set eyes on his friend again. (The poor invalid lingered for six months, dying in November 1813. Messages were sent to home to Scotland; and in his last days, Frank had spoken of the friendship and kindness he had received from his former messmate, entreating 'his relations, and especially his mother, to discharge the debt of gratitude which he owed him by treating him as a son, in requittal of his having, so long as he had it in his power, treated him as a brother'.[5])

Sickness also took its toll aboard *Illustrious*. Two men had died on the passage round the coast and in Madras five others had to be sent into hospital on shore. To the great relief of all on board, the ship's turn-around was quickly accomplished and within a week Captain Skene had put to sea again, bound for home. Sailing conditions were good, though water rations had been reduced to five pints per man per day, and, with only brief calls at the island garrisons, Skene hurried west – there was not a moment to lose. From the Cape of Good Hope, where she embarked prisoners from a captured American whaler, *Illustrious* made for St Helena, the Navy's largest transhipment centre in the southern Atlantic, to lead a convoy back to Britain. There was much for her officers to do, readying ships and men for the voyage. Sailors considered too ill to stand the passage were put on shore; and supplies of bread and strong beer were obtained for the remainder. Fresh stores, including lemons, onions and wine from South Africa, were taken on and decks and yards smartened up since there were ceremonial duties to perform, with receptions on board and great gun salutes, before HMS *Illustrious*, with fourteen sail in company, weighed anchor on 31 August.

The master's mate on the ship conducting the convoy of over a dozen vessels on ocean passage had hardly a moment to himself; constant vigilance was required if they were not to lose the slower, less agile participants. On one occasion in mid-Atlantic, in ever increasing winds, *Illustrious* had to take in tow a distressed south sea whaler; Clapperton had charge of the operation, a difficult and dangerous manoeuvre for all involved even had the sea been calm and the weather mild. Eventually, on 31 October 1813, in moderate gales and squalls, HMS *Illustrious* bowled past the Lizard and up the Channel. Ships left the convoy at Portsmouth; prisoners were discharged and supernumeraries taken on at the Downs. Captain Skene then sailed back to Spithead and at the end of November, seven months after leaving Bombay, finally brought *Illustrious* alongside the quay at Portsmouth. Midshipman Clapperton was once more at their Lordships' disposal.

On return home, Alexander Skene was appointed flag captain to Vice-Admiral Sir Alexander Cochrane, lately made commander-in-chief of the North Atlantic station, and given command of the flagship, HMS *Asia*, shortly to be deployed to Bermuda. Skene entered Clapperton's name for the Atlantic fleet and the young petty officer was happy to be asked to accompany him to the new front, where undoubtedly lay the best prospects of action, promotion and eventual command.

Meanwhile, Skene had Clapperton detached on two months' training duties at the Portsmouth dockyard, one of a handful of promising junior officers to be instructed in a modern form of cutlass drill, following which they would pass on their skills to trainers on board other ships. It was a rather curious initiative at a time when the real need was for investment in improving the fleet's naval architecture and gunnery, both of which were being rapidly overtaken by innovations in the American navy. In London, however, proficiency in arms was still measured against the expertise of the French military, and doubts had been expressed about the quality of British naval swordsmanship. Such concern was hardly shared by the squadrons operating around the world (and certainly not by Hugh Clapperton), but the Admiralty felt obliged to do something; they therefore hired Harry Angelo, a London sword-master, to set the Royal Navy to rights.

Maître Angelo's methods as an instructor were well known to the armed services and to Whitehall and his fencing skills were much lauded by fashionable society. His drills, however, proved more effective as gymnastic exercises than as preparation for battle. There existed a fundamental flaw. The British forces used a cutlass of the broadsword type – an instrument of percussion – as did the armed forces of all other nations; no one used the point. Angelo was a past-master with the stick, but a single stick was of little use against the shock tactics of a charging cavalryman or dragoon, let alone a roaring, rampaging sailor. Nevertheless, Angelo was sent to Portsmouth to set up the new programme (and indeed held the post of instructor there for many years). Clapperton spent two months learning the moves and exercising with the master himself. There was no time for home leave in Scotland.

At the end of January 1814 he received his orders; he was posted to the Great Lakes of Canada to join HMS *Montreal* as master's mate under Captain George Downie, senior captain on the Lakes and second in command to the commodore. War with the United States had reached a critical point and there was an urgent need for officers and men to man the new ships being built that winter. Over the past eighteen months, on land and at sea, Britain and her allies had been up against an aggressive and impressive enemy, and they were severely outnumbered. For Americans, the conflict constituted a second War of Independence; for the Canadians it boiled down to a simple matter of survival.

At the end of 1813, freed from military commitments in Europe, Britain was at last in a position to send substantial and experienced troops to the land war fronts in Canada. At the same time the Admiralty reorganized the Atlantic station, creating as separate commands a northern and a southern station on the Atlantic seaboard, with a third on the Great Lakes. Royal Navy flotillas on the Lakes were tasked with providing support for the land forces, and the Atlantic squadrons were ordered to tie up America's ships in diversionary operations on the eastern and southern seaboards.

Hugh Clapperton was entered as a supernumerary on HMS *Asia* for a passage to join his new ship on Lake Ontario. Alexander Skene immediately set him to work as cutlass drill-master on the flagship, charged with passing on his skills to the ship's junior officers and marines. According to Archibald Blacklock, assistant surgeon on board *Asia* (who also hailed from Dumfriesshire), the burly Clapperton proved a diligent and very effective instructor; his appearance on the quarterdeck fixed the attention of all the crew: standing five feet eleven inches tall, having great breadth of chest and expansion of shoulders, and otherwise proportionately strong, 'a handsome, athletic, powerful man'.[6]

Captain Skene, himself 'a beautiful musician'[7], enjoyed putting on social entertainments and Clapperton was an enthusiastic contributor, painting scenery for the ship's theatricals, sketching views and penning caricatures. He was said to be the life and soul of any party in the wardroom, an excellent table companion, known for his amusing tales and witty conversation. Blacklock recalled that one evening quantities of smoke were seen coming from the gunroom; the officers' quarters being positioned directly over the after magazine, the alarm was energetically sounded. While the crew raced to their muster stations, Clapperton remained seated at table, calmly finishing a cigar. The blaze having been extinguished, he was asked why he hadn't joined a fire-fighting party. He pointed out that as a supernumerary he had not been assigned a particular station; he had had no intention of getting in the way of those who knew what they were doing, and if the ship blew up – which had seemed to him very likely – it would not much have mattered where he was.

On arrival at Bermuda, headquarters of the Atlantic station, Clapperton held himself ready for a transfer to the Great Lakes. Another possibility arose, however; Captain Skene told Clapperton that Admiral Cochrane would be pleased to have him remain on *Asia*'s quarterdeck as flag lieutenant, an appointment offering the prospect of speedy receipt of his lieutenant's commission. But Clapperton was not to be tempted; his heart was set on earning his promotion in action, with the chance of eventual command of his own ship, however small. And so, on 17 April 1814, he set off on board HMS *Ramilies* (Sir Thomas Hardy), a seventy-four gunner carrying two hundred American prisoners of war and a number of refugee slaves, bound for Halifax.

Clapperton had last visited the port as an apprentice on board SS *Postlethwaite*; he found the atmosphere much altered. Halifax had been developed as the Royal Navy's principal base on the North American coast, and throughout the previous winter massive reinforcements of seamen, marines, artillery, equipment and stores had been arriving from Britain to be transported up the River St Lawrence the moment the thaw set in. Clapperton was given a passage, involving several changes of vessel, and five weeks later reached Kingston, the Royal Navy's headquarters establishment on the Great Lakes. It was indeed a new world.

Chapter 4: Canada 1814–1817
occurrences incidental to maritime life

The War of 1812 – Nottawasaga in winter
schooners on Lake Huron – survey and transport duties – a foolish design
a lieutenant's commission and command – demobilization

On arrival in Kingston in the summer of 1814, Clapperton found that the war against the United States was at a turning point. The campaigns of 1812 had resulted in a stalemate and both sides had used the winter to reorganize their land forces and strengthen their navies. When the Americans renewed their offensive in 1813, British forces, aided by an Indian militia, held off General Proctor's attacks in the west, and neither side obtained military advantage. American naval forces outgunned the British squadrons on lakes Erie and Ontario – and razed the poorly defended town of York to the ground (with unfortunate consequences for Washington two months later) – but failed to press home their advantage. In the east, their land command bungled an attack on Montreal, recalling their large armies less than fifty miles from the objective. And the British commander-in-chief, General Sir George Prevost, evinced equal incompetence in forfeiting the opportunity to take control of Lake Ontario, by ordering the fleet to withdraw from Sackett's Harbour just when victory in battle had been secured, and later by turning down Commodore Yeo's proposal for a pre-emptive strike over the ice the following winter. Control of the lake came only with Yeo's successful attack at Oswego Bay in May 1814.

At the British naval headquarters, however, morale was high. Kingston itself was growing rapidly in both size and importance, its civil and military population urgently engaged in construction-programmes, port improvements, shipbuilding and the necessarily hurried turn-around of stores and men. An army of eleven thousand regular troops, veterans of the Spanish Peninsular War, was set to advance southwards into New York State and, determined to deal once and for all with any further opposition at sea, the Royal Navy was about to launch several well-equipped new ships on Ontario and Erie, including the 112-gun three-decker *St Lawrence*, twice as large as any American armed vessel afloat on the Great Lakes.

Hugh Clapperton reported aboard HMS *Montreal*, flagship of the squadron on Lake Ontario; her Scottish commanding officer,

Captain George Downie, had arrived on station earlier the same year and had already earned an enviable reputation. *Montreal* sailed at the beginning of July, her squadron ordered to hold the remainder of the American fleet in check and prevent any interference with the transport of men and supplies round the lake. With a complement of two hundred and forty men, she was one of the largest ships on the Lakes, and had recently been upgraded and re-equipped. Manoeuvrability had been considerably improved by the alteration of her heavy brigantine rig to fore-and-aft rigging; and her short-range weapons, of little use the previous year against the lighter, faster American lake schooners, had been replaced by six long 24-pounders and twelve 18-pounders.

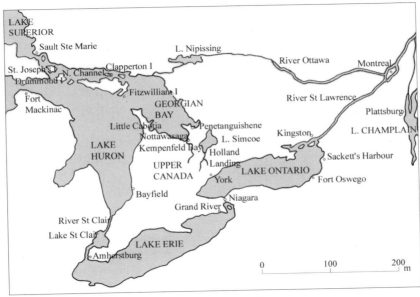

Map 1 The Great Lakes of Canada 1814-1817

Montreal took up station on the southern shores of the lake but to the frustration of the squadron in general – and of *Montreal*'s master's mate in particular – the American navy made no attempt to break out. And while Clapperton was settling into his berth, George Downie was recalled to assume command of the squadron on Lake Champlain. Clapperton remained on board *Montreal* on blockade duty until September, when the successful land campaign in the east effectively brought armed hostilities in North America to an end – although the Royal Navy had suffered an unnecessary defeat on Lake Champlain when Prevost compelled Downie to go into action before his ships were ready for sea and in the face of adverse wind and approach – Downie was killed in the fighting.

At Kingston, meanwhile, Yeo had launched his new 112-gun leviathan and there were other powerful ships on the stocks. The US Navy knew better than to take on such a formidable foe, and hostilities on Lake Ontario came to a close. The Royal Navy was underemployed, and in the autumn *Montreal* was relegated to transport duties (primarily the translocation of men), tasks that offered Clapperton neither excitement nor satisfaction. Transporting troops on small ships of war was justly unpopular with both services but particularly with naval officers, for there was insufficient room below to permit their usual mess accommodation and on deck crews were cramped for space to sail their ships and fight their guns.

The war might well be over but the peace had yet to be won. Having made safe Canada's southern boundaries, the British had still to secure the west where for years they had suffered persistent interference from the Americans. Commodore Yeo was keen to strengthen the fleet on the Upper Lakes (above Niagara), especially on Lake Huron where in August 1814 the Royal Navy had very nearly forfeited control. He decided to dispatch military units to take over transport operations on the overland trail to Georgian Bay, and to make a start on the construction of a naval dockyard at the sheltered, deep-water harbour at Penetanguishene, where a new 36-gun frigate was to be built as the nucleus of an expanded flotilla on Lake Huron. In the meantime, a small naval detachment was to be posted to the makeshift harbour at Nottawasaga to re-build a damaged blockhouse and to guard throughout the winter the Navy's only vessels on the lake, the schooners *Confiance* and *Surprize*. Yeo obtained approval from the Secretary of State for War and the Admiralty for release of men and resources, and put Captain Edward Collier in command of combined operations on the western front. And in November 1814 Hugh Clapperton joined a one thousand-strong pioneer force on the western rim of British-occupied Canada, a vast, uncharted and unbounded region where water provided the only means of communication, transportation and supply.

In the winter round of deployments, Clapperton was appointed acting lieutenant and second in command of HMS *Confiance* on Lake Huron, the appointment to take effect from February 1815. Meanwhile he was posted to join Captain Collier on HMS *Niagara* at York, where his main task was to supervise her complement of gunners, shipwrights, carpenters and boatmen in the dismantling of HMS *Princess Charlotte*, an ageing frigate laid up in ordinary; her spars, sails, rigging and fittings, her great guns weighing two tons, the massive iron capstans and anchors and her stores had all to be made ready for transportation overland to Georgian Bay to fit out the new frigate. By the end of January 1815 preparations were well advanced and Collier travelled to Penetanguishene to oversee progress there, dispatching Clapperton to inspect the small depot and the two schooners at Nottawasaga.

Mid-winter travel in a region habitually receiving some of the heaviest snowfalls on the continent was a gruelling business. The road the sappers were working so hard to improve remained little better than an ill-defined forest track, quite impassable by horse-drawn sleigh, the customary mode of transport between the bases around the wintry shores of Lake Ontario, and Clapperton and his men set out on foot, hauling their own sledges. Once arrived on Lake Simcoe, however, the going was a little easier, the ice having set, and Clapperton put up overnight in a recently erected log-house at the small depot of Kempenfeld Bay where he found the supply teams charged with bringing up the heavy equipment for the new frigate effectively stranded and in a very bad way (their oxen starving, food stores low and long since out of rum). From Kempenfeld Bay they trudged the nine miles of narrow Indian trails to the Nottawasaga River at Willow Creek, and there they bivouacked in makeshift staging-huts built of spruce boughs, bark and buffalo hide, lit a large fire and once again lay down in their day-clothes to sleep.

Collier's men in Upper Canada were breaking new ground. Canadian settlers had yet to penetrate the region in any numbers, earlier attempts to open trading posts to serve the remote bases and the Huron Indian market having been abandoned during the war. At Nottawasaga there was only the naval blockhouse, where the guard detachment had been subsisting in wretched conditions, pinned down by huge snowfalls, their food supplies virtually used up; the lake's ice-bound shore offering neither protection nor sustenance, Clapperton decided to take them back to Lake Simcoe as soon as possible.

They waited four days for the snowstorms to abate and then started out, having breakfasted on one biscuit apiece. Some two miles from the blockhouse, exhaustion overtook a ship's boy in their party; according to the storekeeper, Jacob Gill, the others gathered round, their anxiety and desire to help the lad manage even short distances deflecting their minds from their own plight.[1] Having stumbled another ten or twelve miles through a blizzard, the youngster declared he could go no further; but their entire provisions consisted of one bag of meal, and Clapperton knew that they must keep on the move and reach Kempenfeld Bay with the shortest possible delay. The guard were too numbed with cold to help, so Clapperton hoisted the boy onto his back, holding him there with his left hand and supporting himself with a stout pole in his right. In that manner he had covered another eight or nine miles when he sensed his charge relaxing his hold; the poor boy was dying and soon after breathed his last. Clapperton urged on the remainder as fast as ever they could go, over Lake Simcoe and back to York, in the bitter cold for which they were so woefully equipped, stockings and shoes completely worn off their feet, bodies emaciated from lack of food. Clapperton himself escaped lightly, frostbite affecting only the first joint of his left thumb, 'which ever after continued crooked, and on that account was called "Hooky", both by himself and his friends'.[2]

Back at York, he had returned to supervisory duties on board *Niagara* when reports arrived of the formal declaration in Ghent on Christmas Eve 1814 of a truce between Britain and the United States. Celebrations were in order but for Hugh Clapperton they were tinged with anxiety over his career prospects; he may well have recalled somewhat ruefully his refusal of the proffered staff appointment on Admiral Cochrane's quarterdeck. Colleagues and friends were also inclined to melancholy reflection, one observing that the report 'threw a damper on my spirits'.[3] Their fears were groundless, however; the high command in Kingston intended to maintain the Great Lakes squadrons on a fully operational footing during the post-war negotiations on borders and armament.

On 1 March 1815, General Sir Gordon Drummond, whose small force of British regulars turned the tide of battle at Lundy's Lane in 1813 when American forces had threatened to break through into Upper Canada from the Niagara Peninsular, took over as governor and commander-in-chief (the inept Prevost returned to England in disgrace); and on 20 March a new naval commander, Sir Edward Owen, arrived to replace Sir James Yeo. Captain Owen embarked immediately on a thoroughgoing reassessment of the Royal Navy's Canadian assets, ably assisted by two deputies – the popular commissioner in charge of shore establishments, Captain Robert Hall, and Edward's own younger brother, Captain William

Fitzwilliam Owen, who arrived in April with a brief to review the Navy's sea-going operations; appointed Chief Hydrographer to the fleet, William Owen effectively acted as his brother's second in command.

On receipt of Collier's report that it would take a good eighteen months to move the heavy material overland from York to Pene-tanguishene, Sir Edward Owen decided to cancel the project to build the new frigate and instead to reinforce existing depots.[4] Nottawasaga would serve as the Royal Navy's principal base on Lake Huron. Two new schooners were to be constructed at the dockyards on Lake Erie and, meanwhile, *Confiance* and *Surprize* – the two schooners captured from the Americans the previous year – were to be made ready to move troops and supplies up to Fort Mackinac and St Joseph's Island as soon as the ice melted.

Hugh Clapperton received confirmation of his own posting as acting lieutenant and first officer on HM Schooner *Confiance*, and on 20 March was ordered back to Nottawasaga to get her ready for sea. Before leaving York, however, he sent his acting orders from Sir Edward Owen to his uncle Samuel in London, to have them laid before the Board of Admiralty as a basis for confirmation of his lieutenant's commission.

The journey to Georgian Bay in late March was weary work. The first thaw had turned the trail to a quagmire and storms had brought down trees all over the track; and surface ice on the rivers and lakes melted during the day and closed over again at night, making for treacherous travelling conditions. At Holland Landing Clapperton and his men were provisioned for the journey over the ice to Kempenfeld Bay with just two days' food supplies and two blankets each. They halted for the night in a newly-built log cabin, 'a sort of public house'[5] where a good fire helped the travellers to dry out; but after the night's deep frost, the ice next morning was so glassy smooth that they had to cut up their precious blankets to make wrappers for their shoes to gain a better purchase. From the Kempenfeld depot, Clapperton pressed on to Nottawasaga.

Winter still held Nottawasaga in its grip. Clapperton and other newly arrived officers took up quarters as best they could in a number of barely habitable new log-houses scattered around the depot. There were few activities on which *Confiance*'s complement of two dozen sailors could be gainfully employed; the ground was too hard for construction work, and preparation of the schooners was out of the question. Parties of men were endlessly engaged in breaking up the ice at the bar and clearing the river of sunken logs. And when work on the schooners could eventually begin, they were found to have suffered severely from lack of attention throughout the winter: decks leaked, rigging had rotted and, with no canvas available, serviceable sails had somehow to be contrived.

Provisions were in short supply; hard tack, flour, beef and pork and other basic stores had to be hauled along the rutted track from Holland River and luxuries such as butter, sugar and peas, cheese, chocolate, coffee and tobacco were nigh impossible to come by. Beer and wine were unavailable, and rum rations had to be docked from the men's pay – they learned to distil a maple-leaf spirit instead but, thin and mean, it was thought a very poor substitute. Clapperton's was a tough and unruly crew. A number of the men had been pressed from the towns around Lake Ontario and service in the Royal Navy in peacetime held little appeal; discipline was not easily imposed and only the remoteness and the inhospitable climate prevented desertions. Not only was there nowhere to go beyond the establishment, there were no regular pay-days either (pay was brought up from Kingston only twice a year).

Officers and men learned to fish through holes cut in the ice. To vary the diet Clapperton went out to hunt for game, or exchanged pork and ship's biscuit for wild duck and sugar brought in by Indian families subsisting by tapping the maple forests behind the depot. As the weather warmed, it was his practice to have the ice broken daily on a small pool in which he could bathe; it became known as Clapperton's bath. Entertainments were few and simple – by day, competitive tree felling, snow-shoe racing and snowball battles, and in the evenings whist and talk and drink, with the outside possibility of getting down to Holland Landing to visit the establishment's mess or the small hostelry there.

When the new sailing season began, command of *Confiance* was taken over by Lieutenant Miller Worsley, an officer already celebrated for his actions on the lake the previous summer when he defended his ship the *Nancy* against attack by three American schooners; he had had to scuttle her in the Nottawasaga River, but then had his revenge when he subsequently carried two of the American schooners in a daring boat raid. And a remarkably able eighteen-year-old, Lieutenant David Wingfield, who had already spent nine months as a prisoner of the Americans, was confirmed in command of *Surprize*. Operating in tandem out of Nottawasaga, the two single-deck, seventy-foot schooners embarked on a series of passages moving supplies to Fort Mackinac, a journey of three hundred miles. *Confiance* turned out to be a less than satisfactory ship, slow and awkward to manoeuvre; to afford more working room on deck Clapperton and Worsley dismounted the 24-pounder swivel gun, returning unwanted powder kegs to York.

Owen's pioneering force laboured long and hard. The narrow inlet at Nottawasaga offered no shelter from the north-westerlies and either the ships had to be hauled over the bar into the river (planks were damaged and rudders and pintles were broken) or the stores had to be loaded onto bateaux and put on board the schooners well offshore. Storms continued into May, sometimes bringing freezing rain which caused the running gear to ice up dangerously on contact; but following the almost overnight transformation from spring to summer, day-to-day conditions became increasingly easy.

They lived off excellent lake fish, bass and trout weighing up to thirty and forty pounds, experimenting with different methods of cooking them other than in salt pork fat in the old kettle lid that served as a frying pan. If they ran low on biscuit and meat, there were partridge and waterfowl, bear cubs and racoons to add to the pot, and cherries and other berries from the woods for those prepared to brave sand-flies, mosquitoes and venomous snakes. They planted sweet potatoes and learnt to make maple syrup; and on Michilimackinac they shot pigeons (migrating in their millions over the land point). Clapperton took his turn leading the regular runs down the improved trail to Holland Landing, and sometimes to York, to collect supplies; and for purposes of recruiting labour he had regular dealings with the Indian communities at the lake establishments. While those calling at St Joseph's Island from the interior were generally liked and admired, the Indians resident at Nottawasaga were not so agreeable; they proved less amenable, presenting themselves for duty as guides and labourers only when it suited their pleasure or convenience.

By June it was evident to the British naval command that under the proposed treaty arrangements Fort Mackinac would be handed back to the Americans, so *Confiance* and *Surprize* were detailed to move men and stores from Lake Erie to the site identified for a new base on nearby Drummond Island. Clapperton's unwieldy vessel was worked hard; she often had to be winched over the bar at the St Clair River, requiring regular heaving down for caulkers and carpenters to come at leaking seams. The monotony of their tasks dulled the men's spirits, and the constant delays and the tedium of compiling seemingly endless inventories of stores were trying for *Confiance*'s officers.

Twelve months from Clapperton's arrival on the Great Lakes there was still no word of his long-awaited lieutenant's commission; but in July his optimism was rekindled when Captain William Owen appeared on Lake Erie to survey the Navy's assets on the Upper Lakes, and repaired on board *Confiance* to put her through sailing trials. As second in command, Clapperton was actively involved in all aspects of the assessment, and he discovered much common ground with Captain Owen. William Owen, 'a beloved despot'[6], pompous but brilliant and never afraid to speak his mind, was an ardent admirer of Nelson, a stickler for rules and deeply committed to the Royal Navy. After service in the Mediterranean he had embarked on a career in hydrography and exploration in the East Indies. He later joined Sir Edward Pellew's squadron campaigning against the French, and in 1808 had been captured and held prisoner on Mauritius until the island's relief in 1810 in the action in which Clapperton had participated. Owen had also remained in the east until 1813.

William Owen shared her officers' low opinion of *Confiance*'s sailing capabilities, 'making no way whatever by working against even the most favourable breeze'[7]; in his view both *Confiance* and *Surprize* were most unsatisfactory acquisitions, and he therefore recommended to his brother that two better designed and more capacious schooners should be built immediately and added to the fleet. He remained on *Confiance* long enough to reconnoitre Lake Erie's northern coastline for likely harbour sites, a voyage affording Clapperton both an important introduction to survey work and a welcome opportunity to press his case for preferment and his lieutenant's commission in higher quarters.

William Owen reappeared in September and sailed again on *Confiance*, accompanying his brother Sir Edward on a tour of inspection of the Huron establishments; he remained on board for a further two months, accompanied by two young nautical surveyors from Kingston, to chart the coast and islands of southern Georgian Bay, and Clapperton found himself recruited to the task. In October, when Owen was inspecting the broad and sheltered bays on the coast of Little Cabotia (Bruce Peninsular), Clapperton was sent to examine the Great Sound of Nameyquitong (Sturgeon Sound); and the following month, when Owen needed extra help to survey the rocky coastline from Christian Island to Nottawasaga, he 'sent Mr. Hugh Clapperton, Mate of the Confiance, with Mr. Aldersley, Quarterman of the Shipwrights, in a boat first into the bay in the main opposite the Beckwith Isles and thence into Christian Bay from which to coast the bay of Nottawasaga to the river... On the 15th A.M. the boat returned and brought me very good sketches of the bays and coasts examined by the above named officers.'[8] *Confiance*'s first officer had favourably impressed the influential visitor; and, on leaving Georgian Bay to return to Kingston at the end of November, William Owen promised to help promote Hugh Clapperton's cause in the matter of his delayed commission.

Clapperton returned to the painstaking business of preparing the shore bases for the winter. In September he was loaned for two months to HMS *Huron* (sent up from Lake Erie) to collect and deliver parties of naval carpenters and shipwrights and an Indian interpreter to the construction projects at Penetanguishene and Drummond Island. By the end of October, however, the level of water on the lake had fallen to the point where it created problems for loading operations at Nottawasaga, with corresponding risks to vessels at the bar. The sailing season was over and the officers dispersed to winter quarters.

When in November Sir Edward Owen was recalled to London, his patent withdrawn given the unlikelihood of any resumption of hostilities, his brother became the acting commander of all naval vessels on the Great Lakes. New orders went out to the fleet, and Captain William Owen sent for Hugh Clapperton to be second in command of HMS *Star*, a brig placed at Owen's personal disposal and based at Kingston. While awaiting further news from London, Owen resolved to seize advantage of the later arrival of winter further south to continue the survey of Lake Ontario, intending to sail with *Star* whenever he could to supervise the work personally. Clapperton joined her on 9 November 1815 and went straight to sea as second officer and acting lieutenant.

Star was a sturdy vessel three times the size of HMS *Confiance*, well-equipped, pierced for fourteen guns and carrying a crew of seventy-five men and a contingent of thirty-five marines. Hugh Clapperton found himself part of a team of gifted officers whom Owen, unwilling to wait for trained hydrographers to arrive from England, had recruited locally – lieutenants Alexander Becher, Emerich Vidal and Henry Bayfield, and John Harris, master. Ashore they messed together at Hydrography House, Harris's wife doing the cooking and cleaning; and in their spare time Vidal, Harris and Bayfield walked and sketched in the environs of Kingston, while Owen made notes on birds he had seen during survey work.

Kingston offered junior naval officers all manner of agreeable entertainment. They shot game in the woods, kept pets, cultivated garden- and house-plants, and attended evening backgammon and whist parties and many a formal dance at the houses of the well-to-do. Rowdier amusement was to be found in the town's many taverns and hostelries. According to Bayfield, the small group of survey officers formed a very close-knit community and kept in touch for many years; he recalled 'the winter of 1816, with all its labours, as the happiest of my life'.[9]

Clapperton would surely have agreed. For him the end of that same winter saw the fulfilment of one of his dearest ambitions, his first command, even if with only acting rank. On 28 May 1816, he returned to Lake Huron to go on board HMS *Surprize*, 'Lieutenant and Commander'.

The easy camaraderie among the young naval officers on the Lake exactly suited Hugh Clapperton. HMS *Sauk*'s commander, The Honourable Adam Gordon, was also a Dumfriesshire man and, like Clapperton, had served before the mast from 1804 to 1809 in the Mediterranean (where he had been taken prisoner). He had arrived on the Lakes as a midshipman three months before Clapperton and, rather better connected back home, had been promoted acting lieutenant in April 1815 and confirmed in July of the same year. Lieutenant Henry Kent from Lanarkshire, another companion from the previous year, was also present, currently commanding the newly-built schooner *Tecumseth*. And a particular friend of Clapperton's was the surgeon of *Tecumseth*, James Kay, who hailed from Edinburgh and who had arrived on the Upper Lakes in 1815. They had first come across each other at an officers' party ashore; on that occasion, taking Kay for a new recruit, Clapperton had lectured him in the ways of the Royal Navy and the importance of keeping up appearances, jokingly decorating him with a watch ribbon. Already of considerable standing in the service, Kay had taken the jest in good part, cheerfully accepting Clapperton's apologies when the latter was apprised of his error.

In 1816 the spring thaw was late, and at the end of May the lake was still covered with ice for several miles from the shore. There was much to be done to make good the depredations of the winter. Equipment sent from Kingston had arrived damaged; the depot was littered with ordnance destined for Drummond Island; a flotilla of small boats (eight bateaux, a skiff, a jolly boat and several gigs) had to be readied for work in the bay and several overland journeys were necessary to collect supplies from York.

In the summer of 1816, aged twenty-eight, self-confident and answerable directly to no one at the lake, Hugh Clapperton rather cut loose. He was constantly on the go, and liked to row himself back to the ship to see if he could surprise the watch. After dining on shore he customarily swam back to *Surprize* (fully dressed) rather than call for a ferry, a practice which, according to Adam Gordon, nearly cost him his life when an unexpectedly strong current took him well past his ship; he was unable to bear up against the stream but fortunately his cries were heard by men on board *Sauk* who launched a boat to pick him up. Clapperton was forming his own style of command; he rarely ordered floggings, resorting instead to withholding grog as a means of punishment. With no prospect of armed action ahead, and faced with demobilization once the treaties were confirmed, he increasingly followed his own inclinations and pursuits. And the absence of confirmation of his commission had begun to rankle (the submission forwarded to the Admiralty by his uncle had been declined because a large promotion had just gone through). The apparent lack of official appreciation allied to a tendency to see himself as above the law conspired to land him in hot water with the authorities in Kingston.

Clapperton had made a point of cultivating acquaintanceships outside as well as within the naval establishment. According to his friends, he adopted the Huron badge, and very nearly married an Indian princess; whatever the truth of the matter, he had many Indian friends and was undoubtedly a ladies' man. Passionately interested in hunting and always on the lookout for adventure, he made rather a fuss of the local Indian community, exploiting the availability at the depot of so-called Indian presents – merchant goods deployed by the Indian Department as currency, fees and gifts at administrative posts around Lake Huron. Ever adaptable, innately generous, blithely careless with money (his own as well as other people's), he interpreted the system very freely, lavishing supplies and presents on those chiefs whose company he enjoyed, treating them to feasts and entertaining them by firing off rockets. The extent of his extravagances, however, led to a deficiency in his accounting to the Victualling Department, in repayment of which regular instalments were still being deducted from Clapperton's half-pay after demobilization in 1817.

Friends and relatives later maintained that Hugh Clapperton had entertained the 'romantic and foolish design'[10] of quitting his naval career to settle down in Upper Canada. Such a possibility must have crossed his mind. Staying on to turn backwoodsman was a real option, one which a number of his colleagues including his squadron commander, Captain Edward Bouchier, were actively considering and later acted upon; and Clapperton undoubtedly possessed the necessary aptitudes.

Opportunities for civilians to make a good living on the shores of Georgian Bay were on the increase. A small but growing number of traders and adventurers, together with Indian merchants and chiefs, had made it their business to develop good relations with the commanding officers at the new British bases. On Lake Huron's shores, the would-be pioneers had been joined by a handful of people, among them a fair number of Scots, formerly employed by the Northwest Company or attached to the garrisons at Mackinac and St Joseph's Island, and one or two enterprising veterans of the military campaigns in Niagara. They had begun to settle down and form a local community, and not a few had married Huron girls. A prominent personage at that time was Mrs Johnstone, wife of the tavern keeper Thomas Johnstone. She was the first European woman to settle in the region and had run a flourishing business in canteen supplies (principally baker's goods and whisky) from her husband's tavern, first at Holland Landing and then later at Penetanguishene. The Johnstones were Freemasons; and in all likelihood Clapperton participated in the local lodge's activities – there were a number of lodges in the Royal Navy, and his family had a strong Masonic tradition.

During the course of the summer of 1816, however, command of *Surprize* and the cheerful company of his peers served to reinvigorate Hugh Clapperton's commitment to the Royal Navy. Even more encouraging was the assurance given him by Captain William Owen, who had asked to be transferred home in order to follow a scientific career and to participate in the formation of the Admiralty's Naval Surveying Service; Owen promised Clapperton he would personally take up with the Board the matter of the long delayed confirmation of promotion.

At the end of October, upon the hospitalization of her captain, Lieutenant John Kingcombe, Clapperton was ordered to assume command of HMS *Confiance* and take her down to Lake Erie for the winter. It proved an eventful passage. Autumnal gales were raging and *Confiance's* main mast split during a heavy squall on the way south. Water levels on the lakes and rivers were already critically low, so low that Clapperton had to have his ship hauled over the middle shoal of rapids at the entrance to the St Clair River. Then she grounded at the harbour bar, and anchors had to be put out and warps taken ashore to get her safely alongside a dock. Eventually the gales blew themselves out and a week later, with a new main mast and carrying fresh supplies, *Confiance* set sail for Mohawk Bay and the depot at Grand River.

Clapperton spent the month of November on a series of short passages between depots on Lake Erie, where the new commodore, Sir Robert Hall, came aboard for his first tour of inspection on the Upper Lakes. While access to a wide range of support facilities at the lake's shore establishments rendered practical command of *Confiance* relatively easy, the ship's proximity to urban life offered an already rebellious crew irresistible temptations – Kingcombe had been unwell for some time with a lingering fever, and the men had become increasingly unruly. There were several instances of serious drunken and riotous behaviour, some theft from the stores (punished by thirty lashes) and a number of desertions. Clapperton had to list and sign for those who ran, employing the traditional rubric (used of himself in HMS *Gibraltar*'s muster book in 1806 when he had swum from her to a privateer at Plymouth) 'In my opinion – deserves no relief'. Determined to brook no nonsense, he waded in, restoring the ship to her proper condition and her crew to their duty, *Confiance* soon becoming 'proverbial for its good order as it had hitherto been for its irregularities'.[11]

At the end of that month he handed over his command to Captain Daniel Pring, a former squadron commander on Lake Champlain, remaining on board as second in command to oversee the winter refit. All hands were employed in heaving down the schooners; parties of men were engaged in picking oakum, and others were employed on the construction of Durham boats (small work-boats for the establishment). Once repairs on board had been completed, the ship's carpenters were dispatched to naval establishments along the coast to work on the many building projects in train.

Meanwhile, in London, William Owen had been every bit as good as his word; between them, the Owen brothers had stirred the Admiralty Board into action. In February 1817, four years after passing the examinations, Hugh Clapperton at long last received official news of his gazetted commission. He had been confirmed lieutenant for rank in the December of 1816 and the promotion had been formally backdated to 20 March 1815, the date on which he had been appointed acting lieutenant on board HMS *Confiance*. And the welcome intelligence had reached him in the very nick of time.

The treaties between Britain and the United States had been completed and in March 1817 the British naval high command in

Kingston was awaiting only the final detail of the arms limitation arrangements. And at the beginning of May orders arrived from London regarding the decommissioning of the flotillas on the Great Lakes: by 30 June 1817 the majority of the bases were to be closed, and the fleet put in ordinary. Under the listing of assets agreed, the naval forces of Britain and America were confined to one vessel each, not exceeding one hundred tons and armed with one cannon, on Lake Ontario; to two such vessels on the Upper Lakes, and another on Lake Champlain. The vessels were described as having the role of guardians of the main, a sinecure involving only the occasional guard duty, their principal task being transportation. All other craft were to be dismantled and no new armed vessels built. The Royal Navy's sole shore establishment on Lake Huron would be located at Penetanguishene.

HM Schooner *Tecumseth*

In the spring deployments, Lieutenant Hugh Clapperton RN was assigned to serve with Captain Collier and in May 1817 he accompanied the squadron commander on board HMS *Tecumseth,* bound for Nottawasaga. Clapperton sailed as First Lieutenant, Henry Kent had the command and James Kay continued as the surgeon on the Navy's finest schooner, its designated vessel on the Upper Lakes. Constructed of best Ontario oak, *Tecumseth* was the apotheosis of the armed lake schooner, an elegant pocket battleship intended to outperform the American schooners whose long-range cannon had so comprehensively defeated the British in 1813. Fore-and-aft rigged, she carried a massive sail area for her size, and she was armed with two long 24-pounders on circular stands with a shower arc of 300° and a range of two miles, and two 32-pounder carronades designed for smashing at ranges of up to one mile.

Nottawasaga itself was a hive of activity as the fleet prepared to shut down the base and move all its equipment and stores to Penetanguishene. The first parties of sailors were taken back to Lake Erie for a passage home and a number of men ran, preferring the uncertain life of a backwoodsman to unpaid demobilization in England. In June, after a passage to Drummond Island, Clapperton assisted in the final closure of the depot which he had first visited on foot in the depth of winter two and a half years previously. And on 27 June *Tecumseth* sailed from Nottawasaga for the last time, carrying timber and planking and the remaining seventy-eight men to be redeployed to the new garrison. Half the naval complement on the Upper Lakes had already taken passage for Kingston, bound for England; and Hugh Clapperton had received his own orders to return home. The Captain's log records, '28 June. AM Light Breezes and cloudy with small rain at times. Day light saw H.M.S. <u>Surprize</u> and discharged Lieut. Clapperton to her for a passage to Grand River.'

Fittingly, Hugh Clapperton's last passage on Lake Huron was made on board HMS *Surprize*, the ship which had been his first command. She sailed for Lake Erie later that day, in company with *Tecumseth*, neither schooner carrying equipment, supplies or even ballast, just officers and sailors homeward bound at the end of a long and arduous tour of duty. When *Surprize* entered the bar of the St Clair River, at 3 p.m. on 30th June 1817 in six foot of water, Clapperton bade a final farewell to Lake Huron.[†]

[†] Working his way round the islands (34,500 of them excluding 'rocks without verdure'), bays and passages of Lake Huron in a series of surveys carried out between 1817 and 1824, Henry Bayfield named many after old friends in the squadron and others whom he wished to honour: Fitzwilliam Island and Yeo Island are situated off the southern tip of Manitoulin Island, Point Wingfield is to be found in Cabot Bay, and Owen Sound, Melville Sound and Barrow Bay on Bruce Peninsular; in North Channel, by Manitoulin Island, lie Bayfield Sound, Vidal Island and Elizabeth Island (named after Betty, Bayfield's mistress in Kingston). And adjacent to Elizabeth Island is a long, low, forested island, inhabited today by one family which for three generations has farmed the land and manned the lighthouse: Clapperton Island.

In July, with James Kay and other companions from the Upper Lakes squadron, he continued the return journey, going on board HMS *Prevoyante* at Quebec for the passage to Britain, and on 27 August 1817 he reached Portsmouth where he was demobilized and placed on half-pay. And so he returned to Scotland, tried and tested in all conditions at sea, and secure in the knowledge that his lieutenant's commission had been well and dutifully earned,

Love of glory supports the energies drawn forth in battle; but fortitude is, perhaps, more truly and extensively tried in lingering blockades and pestilential climates, in the noise of many waters, and the darkness of the moonless gale; and, indeed, in most of the occurrences incidental to maritime life.[12]

Chapter 5: Scotland 1817–1821
a gentleman of excellent disposition

Return to Scotland on half-pay – rural pursuits in Lochmaben
Edinburgh and the natural sciences – Dr Walter Oudney
the exploration of Africa – John Barrow's projected expedition to Borno

On his return to Scotland in the autumn of 1817 Hugh Clapperton settled first in Edinburgh. He had been away for fifteen years and with the exception of an aunt at Thorniethwaite no close kin were left in Dumfriesshire.

Hugh's brother George had died in 1811, just three years after joining their father's medical practice, and George senior had followed him to the grave five years later. Brothers John and Alexander had died abroad – John, a lieutenant of Marines, fell on active service in the West Indies in 1804 and Alexander perished on the coast of West Africa after several years' service as a surgeon on a slave ship. Nor, as far as Hugh was aware, had William survived; William had qualified as a naval surgeon in 1804, serving in the combined fleet at Trafalgar. Nearest in age to Hugh, Charles had joined the Royal Marines and made his home in the south; he was based at Chatham, as was their uncle Samuel. And Margaret, who had earlier returned from Thorniethwaite to Annan to act as companion to the family of banker James Scott, had since gone to live in Edinburgh; she had not married.

Local families with whom Clapperton had been friendly as a boy had suffered similar losses and dispersals. One of the Dickson boys had died at sea and another, Thomas, having taken a degree in medicine, was working in the West Indies. The Irving brothers had also left home; John was serving as a medical officer in India, and Edward, who in 1815 had become a licensed preacher in Kirkcaldy, had gone to live in Ireland.

The transition to a civilian life ashore was not easy. The Royal Navy had suited Clapperton very well. It provided him with a satisfying career, and he had found what amounted to a replacement family, a close-knit community with well-defined rules, offering the comfortable camaraderie of like-minded colleagues. He would have given much for further deployment, especially to stations offering good prospects such as the expanded Africa squadron then engaged in operations aimed at wiping out the

Atlantic slave trade. Realistically, however, with Britain's armed services reduced to a tenth of their war-time strength, the chances of a recall to naval service were very slim. He had no wish to return to the merchant marine, nor had he the capital with which to buy his way into ownership in that sphere; and unfortunately, unlike his many acquaintances in the medical branch, he lacked any particular qualifications for a civilian career. Making the best of things, therefore, he took up lodgings with James Kay in a house in Edinburgh's Old Town and found his shore bearings quickly enough.

The Scottish capital's economy was healthy and its lively social atmosphere, the proximity of the busy naval base at Leith and the company of a group of friends and acquaintances with common backgrounds made life in Edinburgh an enjoyable prospect. James Kay introduced him to people with whom he had studied at the University there, of whom quite a number had taken their first career steps in the surgeons' branch of the Royal Navy. Several other colleagues from the Great Lakes squadrons were also in Edinburgh, together with a few whom Clapperton had known in the East Indies; and Francis Mackenzie's name cropped up again.

Frank Mackenzie's mother, the Dowager Countess Seaforth, was anxious to meet Hugh Clapperton, the last person to have known her son well and she had asked a cousin in the Navy, Lieutenant Granville Proby, for help in locating him. Proby tracked him down and told him that Countess Seaforth would like to see him and present him with some of Frank's personal possessions. Proby's rather patronizing approach jarred on Clapperton who responded ungraciously; but the Countess, who had recently lost her husband and two sons in a very short space of time[†], was not

---

[†] According to legend, the extinction of the line of Caber Feidhs, the traditional chiefs of the Clan Mackenzie, had been foretold in 1678 by the Highland seer Coinneach Odhar. Widely known in Scotland, the prophecy held that when a deaf and dumb Caber Feidh lived at the time of certain other great highland lairds – of whom one should be buck-toothed, another hare-lipped, a third half-witted and the fourth suffer from a stammer – his sons would predecease him, the chieftainship would go to another branch of the family and a white-coiffed girl from the east would inherit the lands. Lord Seaforth was deaf and had a speech impairment, the other figures described in the prophecy were easily recognizable, and of the Seaforths' four sons, two died at an early age. In 1814 news reached Brahan Castle of Frank Mackenzie's death in Madras, and later the same year the Seaforths' eldest son, William Frederick, recently elected to Parliament, suddenly fell ill and died. Lord Seaforth slipped into a decline and in January 1815 followed his sons to

to be denied. Determined to honour her youngest son's debt of friendship, she tried again and Clapperton, persuaded by James Kay to be more open and agreeable, called on her and became a not infrequent visitor to the family home. Though at first ill at ease in the drawing rooms of Edinburgh's New Town and wary of the fuss his would-be benefactress made of him, over the next three years he enjoyed a pleasant association with the Seaforths, a family of considerable influence in the Scottish capital. He became acquainted with Lady Mary Hood Mackenzie, Admiral Hood's widow, and her sister Caroline – who are said to have commiss-ioned Henry Raeburn to paint Clapperton's portrait – and with Henry Mackenzie, the grand old man of Scottish letters who had married another Seaforth daughter. Countess Seaforth tried to shower him with gifts and mementoes (Frank's books, gold watch, chain and seals), but he remained chary of becoming beholden to her and her family, mindful of the earlier shipboard accusations that his prime object was to exploit the connection.[1]

In Edinburgh, however, though his friends were moving on with their lives, he could find neither direction nor purpose. A dark, grey town, Auld Reekie in mid-winter could be a bleak and depressing place. Entertainment was expensive and he had great difficulty making ends meet on his half-pay (a modest enough amount in all conscience, and considerably reduced by deductions at source to cover his extravagances on Lake Huron). At the turn of the year Clapperton decided to retreat to Annandale, taking up an invitation from his maiden aunt at Thorniethwaite. Lochmaben offered a homely environment, cheap living, pleasant company and rural sports, and anyone in Dumfriesshire whose acquaintance he wished to renew would be within easy reach. A return to life in Annan town was never a serious alternative (he had no desire for further dealings with his step-mother or her children[2]) but the venerable Bryce Downie, now aged sixty and completely blind, still lived in his old school house and participated actively in the Burgh's Council, and Clapperton's most important patrons from his youth, the Dirom family and banker James Scott, were also there as were other old family friends, among them the Irvings and the Dicksons, and the Nelsons of Port Annan who were now engaged in building ships for the East Indies trade.

---

the grave; the chieftaincy passed to a remote cousin and the estates were inherited by the eldest daughter, Lady Mary Hood Mackenzie.

When Hugh Clapperton had selected Lochmaben over Annan, financial reasons were of course a major factor but his choice also represented the final break with the difficult years of boyhood; and after a long absence he would have found little common ground with the new generation in charge of the Burgh's affairs. The town of Lochmaben, however, held to old-fashioned ways; and the returned sailor was well known and welcome there. In childhood it had been his second home and his grandfather's memory was still warmly cherished (though the house had been sold by the family in 1813), even if few close relatives continued to live in the Burgh. None of his paternal uncles had stayed on in Lochmaben, and his mother's brother, John Johnstone, had fallen on active service in 1795. Of those Johnstone cousins who had also been tenants at Thorniethwaite, Clerk had died in 1803 and only one of his three children survived. Hugh's aunts had continued to live in the family home, the eldest, Martha, overseeing the estate until her death in 1815; the farmland was then let again and the family income allowed her surviving sister to remain there.

Hugh Clapperton was glad to take up residence in the comfortable house, though he was hardly a natural fit in such a sleepy backwater; but country life was above all affordable and he settled down to a round of rustic pursuits. There was good shooting and excellent fishing. Of the seasonal parish sports (quoits in summer and curling in the winter), curling held a traditional place close to the heart of most Clapperton men and Hugh had inherited one of Lochmaben's most famous stones, the Hen. A huge, speckled lump of granite, the Hen had been discovered in a cleugh (rocky ravine) at Thorniethwaite three-quarters of a century earlier and carried to the town in a plaid; it had been honed and polished for generations before coming into the possession of the Clapperton family. When the Hen settled on the ice she clocked, that is to say she could not be disturbed by even the severest blow from another stone; she was used in all parish spiels but never in away matches, out of fairness, it was claimed, to opposing teams.

Sir Richard Broun, local landowner and author of a memoir of curling in Lochmaben, recorded that the inexperienced Clapperton was an indifferent player; when the President of the Society first courteously invited him to join in a match, the playing skippers refused to start unless he and another naval novice were put out of the teams. Noticing Hugh standing aloof (his hands jammed into the pocket of his sailor's jacket and whistling loudly the while), the President attempted a conciliatory remark,

Upon this Clapperton, in an attitude of proud contempt, and pulled up to his height, advanced with the air and gait of the quarterdeck to a respectful distance; then throwing up his hand *a la mode navale* he demanded in a key different from his usual one, 'Am I to play today, Sir, or not?' – 'Certainly, Clapperton,' was the reply, 'You shall play if I play'. Upon which, making a salam with his hand, as if he had received the commands of his Admiral, he strided back to where his stone – (the Hen, which had belonged to his grandfather of antiquarian memory) – and besom lay and seizing upon the former with an air of triumph he whirled her repeatedly round his head, with as much ease apparently as if she had been nearer seven than to seventy pounds, He then placed her upon his shoulder and marched off to the loch.[3]

His team won and he himself 'played with his colossal granite some capital shots'. Broun records that all the Clapperton men were athletic players, particularly Hugh's uncle Sandy who had used the Hen because no other curler on the Lochmaben ice was able to, and Hugh lived up to the family name. On one occasion, 'whilst playing in a Bonspiel with Tinwald, being challenged by his Skip just whilst in the act of throwing the Hen, he actually held her in the air at arm's length, in the same position, until the orders countermanded were again repeated'.[4]

Again following family tradition, Clapperton joined the local Masonic Lodge. In 1777, the year after the Lodge's foundation, his grandfather Robert had been elected Grand Master, a position he held until his death. Hugh himself was passed into the Fellow Craft on 18 October 1818 and two weeks later was raised to the degree of Master Mason – an unusually rapid progression which probably related to attendance at meetings during active naval service – making appearances about once a quarter until October 1819. A number of retired armed service officers who had settled in the town were also Freemasons, among them Dr William Rae, a former naval surgeon two years older than Hugh Clapperton, and Royal Marine Captain William Ferguson, scion of a prominent Lochmaben family, who had retired on half-pay in 1814. William Rae had served in the East Indies and the Mediterranean and was now practising medicine in the Burgh; he had married a local girl, Margaret Bell, and was the father of a young family.

While Hugh went to some trouble to fit in with the more serious side of life in the town (he was one of the founding contributors to a new library, and even undertook studies in French) he didn't lack for informal entertainment – social gatherings and long nights filled with talk and drink. William Rae and his other friends no doubt introduced the belles of Lochmaben to Clapperton, who was probably viewed as quite a catch. The following year he was known to be pursuing one Martha Bell (one of Mrs Rae's relatives perhaps); the relationship progressed and at the turn of that year she announced her pregnancy. But Hugh, though he conceded paternity, had no intention of settling down.

In Lochmaben he was regarded as something of an oddity. The formalities and etiquette of country-town life did not sit so easily with a man accustomed to dropping in on friends without warning and at unsociable hours. Such mild eccentricity was symptomatic of Clapperton's intrinsic need for independence, within which, however, lay an essential paradox – it also mattered a good deal to him that he be recognized and cherished, and he really wanted to belong. Rejection of the love affair and the abrupt abandonment of Martha and their child (a son born on 24 June 1820 and named Duncan by his mother[5]) had no basis in the conventionalities and everything to do with a profound personal restlessness. However, failing a return to naval service, Hugh Clapperton could not have said what it was that he did want. He had accepted all that the town of Lochmaben had to offer, but in the end it was not enough. To a headstrong and self-centred thirty-two year-old, attuned to open horizons and adventure, the claustrophobia of middle-class rural society proved unendurable. He abruptly abandoned it all to return to the capital.

Back in Edinburgh at the end of 1819, Clapperton again took rooms with James Kay, at 47 Bristo Street on the fringes of the Old Town, an area of small streets and wynds offering cheap lodgings for new arrivals in the professions and students at university and medical school. Hugh's sister Margaret lived at Portobello and two cousins, Alexander and Thomas, were also resident in the city, both merchants and reasonably well connected in the banking and trading-house communities. But, while happy to associate with people from different walks of life, Clapperton was always most at ease among former shipmates and their particular circles.

Convivial evenings were habitually spent at John Barclay's Nelson Tavern in Adams Square, where steady drinking sessions and unruly merrymaking on occasion led to a confrontation with the law, which was not known for viewing sympathetically the commotions generated by beached naval officers, and Hugh was fortunate to have got out of one minor scrape with little more than an official wigging. Locked out of his lodgings in the early hours of the morning, he spotted a painter's ladder lying nearby and used it to climb in at his window; but when he threw the ladder down the noise attracted the attention of the night-watchman who called for reinforcements before investigating. Clapperton woke his landlord, imploring him to reassure the authorities that all was well and to send them away. The police, however, insisted on a thorough search and Clapperton jumped into bed, boots and all, feigning innocence. All might have been well had he not left his overcoat lying in a puddle of rainwater under the windowsill. He was accordingly marched to the police station – three men were needed to carry the ladder – but he 'got off on paying a trifling sum, and the housepainter was ordered to chain his ladder to the premises in future'.[6]

Constraints were indeed mainly fiscal. Received quarterly, Clapperton's half-pay disappeared in next to no time and he frequently had to turn to his friends to borrow money; according to Kay, he did so quite without embarrassment or shame, as if he were doing them a favour. When he himself had money he was always ready to respond sympathetically to an appeal. On one occasion, to the considerable amusement of friends, he had been thoroughly duped by a popular preacher working at the temporary chapel belonging to a dissident sect. The man had invited him out for a splendid lunch, accompanied by plenty of good wine, after which he had disappeared, leaving Clapperton to foot the bill.

His determined pursuit of city pleasures might have continued indefinitely and ended disastrously, but fortunately his attention was gradually drawn to more serious interests. Though some of his naval friends were fellow drifters, others were already treading new career paths in the medical world and at the university, and Edinburgh at that time offered more original intellectual stimuli and wider opportunities than any other city in Britain apart from London. In the early 1820s, the Scottish capital was one of the leading centres of the new Enlightenment, a remarkable movement driven by amateurs and professionals alike. The city's philosophers and scientists were respected throughout the world, and every country felt the influence of her literary achievements. Edinburgh's periodicals and journals were at the forefront of political energy and her medical school was second to none, while the architecture of Robert Adams' New Town was amongst the finest in Georgian Britain.

Though neither politically nor intellectually inclined, Hugh possessed an enquiring mind and readily participated in the wide-ranging debates which were the daily fare in every lodging and hostelry and addressed with passion in print: the abolition of slavery, prison reforms, falling wages and rising unemployment, radical political uprisings in Glasgow, the potato famine in Ireland and the ensuing mass emigration. His innate sympathies were aroused, and on the subject of abolition he was better informed than many. Two of his older brothers, George in the late 1790s and Alexander after the turn of the century, had had experience of the trade in slaves across the Atlantic when serving as surgeons on Liverpool ships transporting the so-called black gold; and in the mid-1770s his uncle and namesake had published (anonymously) accounts of the horrors of the traffic and an attempted uprising on board.[7]

Great strides were being made in the natural sciences, in mineralogy, geology, botany and the other disciplines that had emerged as subsidiary branches of Edinburgh University's schools of physics, anatomy and medicine. Lectures were usually over-subscribed, attended both by ardent students and by members of the general public eager to hear renowned professors advance their theories and introduce new material for discussion. James Kay had become an active member of the Linnæan Society which in addition to engaging in theoretical work conducted regular excursions into the nearby countryside and to the Highlands, to collect specimens of fauna, flora and minerals.

A particularly close friend (and Bristo Street neighbour) already deeply immersed in matters of scientific enquiry was Dr Walter Oudney. Two years younger than Clapperton, Oudney had studied medicine at Edinburgh University before joining the Royal Navy in 1810 as an assistant surgeon. He had served on a number of stations, including a short spell in the East Indies, and was pro-moted surgeon in August 1815. On return to Edinburgh after the war he immediately took up work as a doctor in order to be able to care for his widowed mother and two sisters, while continuing medical research in his spare time. He had earned a good reputation, publishing articles in the *Edinburgh Medical and Surgical Journal*, and had worked in collaboration with Scotland's distinguished Royal Physician, Dr Robert Abercrombie. Concurrently with his medical investigations, Walter Oudney had embarked on research in natural history, joining the Wernerian Society and soon taking a special interest in botany, particularly grasses. He participated in field expeditions, wrote learned papers for the Linnæan Society and cooperated with other scientists in arranging the plates for a botanical studies project at the university's library – and by 1820 he was already considering giving up medicine to devote himself full time to the study of botany.

Intrigued by his friends' commitment, and impressed by their meticulous approach to their work, Clapperton also began to take an interest, his grandfather's name and standing in Edinburgh's prestigious Society of Arts, and his own connections to current members, among them General Dirom and the Seaforth family, providing additional motivation. And through Kay and Oudney he became acquainted with the leader of a small band of dedicated amateur botanists, Dr James Robinson Scott, a lecturer at the university and former surgeon in the Royal Navy; however, the person whose fields of endeavour appealed most to Hugh Clapperton was their patron, Robert Jameson.

Regius Professsor of Natural History (from 1804 till his death in 1854) and Keeper of the University Museum in Edinburgh, Jameson was a towering figure of the Scottish Enlightenment. A tireless field worker, author and editor, he was also a charismatic teacher under whom, among many others, the marine naturalist William Scoresby, Edward Forbes, the father of oceanography, and Charles Darwin had been attracted to study. His greatest passion, however, was his museum, widely acknowledged to be second only in importance to the British Museum and for which he spared neither pains nor expense in acquiring new specimens, purchasing collections from similar institutions and coercing the great and the good at home and abroad into contributing to his work.

In London, Robert Jameson had established a close personal and professional rapport with John Barrow who, from his position as Second Secretary at the Admiralty, had become the prime mover in a series of official expeditions to probe the Polar regions for a north-west passage from the Atlantic to the east, and to explore the interior of west and northern Africa to identify the course of the River Niger. Moreover, in 1819 Professor Jameson had been instrumental in the award to Barrow of an honorary degree at Edinburgh University in recognition of his contribution to its work of science and discovery, an honour which cemented the relationship between the Royal Navy and Scottish men of science.

For Hugh Clapperton, journeys of exploration represented the most absorbing aspect of the expansion of interest in the natural sciences. A number of the participants had been Scots, and not a few were Edinburgh men. Several members of current expeditions to the Arctic had studied under Jameson; and the heroes of past exploits in Africa – the Selkirk doctor Mungo Park on the River Niger and James Bruce in east Africa – were household names. And to a greater extent than most people in Scotland, Clapperton and his naval friends possessed if not actual experience of the more remote regions in the scientists' sights then at the least a fair idea of the hardships and dangers to be met with. That the latest attempts had been organized from the Admiralty only lent the enterprises additional allure.

The Royal Navy boasted a splendid tradition of participation in scientific exploration and its officers on shore in Scotland eagerly kept abreast of news from abroad. Africa had particular resonance for Clapperton whose squadron commander on the Upper Lakes, Captain Edward Collier, had been promoted commodore of the naval station's busy anti-slavery squadron; and his friend and patron Captain William Owen was preparing a major expedition to survey the vast continent's coastline.

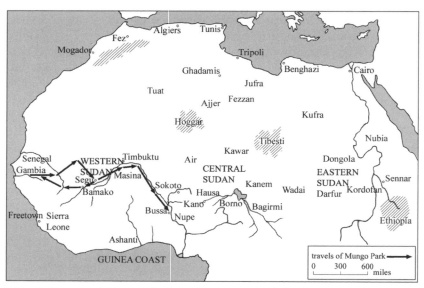

Map 2 Travels of Mungo Park in Africa north of the Equator

In 1820, the focus of attention in Africa was on the region lying between the Sahara and the tropical forests of the Guinea Coast, known as the Sudan (Arabic, *bilad as-Sudan*, land of the blacks), and on identifying the final course of the River Niger. There was understandable excitement among Edinburgh's natural scientists when in the October of that year Barrow let it be known that he was planning another venture into central Sudan, starting from Tripoli. Previous expeditions into the interior of Africa had been covered in detail in a regular flow of articles in Edinburgh's newspapers and in the leading journals of the day. The first missions, organized by the African Association (founded in June 1788 by a group of scientists led by Sir Joseph Banks), had ended in disaster and death, serving only to increase the mysteries surrounding the River Niger and the fabled city of Timbuktu, and to highlight the apparent inaccessibility of the Sudan. The Association's next geographical missionary, however, had fared rather better. Mungo Park's first heroic journey, during which he finally sighted 'the long sought for majestic Niger, glittering to the morning sun, as broad as the Thames at Westminster and flowing slowly to the Eastward'[8], was a landmark event and a decade and a half later the public continued to puzzle over the unfortunate end to his second journey at the Bussa rapids.

Following the Napoleonic wars, the British government took over the initiative but their first attempts, launched from the west coast, were similarly bedevilled by sickness, accident, the hostility of suspicious local leaders and the jealousy of resident Arab merchants. The Royal Navy then assumed the helm and fresh approaches were tested when John Barrow became interested in the riddle of the River Niger and in 1816 sponsored an expedition, led by Captain J.K. Tuckey RN, to ascend the River Congo to establish whether it and the Niger formed a single watercourse. A new, shallow-draught sloop with a wood-burning engine was commissioned for the purpose, but navigation proved problematic and fever took its inevitable toll. Some two hundred and eighty miles into the interior Tuckey was forced to turn back, and three days later he died; of the fifty-six men who had left England, twenty-one never returned. The miserable failure of that mission resulted in a shift of focus to a trans-Saharan gateway (thought to be a somewhat healthier option) when Barrow's attention was drawn to the possible viability of an overland route from Tripoli across the Sahara to Timbuktu and the River Niger.

In 1817, Commander W. H. Smyth RN, engaged on a survey of the coast of North Africa, called at Tripoli to collect ancient stones and monuments from Lepcis Magna for transport to England (gifts from the Pasha in Tripoli for the Prince Regent). After his visit he had reported to his admiral the offer of Yusuf Pasha Qaramanli to protect British travellers in his own territory and beyond into the Sahara and Sudan. Smyth had also been impressed by the views of the British Consul-general in Tripoli, Hanmer Warrington, who appeared to enjoy considerable influence with Yusuf Qaramanli. There was an encouraging coincidence of interests: Britain wished to investigate the interior of Africa beyond the Sahara and the Pasha hoped to maintain his independence from the all-powerful Ottoman Porte by currying favour with the British.

In London, John Barrow was keen to exploit the opportunity since Lord Bathurst, Secretary of State for the Colonies and War, seemed as 'favourable for the undertaking'[9] as the Pasha in Tripoli; and the following year the Second Secretary was able to dispatch a small team to Africa – a twenty-nine year-old Scottish surgeon, Joseph Ritchie, and George Lyon, a young naval captain, accompanied by a shipwright from the Malta dockyard, John Belford. In the summer of 1819 they reached Murzuq, capital of Fezzan, but there they ran out of funds. Marooned in one of the unhealthiest places in the Sahara, Ritchie sickened and died, Belford became semi-blind, and Lyon aborted the mission.

George Lyon had learnt a great deal about travel and conditions in the interior and on return to Tripoli in March 1820 he wrote a lengthy dispatch on the slave traffic, the miseries of which he had personally witnessed. Of particular interest to geographers in Britain, however, was Lyon's report that, according to merchants of Borno, the Niger flowed past Lake Chad and 'that by one route or another, these waters join the great Nile of Egypt to the south-ward of Dongola'.[10] Borno henceforth replaced Timbuktu as the main focus of attention and John Barrow, convinced that the rivers Nile and Niger were one, at once set about preparing a further mission. In August 1820, Consul Warrington having announced his own readiness to organize and participate in an expedition, Barrow invited Professor Jameson in Edinburgh to recommend someone to lead its work of scientific enquiry. Jameson considered Dr Walter Oudney to be just the man for the job and asked James Robinson Scott to approach him.

Intent upon establishing a reputation upon which to base his bid for a lectureship at the university, and keen to undertake new research further afield, Oudney was immensely attracted by the idea. Furthermore, having recently become aware that he might be consumptive, he believed that a change of air and travel could only be beneficial to him.[11] He therefore enthusiastically applied for the post, requesting only sufficient emolument to support his mother and his two sisters. Jameson backed the application and James Scott confirmed to Henry Goulburn, Under-Secretary at the Colonial Department, that Oudney was 'abstemious to a degree' and 'a good active little walker; as to horsemanship, I cannot say, but a few falls at the Edinburgh Riding School may be of service to him'.[12] In November 1820, all references having proved satisfactory, Dr Walter Oudney received a formal invitation to volunteer his services; he was officially engaged by the government two months later and required to hold himself in immediate readiness.

Meanwhile in London, Barrow continued to promote his plans for the new expedition and when in March 1821 it transpired that Hanmer Warrington did not in fact intend to take an active part in the proposed expedition, the Second Secretary cast around for another officer to accompany Oudney. Once more he consulted Jameson and Scott in Edinburgh. They in turn spoke to Oudney, who 'felt glad at the prospect of having a companion' and made his immediate recommendation,

> My friend Lieutenant Clapperton RN, a gentleman of an excell-ent disposition, strong constitution, most temperate habits, is exceedingly desirous of accompanying the expedition. He wishes no salary, his whole object being love of knowledge. He possesses strong natural powers of mind & is an acute observer of nature. I have known him long and intimately & I think he will be a great acquisition.[13]

Chapter 6: London 1821
no exertion of mine will be wanting

Appointment to the Borno Mission – Lieutenant Dixon Denham
confusion in Whitehall – Malta — arrival in Tripoli

Word of Dr Oudney's choice of companion was passed to the Admiralty and Barrow signalled his approval. Hugh Clapperton, who was well known to Robert Jameson and his associates and creditably spoken for elsewhere in Edinburgh, duly forwarded his application to the Colonial Department,

> I am very desirous of being appointed to accompany my friend Dr. Oudney on the intended mission to the Interior of Africa – I am endowed with good health and a vigorous constitution which has been sufficiently tried by active service in very different climes – Dr. Oudney has known me long & is of the opinion that I would assist him greatly in his scientific research in that ill known country – My situation in the Navy has often brought me in contact with uncivilized tribes and in my intercourse I have always had the good fortune to insinuate myself into their good opinion – Should my service be accepted no exertion of mine will be wanting in the great cause of discovery – I would thank you to inform me as soon as possible of your determination
> I have the honour to be, Sir, your Most Obt. Servt.
> Hugh Clapperton, Lieut. R.N.[1]

John Barrow, Second Secretary at the Admiralty and a born bureaucrat, was not a particularly agreeable man. Clever and self-made, he had held his post for ten years, and would do so for another twenty, by kow-towing to his superiors and harrying his inferiors. Small, lean and ascetic, he devoted himself unreservedly to his work, to his great personal hobby (the geography, history and customs of remote and unfamiliar regions of the world) and to writing lengthy articles for his friend John Murray's *Quarterly Review*. He was keen to have an officer of the Royal Navy involved in the new mission, partly because he intended that the expedition should navigate down the River Niger but equally to increase his own *locus standi* in a mission officially sponsored and funded by the Colonial Department, an expanding rival government office. Barrow envisaged that the mission to Borno would leave Britain within a month or two in order to travel across the Sahara in the cooler weather and, allowing for the transit of the desert in both directions, he anticipated the expedition would last some three years. Consul-general Warrington was already preparing the way with Yusuf Pasha Qaramanli who had promised an armed escort to the Sudan; and also at the mission's disposal in Tripoli would be the equipment discarded by George Lyon.

Walter Oudney and Hugh Clapperton set about examining such information as was available, pouring over the maps and debating existing hypotheses[†] with their friends. George Lyon's recently published *Narrative* of his travels was an obvious first point of reference; and they paid particular attention to the work of James M'Queen, a Glasgow newspaper editor and amateur geographer who was currently preparing for publication his own thesis on the final course of the River Niger – which he firmly believed to have its termination in the Bight of Benin.[2] However, nearly all reports from indigenous sources continued to refer to a single watercourse between Timbuktu and the Nile, and Lyon's findings appeared to confirm those accounts. In anonymous articles (penned by John Barrow) the *Quarterly Review* argued in favour of the eastward flow and River Nile solution, while the *Edinburgh Review* took up the cudgels on behalf of James M'Queen. But there was general agreement that given her far-flung interests Britain must solve the mystery.

While awaiting official orders, Oudney studied African herbaria and made a start on learning Arabic (and perhaps he took a riding

---

[†] Herodotus was the first to posit a large river flowing eastwards – the origin of a supposed link between the River Nile and the Niger. Mediæval Arab geographers, however, referred to the western course of the Nile of the Negroes, which fitted Portuguese navigators' accounts of the large rivers entering the sea on the west coast. European knowledge of the Niger continued confused until Mungo Park's confirmation of the river's easterly course, which in turn provoked a new debate about its termination. Some held that the Niger flowed into a large land-locked lake, being prevented from reaching the Guinea Coast by a chain of mountains running behind and parallel to the coast from the eastern African highlands to Senegal. Others maintained that its waters disappeared underground to resurface further east in the unexplored swamps from which the White Nile emerged, while Tuckey's expedition had not ruled out the possibility that the Niger and the Congo might yet prove to be one and the same watercourse.

lesson or two). Though he followed his friend's researches with interest and enthusiasm, Clapperton's own preparations were minimal. Never inclined to worry about what did not concern him, he saw his principal task as being to get Oudney safely there and back again; as to the logistics of travel, he was fully confident of his skills in organization, navigation and draughtsmanship and could safely trust in his considerable experience of commanding men.

In external appearance and manner the two men were complete opposites and on the face of it an ill-assorted duo. Clapperton, tall and burly, was an unabashed extrovert and tended to take life as he found it. Oudney was of 'middle size, slightly made and with a pale complexion'[3], with an unassuming manner and grave air, a dry, somewhat withdrawn and taciturn man; his profound feelings of obligation to his family were matched by ardent belief in the loftier virtues and in self-betterment through education. He was a committed scholar who during his service at sea had assembled his medical observations into a faculty dissertation, *De Disenterio Orientali*, and used any spare time to read through the Latin and Greek classics and teach himself French and Italian. His choice of Clapperton for a travelling companion was shrewdly based on a sound understanding of his friend's strengths and abilities and an awareness that each well complemented the other; in common, they had a background of naval service and a firm appreciation of their scientific goals. The alliance of determined scholar with seasoned sailor augured an effective working relationship.

From the very beginning, however, administrative arrangements for the mission were bedevilled by bureaucratic blunderings and negligence. By June, neither confirmation of Clapperton's recruitment nor word of a start date for the mission had come through from the Colonial Department. The chances of setting out on the desert passage in October were evidently receding; Dr Oudney made urgent enquiries of the Under-Secretary, and in early July had to write again to remind John Barrow that they were still awaiting their orders. News of Clapperton's appointment finally came through in August and Oudney replied to Barrow on behalf of his friend, 'Lieutenant Clapperton was away on a tour through Scotland and only returned yesterday. He accepts your proposals and is in high spirits respecting the expedition. I am exceedingly glad that he is appointed for he will prove a valuable acquisition'.[4]

To the two delighted Scots everything at last looked set fair for their departure. How dismaying in contrast then was their discovery on arrival in London in late August that not only had the Colonial Department seen fit to appoint another officer to the mission – at the express request of Lord Bathurst – but that this third officer, an army lieutenant named Dixon Denham, would apparently assume overall command of the venture. Walter Oudney was profoundly disappointed and distressed by the official *volte face*; and Hugh Clapperton was both outraged that his friend's richly deserved position had been usurped and mortified to find that he himself was expected to take orders from a lower-ranking, English army officer.

Dixon Denham

Older than Clapperton by two years, Lieutenant Dixon Denham was well bred, well educated and very well connected. He had obtained a commission in the Twenty-third Royal Welch Fusiliers during the Peninsular War, and from 1812 to 1814 was aide-de-camp to the commander of the Eighth Portuguese Regiment, Colonel Sir James Douglas. Denham served in the army in Spain and Belgium and in 1818 secured an appointment on the staff at Sandhurst Royal Military College. In the autumn of 1820 he had been in personal touch with the Duke of Wellington on the subject of army discipline; and in the spring of the following year, through highly-placed connections, he had had no trouble obtaining a personal interview with Lord Bathurst in order to discuss British exploration in Africa.

Fired by George Lyon's account of his adventures in Fezzan, Denham had begun to see himself as an explorer and following several meetings with Lyon he had pulled together a plan to travel to the Sudan via Fezzan and Timbuktu and presented it in person to Lord Bathurst in March 1821. The Colonial Secretary was duly impressed and Denham much encouraged. The following month he began to take Arabic lessons; and on 12 June 1821, while the anxious Oudney was yet pressing Barrow for news, Denham had been officially engaged by Lord Bathurst to lead the expedition across the Sahara to Borno.

The three officers were summoned to attend together at the Admiralty, where Barrow gave them the gist of their instructions. The general orders were unambiguous. Under the protection of Yusuf Pasha Qaramanli, they would travel to Borno where they were to establish good relations with the Sultan, familiarize themselves with the languages and peoples of the country, and obtain geographical and commercial information for the benefit of future travellers. Thereafter, their objectives were to explore the wider interior and, if possible, trace the final course of the River Niger. Much less clear, however, were the essential questions of overall command and individual duties.

The original scheme agreed between the Colonial Department and the Admiralty had envisaged a two-officer team, a repeat in effect of the Ritchie-Lyon mission to Fezzan. While Barrow would put up nominations, formal recruitment and the responsibility for administrative and financial arrangements and for issuing the mission's official instructions rested with the Colonial Department. The seeds of confusion were sown when the Colonial Secretary personally engaged Dixon Denham to command the mission. John Barrow evidently took it that Denham's appointment could not affect Hugh Clapperton, who would still travel as another string to Walter Oudney's bow. The broader implications of Bathurst's separate initiative were apparently never discussed since, until August, Barrow and Goulburn had each believed that the other was amending the instructions as necessary to accommodate a three-man team, and that all three officers involved had been kept fully informed.

At the Admiralty, the Second Secretary outlined the latest proposals to the three intractable young men. He advised them that Dr Walter Oudney had been appointed vice-consul-designate to Borno; once there, while working to further British commercial interests in the interior, he would also provide a communications and supply base for the mission. And Dixon Denham would take charge of the work of exploration; he would be accompanied by Hugh Clapperton. But Barrow's explanation skated over critical issues: the question of overall command (both during the Saharan crossing and once in Borno), and Clapperton's official ranking in the mission and the exact nature of the duties expected of him.

John Barrow

Without doubt the officer best qualified to take charge of the scientific aspects of the expedition, Walter Oudney was deeply offended by the allocation to him of a minor supporting role in a mission which he had expected to lead (for months afterwards ne could not even bear mention of the word vice-consul). And though inwardly fuming, Hugh Clapperton had perforce to accept that he would accompany (but not necessarily *assist*) Dixon Denham.

Believing that he had Lord Bathurst's personal approval to run the whole expedition, Denham was decidedly aggrieved to discover that Oudney was apparently to be independent of his command; and, in a fit of pique, he roundly accused Oudney and Clapperton of responsibility for the delay in finalizing arrangements (though it was clear to those present that he himself was not yet ready). All three men left the Admiralty in high dudgeon. The two Scots had nothing in common with the arrogant English soldier; the antipathy was mutual and, unfortunately for the new mission, long lasting. Failure to liaise effectively with the Colonial Department meant that Barrow was at least partly to blame for the unhappy state of affairs, but his two naval nominees were duty bound to accept the changes with good grace and, somewhat surprisingly, they appear to have borne him no personal ill will.

Oudney and Clapperton were instructed to make everything ready and get themselves, their baggage and equipment down to Falmouth with the least possible delay in order to proceed to Malta and Tripoli in advance of Denham. From their lodgings in Villiers Street off the Strand they hastily completed their preparations, and each arranged for a nearby firm of solicitors to look after his personal affairs (for which Clapperton also obtained help from his uncle Samuel, currently a major at the Chatham Division of Royal Marines). They were allowed £100 each for a fit out, and on the eve of departure Oudney recounted their progress to James Kay, 'Our worthy friend Clapperton gets on amazingly well. I am in high spirits respecting my mission; from all that I have been able to learn, very little danger, and scarcely any impediments, are to be apprehended. We have got excellent fowling pieces and pistols, and a most valuable assortment of philosophical instruments'.[5] At seven in the morning on 3 September 1821 the two friends finally set out for Falmouth while Denham, claiming he needed more time to complete his preparations, returned to Sandhurst from where it was in fact his intention urgently to lobby for new instructions.

Oudney received his personal orders four days later, on board ship. Lord Bathurst confirmed his appointment as vice-consul at Borno, where he was to gather information on adjacent countries and collect specimens of objects of natural history; he was expected 'in the first instance' to remain in Borno, rather than to undertake any exploration himself, and he would be 'accompanied by two gentlemen' whose object was to explore the interior and, if feasible, trace the final course of the River Niger. Once familiar with the country, Denham was to proceed eastwards from Borno and Oudney would provide him with financial support, 'but you are not to consider him subject to your orders, as he proceeds on a special service under my directions'. And although Clapperton had volunteered his services to accompany Oudney, the orders continued, he could either travel with Denham or assist Oudney in Borno – 'though it would perhaps be most adviseable that they [Denham and Clapperton] should proceed together. This, however, must be an arrangement left to themselves'.[6]

Oudney and Clapperton continued aggrieved and angry. At the eleventh hour the expedition had been abruptly removed from Walter Oudney's control, its structure altered almost beyond recognition; and sailing the following day for Malta they were very conscious that raising objections would henceforth be much more difficult, if not well nigh impossible. On arrival in Valetta in late September 1821, new problems and yet further delays awaited them. His instructions required Oudney to apply to the government of Malta for assistance in getting to Tripoli. The government at Valetta, however, although formally responsible for all His Majesty's affairs in the Mediterranean and North Africa, including those of the Consulate-general in Tripoli, had no knowledge of the planned mission and thus no authority to assist. And although Oudney had also been deputed to hire a naval carpenter from the Malta Dockyard neither he nor the Commissioner was aware of the terms on which such a person could be engaged.

Clapperton turned increasingly morose. Oudney told Kay that they had tried sight-seeing, but 'fretful from experiencing great harassment from individuals who ought to have been forwarding our views, a disinclination to enjoy anything was induced'.[7] That Denham had yet to join them was no concern of theirs (in truth they welcomed his absence) and they resolved to make their own way to Tripoli without delay. Since the Senior Naval Officer, the Hon. Captain Pellew, regretted that he had no authority to put a ship at their disposal, Oudney hired a small Sicilian boat – an initiative endorsed by the Admiral who unexpectedly returned to Valetta on the morning of their departure.

The vessel they hired was a fifteen-ton *spirano*, a coastal fishing boat, and their passage to Tripoli was beset by storms. The intrepidity of his newly arrived protégés clearly impressed the British Consul-general there, and Warrington's good opinion and instant expression of full support for their undertaking did a great deal to dispel the gloom caused by the frustrations encountered in Malta.

Chapter 7: Tripoli 1821–1822
all well and in high spirits

Consul-general Warrington and Yusuf Pasha Qaramanli
arrival of Denham – discord within the mission
preparations for departure for Fezzan

Hanmer Warrington[1] was a man after Clapperton's own heart – genial, optimistic and a dyed-in-the-wool patriot. Brimming with enthusiasm and ideas, the Consul-general was quite ready to use British influence to achieve his own aims, and was wont to take initiatives and consult afterwards. He had obtained his post in Tripoli in 1814 through good personal connections; he claimed the patronage of the commander-in-chief, the Duke of York, but gossip linked his wife to the Prince Regent in whose personal gambling circles Warrington was very much at home. A trusted and influential figure, representing the greatest power in the Mediterranean at the time, he was the doyen of the foreign consuls accredited to the Castle. Though garrulous and on occasion unwise, by dint of his official standing and his personable demeanour Warrington had won the confidence of the Regent of Tripoli, Yusuf Pasha Qaramanli[2], who consulted him on both domestic and foreign affairs.

In Tripoli, enveloped in the restorative warmth of Warrington's welcome and comfortably housed in the elegant villa the Consul had had built for his personal use the previous year on six acres of land at Menshia just outside the capital, Clapperton began to view their prospects in a more positive light; and Oudney pronounced himself delighted by the ardour with which Warrington pursued the mission's interests, 'I cannot speak too highly of the assistance I have received from Mr. Consul Warrington, and of the pleasure with which he received us'.[3]

Reviewing arrangements for the mission's travels, however, Oudney and Clapperton met with immediate disappointment. In London they had been told that Qaramanli would have an escort ready to take them to Fezzan and across the Sahara, but no such arrangement was yet in place. The bluff and amiable Consul had been unable to pin down the wily Pasha; immersed in dreams of a vice-consulate in Murzuq and another in Borno and of the Union Jack being raised on the River Niger itself by his enterprising new

72

friends, Warrington unfortunately lacked the necessary force of character to exploit either his own position or his personal relationship with Qaramanli. Yusuf Pasha had had no difficulty gaining and holding the initiative in what had turned into a drawn-out and complicated affair. It had never been the Pasha's intention to make early disposition for the proposed new British mission and he had long since resorted to apologetic prevarication, at which he was a past-master, while continuing to hold out for more money – and that for a very good reason. The Regency's coffers lay virtually empty.

In the October of 1821, Yusuf Pasha Qaramanli was felicitating himself on an extraordinary piece of good luck: the unexpected opportunity to use Britain's official mission of geographical and scientific exploration to Borno to mask his own imperial ambitions beyond the Sahara. Over the century since wresting control from the Ottomans, the powerful Qaramanli dynasty had developed an independent economy based on revenues from the unquestionably successful activities of Mediterranean pirates, topped up with the income and customs dues derived from the import of slaves and luxury goods from across the Sahara. By the time Yusuf Pasha himself had murdered his way to supremacy in 1795, however, the corsairs were already under mounting pressure from the western maritime powers, and by the end of the French wars the Royal Navy commanded the Mediterranean.[4] He therefore turned his attention to improving his hold on Tripoli's hinterland, focussing on greater exploitation of the lucrative Saharan slave trade and of commercial opportunities in the Sudan.

In the first decade of the new century the Pasha, already in control of the tribes of Tripolitania, had seized Ghadamis, a major crossroad of trading routes in the west. He had appointed as his collector of dues in Fezzan a close friend and ally, Mohamed al-Mukni, who soon doubled the province's contribution to Tripoli's purse. When in 1811 the traditional sultan threatened rebellion, Al-Mukni staged a successful coup in Murzuq, and over the next eight years mercilessly drained Fezzan of its wealth and mounted a series of *razzias* (slave raids) into and across the Sahara to raise tribute for his master and to enrich himself. By 1819, however, Al-Mukni had become wealthy and powerful enough to pose a threat to Qaramanli who therefore dismissed him and propelled a new bey, Mustafa al-Ahmar (a reliable Georgian renegade married to one of the Pasha's daughters), into a further series of *razzias* across the Sahara under his personal direction.

Looking to extend his influence across the Sahara, Qaramanli had also opened relations with Sheikh Al-Kanemi, the powerful leader of Borno, and earlier in 1821 had responded to a call from the Sheikh for armed assistance against the rebellious satellite state of Bagirmi. In exchange for its military support, Al-Ahmar's army had been permitted to raid for slaves and their *razzia* had provided a useful opportunity to gather military intelligence. In the event of success in battle, several strategic options would be open to the Pasha. He could collaborate with Al-Kanemi in other wars, with the prospect of even larger-scale and more lucrative slave raids, or he could take outright control of the Saharan trade corridor linking Borno with the Mediterranean ports and bring Borno into his sphere of dominion as a tributary state. Then again, he might move directly against Al-Kanemi, either by military might or by engineering a coup in Borno, thereby winning a valuable commercial foothold in the Sudan.

Qaramanli was still awaiting news of the outcome of Bey Al-Ahmar's expedition when Warrington announced the imminent arrival of the new British mission. Naturally enough, Yusuf Pasha intended to press for a high cash price for providing his assistance, but that was only one consideration. Of equal importance was the need to find a reliable and effective henchman to lead the escort on an expedition which the Pasha aimed to use for vital military reconnaissance. He was therefore in no hurry to complete his arrangements for the forthcoming mission to Borno.

Negotiations had continued at Qaramanli's pace. Pointing out that an escort one thousand strong would come very expensive, he had first asked for a cash payment of £5,000, and then upped his bid, asking for a loan of £25,000 from the British government, the money to be repaid over several years. The Pasha explained to Warrington that with such a sum he could raise an army of six thousand men with which to take Borno and Hausaland, establish beys there and generate sufficient commercial income to be able to relinquish the traffic in slaves. Warrington rejected any notion of a loan but, without seeking authority from London, increased his offer; he was ready to pay the £5,000 and provide a bonus upon the expedition's safe return. It was settled that the mission would purchase its own equipment and pack animals, and hire servants and camel-men, but the cost of food and supplies for the officers, their servants and baggage animals on the journey would be to the Regent's account.[5] As to a start date, Yusuf Pasha repeated that he could do nothing until the Bey returned.

In the interim, of the most immediate concern to Oudney and Clapperton was the unresolved issue of responsibilities within the mission. Oudney asked Warrington to obtain urgent clarification from London, hoping to have settled the matter before Denham set foot in Tripoli. In response, and addressing his letter to 'Dr. Oudney, Commanding the Expedition to Explore the Interior of Africa'[6], the Consul simply acknowledged that Oudney was in overall charge as far as Borno where he would then take up his post as vice-consul – not the reassurance the doctor was seeking.

The discovery that bills presented to the Treasury by their agents for reimbursement of their fit-out had not been honoured was cause for further exasperation. Oudney fired off a letter to the Colonial Under-Secretary, informing him of their hurt and disappointment and asking for immediate refunds to be arranged.

While waiting for Denham, Oudney and Clapperton returned to their Arabic studies and undertook a number of excursions into the surrounding country to become familiar with local travelling conditions, examine the geology and botany of the hinterland and collect information about the interior. Dismayed to find that little of the equipment left behind by Lyon was of any use, they turned for assistance to two British naval officers, the brothers Beechey, who were visiting Tripoli during a voyage to survey the northern coasts of Africa and who generously supplied cooking gear and other useful articles from their ship. Captain Henry Beechey was particularly enthusiastic about the new enterprise. The previous year he himself had made a journey overland to Cyrenaica with George Lyon (a former messmate) after the latter's return from Murzuq, and he was impressed by the determination of the newly arrived Scots,

> They are both decent fellows and entirely well calculated to travel together. The impetuosity and enterprise of Clapperton is well restrained by the caution and prudence of the Doctor, who is certainly a man of a good deal of information and well acquainted with several of the sciences – they are both very zealous in the pursuit of this object and there really appears to be every prospect of their success.[7]

Bored with life ashore in Tripoli, and intrigued by the possibility that the Niger might lead to the Nile and perhaps to undiscovered antiquities, Henry Beechey at one point entertained notions of accompanying the mission.

In the Consul's comfortable if crowded house – known to all in Tripoli as the English Garden (or simply the Gardens) for its fine collection of ornamental fruit trees – the travellers were much caressed by his large family and personal staff. Warrington's amiable eldest son, Frederick, had increasingly adopted the local lifestyle; a considerable Arabist, he acted as his father's interpreter and oriental secretary. Having travelled quite widely in Tripoli's hinterland, he proved a valuable source of information and advice to the new mission, as indeed did the efficient Vice-Consul, John (Giacomo) Rossoni, and the Consul's factotum, Angelo Ricci.

The Gardens brought Oudney and Clapperton into contact with all manner of influential and helpful members of Tripolitan society. The former Foreign Minister, blind eighty-year-old Sidi Mohamed D'Ghies, whose son was ambassador at the Court of St James, offered sage and welcome counsel; and Clapperton much enjoyed the company of the Danish Consul Johan Carstensen and his wife and the many other diplomats who liked to frequent the Consul's hospitable home. Another regular visitor, and very well up in Tripoli's affairs, was one Dr John Dickson, a former naval surgeon and for ten years surgeon at the Pasha's court, whose meticulous meteorological journal Oudney considered worth sending back to Professor Jameson. Most significantly for his new visitors, however, Warrington courted influential Arab merchants, many of whom knew the interior well, and held himself ready to intercede with Pasha Qaramanli on behalf of those in difficulty or politically oppressed, even outlaws seeking refuge. At the Gardens and at the Castle, Oudney and Clapperton thus had ample opportunity to converse with renegades[8], Traboleze merchants, *marabuts* (holy men), visiting traders and tribesmen from the interior and with all manner of other travellers, informants and supplicants.

The man with whom Clapperton found most common ground, however, was a twenty-four year-old former midshipman attached to the Consulate, John Tyrwhitt. Having run up very large debts while on naval service and brought down upon himself the extreme displeasure of his family, the young man had been foisted upon Hanmer Warrington by his father, John Tyrwhitt senior, Marshal of the Court of Admiralty in Gibraltar, to whom the Consul owed considerable sums of money (borrowed to repay old gambling debts and to support his personal expenses in Tripoli). Though entirely wanting in financial acumen, young John was a straightforward and most agreeable fellow, an incorrigible extrovert who happily attached himself to Oudney and Clapperton.

Dixon Denham appeared on 19 November, bringing with him William Hillman, a naval carpenter from Deptford, whom he had recruited at the Malta Dockyard. And once again the three officers were off on the wrong foot. For Denham, empowered by London to offer a wage (£120 a year), the recruitment of a carpenter had presented no difficulty whatsoever and his scornful dismissal of their own attempts to recruit a suitable man in Valetta rankled with Oudney and Clapperton. More disquieting, however, were his assertions about chains of command within the mission.

Denham showed his colleagues the orders he had received in London. The document stated that his principal objective was to be the exploration of the country south and east of Borno with a view to tracing the final course of the Niger and (in instructions bearing the hallmark of Barrow's private convictions concerning the geography of the interior) allowed for Denham to return home via Egypt. It confirmed that Oudney would remain independent of all command, although he was required to provide assistance for Denham's travels. But the language employed considerably strengthened the army officer's hand vis-à-vis the duties assigned to Clapperton who, regardless of relative rank, was called upon to *assist* as well as accompany the interloper. Oudney once more appealed to Warrington for clarification but, typically, the Consul again ducked the issue; he regarded Oudney and Denham as joint leaders of the Borno mission and continued to treat with them as such, referring in his official communications to 'the expedition under the direction of Dr. Oudney and Capt. Denham'.[9]

Two further months passed, and the impatient Scots aired for the first time with the Colonial Department the notion of travelling across the Sahara on their own, while acknowledging that 'being under the Pasha's protection we have to conform to his wishes'.[10] However, at the turn of the year, increasingly frustrated by the lack of progress, the mission's officers came to a collective decision to travel forthwith to Murzuq to await the return there of Bey Al-Ahmar. And, hopeful of official approval for the establishment of a vice-consulate in Murzuq and in a calculated attempt to force London's hand, Warrington proposed sending John Tyrwhitt with them to facilitate communications and supplies.

Particular consideration was given to the matter of dress. Should the officers travel as Christians or disguised as Moslems? Received wisdom had it that it was safer to advance incognito throughout the Islamic world, but there were obvious risks involved. Walter Oudney was firmly set against the notion of masquerading as a

Moslem as a matter of principle; he argued that given the Pasha of Tripoli's official support for the expedition such a disguise was neither sensible nor necessary. Warrington was of the same mind but recommended that they take 'Consular British uniforms and various articles of Christian dress which may promote comfort to your selves and give a degree of consequence to the Mission'[11]; Denham was in agreement and, when the Pasha approved their decision, the Colonial Department was informed. As a matter of convenience, however, they adopted Islamic travelling names, Clapperton taking for himself *Rais* (Captain) Abdullah, while Denham travelled as *Rais* Halil. Oudney was known simply as *tabib* (Arabic, doctor); and, perhaps with the help of Angelo Ricci who had become a particular friend, Hillman settled upon Ali.

Prior to departure, Denham put forward a set of standing orders for the desert journey, covering the issuing of stores, the posting of sentries, the punishment of defaulters and the like, but they were advanced in an opinionated and condescending manner which did nothing to endear him to Oudney and Clapperton, both of whom raised strong objections. And the doctor, officially responsible for the mission's funds, was equally sensitive to Denham's gratuitous criticism of his handling of finances during their enforced stay in Tripoli. Internal discord continued to rumble on ominously.

By the beginning of February most of the equipment had been assembled – tents, medicines, writing materials, tea, coffee and other luxuries – together with an ample stock of suitable goods for presents and barter. They had with them the most up-to-date maps from London and Paris, various books of scientific reference and published accounts of relevant travels, including a copy of Lyon's indispensable *Narrative*. The mission was supplied with blank bills of exchange to be drawn on the Consulate-general in Tripoli and held reserve funds of four thousand Spanish dollars in cash (the dollar being worth approximately five shillings sterling).

Yusuf Pasha put at their disposal a *shawsh* (an escort officer of senior non-commissioned rank) to conduct them to Murzuq; the *shawsh*, Ranaimi, was a trusted official who knew Fezzan well. And Qaramanli's staff assisted the officers in engaging freed slaves to be their personal servants. Madi was Clapperton's man, Absalom served the doctor and Denham had engaged Barca, a Bornoese formerly employed at the Castle. They also recruited a major-domo, Jacob Deloyice, a Gibraltarian Jew living in Tripoli, to run their commissariat; Tyrwhitt's servant Angelo also hailed from the local Jewish community. William Hillman, a native of Somerset and a typical old salt (naturally known to all as Old Chips), had charge of the stores. The officers acquired a horse each; two mules and two camels were destined for Hillman and the servants; and two dogs joined the party. Thirty camels had been purchased to carry the baggage, and four camel-men were hired to look after them (it was intended that some of the animals be sold as the mission's stores diminished).

In mid-February 1822, Walter Oudney and Hugh Clapperton, together with the mission's servants, set out from Tripoli. As they rode across the stony plain Clapperton made his first sketch maps of the route and notations concerning wells and landmarks on a pad of squared paper, while Oudney wrote down his observations on the curious structure of the surrounding limestone hills capped with 'a thick bed of columnar green stone, with thick layers of vesicular lava'.[12]

Accompanied by Warrington and Tyrwhitt, Denham followed a few days later, and the two parties met up at Wadi Mimun near Bani Walid, some one hundred and fifty miles south of the capital, to make their final preparations for the journey. In rounding up the accounts, Oudney was dismayed to find that the prolonged sojourn in Tripoli had seriously depleted the mission's resources. He wrote Warrington a bill for a further two thousand dollars, which money the Consul promised to dispatch to Murzuq immediately upon his return to Tripoli. Finally, on 8 March 1822, Hanmer Warrington bade his protégés farewell as they set off for Fezzan and the Sahara, 'all well and in high spirits'.[13]

Chapter 8: Fezzan 1822
a strange looking figure

Merchants of Murzuq – a journey through eastern Fezzan – Wadi Al-Ajal
the Dawada sand sea – an expedition to Ghat – Denham's attempted
flight to England – alarum in the capital – plans to leave for Borno
return to Murzuq of Denham and Abu Bakr bu Khulum

The forty-day road from Tripoli to Fezzan, though on well-beaten tracks, afforded the explorers their first taste of travel over the waterless plains and barren stony plateaux of the Sahara. En route they were overtaken by a sudden storm and sought shelter from the searing winds and choking sand huddled down amongst the animals. Forced marches between wells lasted two and sometimes three days; the inherent dangers of their situation were brought home to them at one particularly dismal spot strewn with bones and desiccated carcasses where, just the year before, two men, their camels and fifty sheep had all perished from thirst and exhaustion only a few hours' march from the next available water supply.

The transition from deep seas to sand seas caused Clapperton few problems and he soon settled comfortably into what would become a familiar daily routine. From the moment of leaving Tripoli he maintained a chart of each day's march, complete with diagrams and notes of the main topographical features, and made regular navigational calculations from which to record the route on the maps he had brought with him.

The maintenance of accurate journals was an important part of the mission's methodology and Clapperton was accustomed to keeping exact naval logs. On the road he used a series of small remark-books, the contents of which he transposed in expanded detail into a main journal as and when time allowed. The remark-books constituted a primary record of incidents and encounters, and contained notes on the weather, the condition of wells, the changing landscape, fauna and flora, and observations on the activities of nomadic tribes. Descriptions of settlements in which the mission stayed for more than one day were usually written up at the end of the visit. And as a rule he wrote up his main journal in two copies, which allowed for the dispatch home of one copy when couriers were available.

Ensuring that the right equipment was always to hand and in good working order, and putting in place the practical routines required for the safe and efficient movement of a large party of men and animals across the desert differed from the usual duties of a master's mate only in context and content. The welfare of the expedition's horses and pack animals and the supervision of the mission's employees assumed ever increasing importance among Clapperton's daily concerns. He was perfectly at home in his new duties, whether keeping his logs, standing watch under the starry skies or calling for all hands at first light. And if Dixon Denham was leery of the breezy air with which Clapperton set about his work, his friend's confident efficiency was exactly what Oudney expected of him, indeed counted upon.

On 21 March they reached Sockna, where they encountered a caravan escorting seventy footsore and despondent female slaves from the Sudan, and one week later crossed the Jabal as-Sawda into northern Fezzan. On 7 April 1822, they arrived at the gathering place of caravans, one day's march from Murzuq, where they donned their best dress uniforms and waited until the governor of the town arrived to greet them in the name of the bey, Sultan Al-Ahmar, and escort them into the town.

The Castle of Murzuq

Passing through the narrow gates – just wide enough to admit a loaded baggage-camel – in the twenty foot-high walls, the British travellers entered the grounds of the fortified castle where they were accommodated close to the Sultan's palace in Murzuq's finest house (in which Ritchie and Lyon had also been lodged). Yusuf Pasha had led them to believe that they would encounter Al-Ahmar at some point on the road, but the Bey of Murzuq had only just begun to prepare his journey to Tripoli with the booty from his latest raid into the Sudan, and their first audience with him was not encouraging.

A red-bearded Circassian in his late thirties who spoke both Italian and Arabic, Mustafa al-Ahmar opined that it was doubtful, so many were the preparations to be made, that the necessary escort of two hundred men could move before the spring of the following year, or perhaps in the winter months at the earliest. The mission's officers tried very hard to change his mind; he remained adamant. They offered financial inducement, to the tune of two thousand dollars. The Bey said he would not go even for twenty thousand dollars; only after he had reported in person to the Pasha would more be known. For the time being, therefore, they were invited to reside under his protection in Murzuq and await his return from Tripoli.

Resignedly, Clapperton and his colleagues settled down and took stock of their surroundings. A small conglomeration of mud-brick buildings, its crumbling castle surrounded by palm groves, Murzuq lay in an airless hollow. Its population had a cosmopolitan character, reflecting Fezzan's central role in the history of the peoples of the Sahara[†]. Alongside the Fezzanis of Berber origin, semi-sedentary Arab tribesmen lived in and around the town, as did small groups of urbanized Tuareg and Tubu people. There was also a considerable black community, descendants of

---

[†] Fezzan had been the homeland of the ancient Garamantians, a Berber people who had penetrated the Sahara, apparently with ox-drawn carts, by at least the first millennium BP. First the Greeks and later the Romans, followed by their Byzantine successors, had traded with and held sway over the country without achieving outright control. Arab peoples occupied it in the seventh and eleventh centuries BCE bringing Islam to the region and introducing the camel. The Sudanic state of Kanem ruled Fezzan in the thirteenth century and again in the sixteenth century but withdrew when the Ottomans took over in Tripoli, leaving a vacuum of power which was filled some decades later when the Walid Mohamed dynasty of Arabs from the west came to Fezzan's aid against expansionist Ajjer Tuaregs and ruled from their new capital at Murzuq until 1813.

immigrants from across the Sahara, and consequently many citizens of mixed ethnic origin. The affairs of the town were run by some dozen members of old-established Arab merchant families (who had seized the best land and controlled all trade) assisted by a handful of renegades and descendants of renegades, known as mamluks, appointed – or banished – to assist the Bey in administering the impoverished and unruly province. The merchants of Murzuq made their living from a precarious but lucrative trade with the Sudan and travelled frequently to Borno and Hausaland where, in exchange for manufactures from Europe and the east, they bought slaves, camels and luxury goods including civet for musk, leather-ware, spices and kola nuts. They derived further income from the control of local trade in corn, dates and natron (hydrous sodium carbonate); but undoubtedly the best pickings came from accompanying the beys in armed raids into and across the Sahara to capture slaves.

Hugh Clapperton made it his business to get to know everyone. From the leading trading families in the town, three individuals in particular earned his respect: Old Hadje Mohamed – a venerable merchant of renegade descent who had three times made the long pilgrimage to Mecca, and previously befriended George Lyon – and the Lizari brothers, Mohamed and Yusuf. Sons of a mamluk long since dead, the brothers had succeeded in remaining aloof from Al-Mukni's predatory operations (though bringing trouble upon themselves for daring to do so). The qadi (head of religious and legal affairs of the town), Mohamed Zyan al-Abidin, was some-one for whom Clapperton also professed admiration, and both he and Denham were impressed by the senior member of another clan of wealthy merchants, Abu Bakr bu Khulum. The oldest son of an Awjila Arab who had settled in Fezzan, Bu Khulum had risen to become chief minister and was known to be a rival for the beyship. And a Tuareg chief from Ghat, Hatita ag Khuden, rather attached himself to them. He too had been helpful to the previous mission, and Denham had brought out a dress sword as a present for him from George Lyon. Of noble Ajjer ancestry and a well-to-do trader, Hatita had particular responsibilities in Ghat for foreign trade and foreigners. He was as cosmopolitan in outlook as his Arab counterparts and like them had travelled to the Sudan and back on numerous occasions.

While the town exhibited a certain vitality and some structure, Murzuq's degenerating outlying regions were in a state of more than usual chaos. The Bey's last *razzia* across the Sahara had not been productive, and to swell his coffers Al-Ahmar was busily rounding up all the available slaves and camels in Fezzan itself. In addition, he had requisitioned every last horse and mule and all food, fodder and supplies in the town and surrounding districts in order to provision his caravan for the journey to Tripoli. Granaries were thus empty and supplies in the market were scarce and very expensive. Life in Fezzan's capital could at no time be described as comfortable and in April day-time temperatures in the mud houses climbed to well over 100° Fahrenheit. No word had arrived from Tripoli, nor had the promised and much needed supply of dollars. Any delight in reaching Murzuq soon faded and tempers grew increasingly short.

Beyond some acquaintance with the people and the language the mission had achieved very little since arrival in Africa. Oudney and Clapperton therefore proposed making a short journey across central and eastern Fezzan while waiting for Al-Ahmar to make his intentions known. The doctor particularly wished to see for himself the geology and flora of areas described by George Lyon and to investigate the rumours of a strange mountain of saltpetre, and Clapperton was keen to get on with the business of exploring, preferably without Denham. Desiring to remain in Murzuq to keep in touch with the Bey, Denham had no objection; and John Tyrwhitt agreed to stay behind with Old Chips at their temporary headquarters, to await messages from Tripoli and to look after the baggage, stores and animals.

The eight-day excursion through the heartland of a country essentially unchanged since mediæval times provided Oudney and Clapperton with a happy respite. They took Madi and Absalom and were accompanied by *shawsh* Ranaimi. In Traghan, capital of Fezzan when it had been a province of Kanem-Borno, Clapperton inspected the town's deep green wells and famous hot springs, and explored its massive castle of baked clay and the monumental tombs at the desert's edge. They also visited Zawila, the ancient spiritual centre of Fezzan founded by the Ibadi in the eleventh century, where the reverent demeanour and gentle manners of the community of scholars who looked after them during their stay met with Clapperton's respectful appreciation.

Between oases their route lay over gravel plains and immense shimmering salt flats. They halted on the way in a number of small settlements, most of them little more than a collection of huts made of palm fronds in the care of the local *kaid* (the petty administrator representing the Bey). In some villages the *kaid* was neither a Fezzani nor an Arab, but a black man, 'of which the Dr's servant and mine were not a little proud'.[1] The local *kaids* shared power with others such as Sheikh Barud, the powerful head of an Arab nomad clan, who owned large flocks of sheep and camels and a thousand slaves.

On one occasion they pitched camp outside a slave village, the inhabitants of which were not in any way to be confused with the miserable wretches transported in irons across the Atlantic. Rather were they agricultural serfs, indistinguishable from the majority of the population of the country in appearance, dress and manners, who worked the land in exchange for some degree of protection against nomadic warriors and the predatory lords of Tripoli and Murzuq. While he expressed some sympathy for their ignorance and generally impoverished situation, Hugh Clapperton was not disturbed by African feudalism.

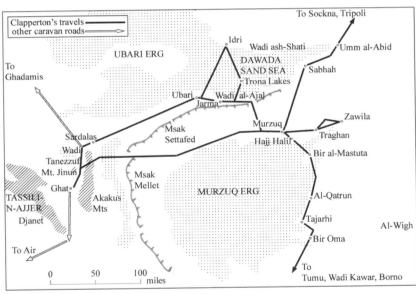

Map 3   Fezzan and Ghat 1822

Fezzan's rural populations barely eked out an existence. They lived in makeshift shelters, tilled their sandy gardens, subsisting on dates and milk from their meagre flocks and finding some relief in *lackbi* (palm wine). Their lands had been appropriated, and their crops, animals and domestic slaves seized, during the grasping rule of two successive beys. In one town, *shawsh* Ranaimi lightly remarked that two years previously he had personally arrested and caused to be strangled eighteen of its inhabitants. He was surprised by Clapperton's obvious distaste. The latter's innate sense of fair play and notion of a just wage for a reasonable day's labour had rendered the sailor increasingly uncomfortable in the face of Ranaimi's persistent bullying of the villagers. Embarrassed by the constant deployment of *teskeras* (formal and legally binding orders from the supreme authority, in this case the Bey) to extort supplies, the two Scots paid their way wherever they could.

The country people everywhere were very friendly, and they flocked to consult the doctor, whose reputation went ahead of him – barrenness, sore eyes, consumption and liver complaints were among the more common afflictions. While supplies lasted Oudney handed out simple medicines or, *faute de mieux*, placebos such as a solution of salt and sugar. Clapperton lent a hand and kept an attentive eye on the proceedings; and he assisted the doctor with geological work. He also recorded his own observations on local customs and festivities (though he did pay the ragged musicians and dancers to go away); and he found time to write to James Kay in Edinburgh to tell him of their adventures, reporting that Oudney was much admired for the blackness of his beard. Oudney added a post-script, 'Clapperton is just the old man. He is a strange looking figure with his long sandy coloured beard and mustachoes. You would smile were you to see him smoking his pipe, and calling to his servant, "Waddy ama simpri", or "fill my pipe"'.[2]

They returned to Murzuq with a better understanding of desert society and convinced that they could travel openly as Christians. No advantage would be gained by joining a large caravan nor, as Clapperton informed Barrow, would there be any need for armed escorts – a large armed force provided by Yusuf Pasha implied close association with the conquerors of the Sahara, setting the mission and its objectives at a serious disadvantage. Their new-found convictions thus only increased their dismay on discovering that Al-Ahmar had yet to leave for Tripoli; slaves were still being seized and brought in from outlying districts (one thousand alone were required for a gift to the Porte), additional taxes were being extorted and the remaining baggage animals rounded up. There could be no thought of an expedition across the desert in the near future; there was no one to conduct it nor were there any camels available to transport it.

When on 18 May the Bey at last set out for Tripoli accompanied by a number of merchants, among them the ambitious Abu Bakr bu Khulum, the British officers talked over their situation. It was clear that one of them must return to Tripoli as soon as possible to report to the Consul and to remonstrate personally with Yusuf Pasha; they were also in urgent need of funds from Warrington to sustain the enforced delay.

The Borno Mission found itself painted into a corner. Given the unfortunate experiences of the hapless Ritchie and Lyon, leaving Tripoli without more certain arrangements for onward travel had been ill-advised if not actually foolhardy. Essentially, their present difficulties could be traced back to Hanmer Warrington's lack of understanding of the realities outside Tripoli. His knowledge of the Sahara and the Sudan was in fact very limited and he was unaware that the Regent had little if any influence beyond the borders of Fezzan. The ingenuous Consul, lulled into accepting at face value statements issuing from the Castle, had been roundly taken in. Belatedly, it had become clear to everyone that neither authorization nor armed escort would be forthcoming until Yusuf Pasha Qaramanli was good and ready, and that no man in Tripolitania or its provinces would dare to move without his express permission.

Since their return from central Fezzan, Oudney and Clapperton had begun to reconsider the feasibility of proceeding to Borno independently of the Pasha's authority, travelling instead in the company of Arab merchants who frequented the trade routes of the Sahara and the Sudan. A political realist, Denham rejected their scheme as both impracticable and extremely unwise, and he volunteered to be the one to return to Tripoli. The two Scotsmen jumped at the offer – Denham was best qualified to get things moving, and they would be glad to have him out of the way.

For his own part, the English officer found the attitude of his colleagues entirely exasperating. In a letter to Lord Bathurst he complained of Oudney's 'natural disposition to suspect a lack of good faith' in those around him but never to express it aloud; and any proposal made by himself to the doctor was invariably 'received with "Thank ye Sir, but I dare say we shall do very well" and generally the contrary system adopted'.[3] Writing to his brother Charles, Denham described Oudney as cold and distant, 'almost Dominie Sampson with more cunning'; Clapperton was 'so vulgar, conceited & quarrelsome a person scarcely ever met with … this Son of War, or rather, of Bluster'. 'They are both Scotchmen and friends', he concluded, 'and to push me off the stage altogether would be exactly what they wish'.[4]

Dixon Denham had fallen foul of the more intractable side of the doctor's companion. Refused his own way on issues to which he was particularly sensitive, Hugh Clapperton became almost impossible to reason with; once convinced that he was in the right he pursued his goals with scant regard for the feelings of others, exhibiting fierce resentment in the face of any criticism, however justified. And he had from the first regarded Denham's presence on the mission as a personal insult. Allied to a typically nautical fondness for drink, Clapperton's wilful behaviour often dismayed even those of a more broad-minded and forgiving disposition – Warrington himself admitted to Denham, 'I never once sat down at Table with Mr. Clapperton without a feeling of dread that something disagreeable would happen before we separated'.[5] Accustomed to his friend's rough-hewn style, however, Walter Oudney paid it no mind.

Accompanied by *shawsh* Ranaimi, Denham set off for Tripoli on 20 May with his servant Barca, and Angelo and Absalom who wanted to visit their families; he expected to be away three months. Tyrwhitt remained in Murzuq with Oudney and Clapperton, ever optimistic that Warrington would yet be permitted to establish a vice-consulate there.

To make profitable use of the wait, Oudney and Clapperton decided to take up Hatita's offer to accompany them on a visit to western Fezzan and his native town of Ghat, an area still beyond European ken. Their Murzuqi friends, however, were concerned about the risks on account of warring Tuareg clans in the region, concerns understandably coupled with consideration for their own skins since the administrators of Fezzan would be held personally responsible if anything untoward happened to the travellers in Bey Al-Ahmar's absence. But eventually Sidi Mohamed Lizari, acting-governor in the capital, was prevailed upon to agree to the expedition. Lizari appointed Mohamed Baba, a Georgian mamluk of some seniority, to be their official escort officer; and Mohamed ben Abd Allah, a Neapolitan renegade who had been attached to Ritchie and Lyon three years earlier, volunteered to join the party. Oudney and Clapperton took both Tyrwhitt and Hillman along with them; and as guides they engaged Mohamed, one of Old Hadje Mohamed's sons, and Hadje Ali, a younger brother of Abu Bakr bu Khulum. Governor Lizari provided *teskeras* for supplies on the road.

Their first stop was at Wadi Al-Ajal; known simply as The Wadi, it lay on the ancient caravan route for pilgrims and trade, connecting

southern and western Sahara with Tripolitania and Egypt. From
the head of the pass the luxuriant valley winding into the far
distance between lofty escarpments was indeed a fine sight and
for a better view they climbed to the summit of a nearby peak,
where they were led by Hillman in the singing of 'God Save the
King' to celebrate the occasion.

The Wadi was populated by Berber descendants of the fabled
Garamantians, and by semi-sedentary groups of Ajjer Tuareg
herdsmen who exchanged their meat and milk for dates and corn
and supplied transport camels and guides for the longer caravan
routes. Huge groves of date palms interspersed with well-watered
agricultural small-holdings attested to the valley's long-established
habitation. At Old Jarma they were surprised to come across a
Roman ruin; Clapperton made sketches of it, but did not pretend
to gauge its purpose.[6] The travellers climbed the valley's lofty
escarpments; and Clapperton sketched the rock engravings and
attempted to decipher the mysterious script (later affirmed to be
Tifinagh, used by the Tuareg). And all about them lay evidence of
the continuing depredations of Tripoli's beys. Village lands had
been confiscated, houses owned by traditional Murzuqi leaders
had been abandoned, date groves and gardens were deserted and
castles and walls lay in ruin or disrepair; in the smaller settlements
the impoverished inhabitants could barely respond to the party's
teskeras with so much as a mess of porridge.

Poor they may have been but the villagers' simple faith (part
Islam, part animism) contrasted favourably with what Clapperton
viewed as the hypocrisy of his Murzuqi companions – Mohamed
ben Abd Allah, the Neapolitan renegade, was 'a notorious liar,
constantly drunk'[7] who in front of the British travellers was ever
ashamed of his expedient and token conversion to Islam. Young
Mohamed ben Hadje was another who got drunk on laqbi; and the
double standards of Hadje Ali bu Khulum – who refused to eat an
incorrectly slaughtered fowl though he happily 'got muzzy on a
bottle of rum which requires no ceremony to go through in drawing
the cork'[8] – similarly grated on the explorer.

As for Mohamed Baba, their official escort and protector, a
Georgian from Tiflis with 'a laughing round face, fair hair and
blue eyes', he openly admitted to being at the time of the coup 'the
person who strangled Hadje Osman & his two sons – & he used to
sit and converse with one of that person's sons who had the good
fortune to be out of the way at that time with as much ease and
freedom as if nothing had ever been done to his unfortunate father

& brothers… it was the Bashaw's orders & you know – says he – they must be obeyed'.[9] However, Clapperton made a point of getting on with him, though Mohamed Baba's hectoring of head-men over the validity of *teskeras* often required his intervention, as did the bickering among camp servants and the frequent squabbles between the mission's employees and outsiders.

Along the roads in Wadi Al-Ajal the travellers' customary fare consisted of *bazeen* (a thick paste of barley flour with gravy, oil or butter), *zumeta* (barley flour mixed with parched dates and cold water) or *fatat* (unleavened pancakes served with gravy, fat or oil). At longer halts couscous formed the standard meal with perhaps a scraggy chicken and bread and wheat; occasionally they procured a sheep, its head traditionally the servants' perquisite, but fruit (melons, figs or grapes) and vegetables were rarer luxuries. They paid their way with little gifts of scissors, thimbles or mirrors, and contributed at the local feasts and ceremonies; and Dr Oudney's medical advice was free to all-comers, although some brought corn, puddings or a chicken in payment.

On arrival in Ubari, the westernmost town in Fezzan, the two friends left Hatita (suffering from guinea worm infestation in one leg) and made an excursion to Wadi ash-Shati, the most northern of the long-settled valleys of Fezzan and the home of nomadic Arab tribes from the surrounding regions. On the seventy-mile journey across the Dawada sand sea, they were accompanied only by an elderly hired guide, Albini, and their personal servants. They sent Tyrwhitt and Hillman back to the capital to see to the mission's belongings and (by paying them to return home) dispensed with the services of their objectionable escort, the two renegades, young Ben Mohamed and Hadje Ali bu Khulum. And the doctor's mule decided to go home by itself, and was last seen running full tilt back along the wadi. (Clapperton set a servant to recover it; if that attempt failed the *kaid* was to send a message to Lizari to allay any fears caused by the return of the riderless beast.)

On 29 June they started out for the sand hills. With neither a clear horizon nor landmarks, navigation was a matter of conjecture and progress through the baking four hundred foot-high dunes was slow and painful. Wading along beside the camels Clapperton suffered considerable blistering to his ankles and bad burns to his legs; his shoes disintegrated and though the soles of his feet held out he was in a fair way to losing all his toenails.

On the third day, Albini lost his bearings so the servants went ahead to look for the path. When at dusk they had not returned,

Oudney set out to reconnoitre, and he too was quickly swallowed up among the dunes. After some little time, growing anxious on his friend's account, Clapperton lit a large fire and repeatedly fired shots into the air until Oudney reappeared. The three of them – Clapperton, Oudney and the old guide – waited up all night in vain. At first light they set off again, Albini once more confidently leading the way, and finally emerged on the rim of the sand sea within sight of the rock citadel of Idri where to their great relief they found their servants awaiting them.

Idri from the south

While Clapperton sketched the outcrop from below, Oudney inspected its basalt columns; and the townspeople took them to see the old Garamantian rock tombs in the escarpment nearby. As usual, the doctor's surgeries were packed, and among the patients attending was a buxom widow who wanted medicine to bring her a new husband. Clapperton jumped to his feet, proposing himself, and was dismayed to find that she took him for an old man. And though he offered to read the Fatiha with her she saw through him, 'oh says she thou art a rogue and thou wilt marry me today and leave me on the morrow – I know travellers'.[10] Henna was customarily used to dye grey hair, and Oudney realized that the widow had mistaken his red-bearded friend for an ancient, 'to my great amusement, and his chagrin. He had prided himself on the strength and bushiness of his beard'.[11]

At the start of their return journey Clapperton fell sick, having drunk too liberally of the polluted brackish water at one of the wells, but he was recovered enough to enjoy a visit to the natron lakes where he watched the harvesting of lake shrimps[12] and in the cool of the evening climbed the high dunes to sketch the view. Back in Ubari again two weeks later they found Hatita recovered in health, and made ready to continue to Ghat. They decided to retain the services of the guide, Albini, who 'by his good temper and inoffensive manners had become a great favourite with us'[13]; he would also cook for them. The camel-men and the hired camp servants repeatedly failed to turn up, however, until Clapperton feigned a return to Murzuq, which brought them running.

The excursion began with a tiring series of twelve-hour marches beneath the jagged escarpment of the Black Messak to the desert dividing Fezzan from the Ajjer Mountains (the border itself was marked by a large stone, and it was customary for all travellers entering Fezzan from the west to make a halt there and jump over the stone, to demonstrate their strength after a long journey and to celebrate their safe arrival). The further they travelled across the desert plain, the greater the distances between wells. Following Hatita's example, Oudney and Clapperton wore the Tuareg turban and, unlike Arab travellers, they journeyed only by day. They rose before daybreak and breakfasted on coffee and, when available, camel's milk. At their brief midday halts they took no food other than a handful of dates, after which they set out again, riding at a steady pace[14] until dark, when they made camp. Their camp fires were of brushwood and camel dung and they dined on couscous or a porridge of wheatmeal boiled with grease or fat; occasional evening luxuries consisted of coffee and pipes, or perhaps a sherbet made of oranges.

Round the fire everyone talked and relaxed; Clapperton and Hatita were comfortable enough in each other's company to compare religions and joke and tease one another without loss of respect. Many were the times that Hatita urged Clapperton to apostatize, promising pretty Tuareg girls in this life and paradise in the next; the habitual rejoinder was that Hatita had never seen Scottish girls, who were even more beautiful, and then the two would rib each other, 'what a rogue you are, Abdullah'.[15]

Mount Jinun

On the way through Wadi Tanezzuft they were joined by a small Tuareg war-party. To Clapperton, the clear moonlight, the mountains, the camp site's acacia tree and a ruined castle nearby all provided a pleasingly romantic back-drop for the proud desert warriors seated around the fire, their spears stuck point upper-most in the ground beside them. Indeed, an aura of myth and mystery wreathed itself about the whole Akakus range; intrigued by the legends attaching to Mount Edinan (or Jinun – the home of the djinns) he recorded one of them in his journal,

> A Kaffle comming from Ghadames had been stopped by one of
> the people [djinns] who had demanded a gun ~ which was paid
> for by a piece of paper with writing on it which the Merchant
> did not understand – this on his arriving at a town in Tuat
> was to be given to a black dog that would come out & meet
> him ~ the Merchant when he got there received the money
> from the dog for the letter & has been rich ever since[16]

The guides believed the shrieking and howling of the wind among the crags to be the eldritch voices of desert sprites; with the help of an empty bottle Clapperton attempted (unsuccessfully) to persuade them of the origin of the sounds. Then, to the alarm and consternation of Hatita, Oudney set out to climb Mount Jinun, desiring a closer look at its geological composition. The mountain was further from the track and the climb more difficult than the doctor had foreseen; overcome by fatigue, he lost his way. To the relief of one and all, however, he at length reappeared, happily unscathed by his sojourn among the spirits.[17]

One day's journey outside Ghat the party halted at the wells of Tinisala, under the spreading shade of a giant tamarisk tree, to prepare themselves for arrival in Hatita's home town. There they buried a store of dates for the return journey, and stood barber to each other. To do the occasion justice, Clapperton attired himself in full naval uniform, and Oudney reported that Hatita, 'anxious that we should shine', had expressly tutored his companion in the deportment expected of him (Clapperton should not laugh or sing, but look as grave as possible) – 'As for myself, I had a natural sedateness, which Hateeta thought would do'.[18]

The travellers received a most friendly welcome in Ghat. From Hatita's descriptions and his frequent references to the Tuaregs' great men, Clapperton had expected to find a court of quite some distinction, and was initially a little disappointed when they met the Sultan, whose dress was no different from the rest of the towns-people, in his very modest palace, 'the room next to the one we sat in was occupied by his horse ~ and one of the young princesses came in during our visit with nothing but a ragged breachcloth on and ran into her father's arms'.[19] But he was very struck by the well-read son of the qadi, and by three visiting merchants of Ghadamis who were impressively up-to-date on world affairs and personally acquainted with all the grandees of Tripoli.

Like so many other Europeans after him, Hugh Clapperton was immediately comfortable among the Tuareg people, favourably contrasting their daily life and demeanour, particularly the open-ness of the women, with those of the Arabs. The evenings were spent talking and laughing with Hatita's bright, outgoing sisters and their circle. And with the help of Hatita and others he made a creditable attempt, the first recorded by a European, to draw up a short Tamasheq vocabulary together with a note on the Tifinagh script. Clapperton's interlocutors were engaged by his cheerful, open manner, obvious interest and good will and they responded positively, regardless of language barriers requiring the presence of an interpreter.

Many were the warm solicitations from Hatita's friends and relatives to prolong the British visitors' stay, with tempting offers to escort them on the caravan road south to Aïr and thence to Katsina or Timbuktu. But, with their colleagues awaiting them in Murzuq, Clapperton and Oudney felt unable to delay their return. They left Ghat on 4 August and the following day climbed out of

Wadi Tanezzuft. His concern for the camels labouring up the gorge nearly brought Clapperton to grief. Spotting a number of ticks on the hind legs of Hatita's maherry he made to remove the insects but 'the offended beast gave me a kick on the breast that sent me reeling against the rock – as much as to say take that for your humanity'. Had it been the near rather than the off hind foot, he observed, '[I would have been] sent to glory before my time and lain at the foot of the rocks until the day of judgement if the Kites and Ravens had not carried me away piece meal'.[20]

They returned to Murzuq using a more direct southerly route, accompanied by a party of nomads heading for distant pastures and a few petty traders bound for the oases of central Fezzan. Once across the plateau into Fezzan they embarked on four days of punishing twelve-hour marches along the arid track lying between the *hamada* to the north and the dunes of the Murzuq sand sea and on to the derelict villages and abandoned date groves westward of the capital. On 11 August they were reunited with Tyrwhitt and Hillman, who were still awaiting confirmation of the promised escort. Denham had reached Tripoli before Bey Al-Ahmar and, when he and Warrington called at the Castle, Yusuf Pasha had reaffirmed his intention to consult the Bey before coming to any decision. And there was further disappointing news. London had refused Warrington permission to open a vice-consulate in Murzuq and Tyrwhitt was to return to Tripoli; his recall was a particular blow for Oudney and Clapperton.

John Tyrwhitt had proved a tower of strength; as Oudney wrote to Warrington, he was 'really the best person we could have got, he is always happy'.[21] Hillman had particularly liked the young fellow, they having shared a bottle or two together (in fact between them they had polished off most of the mission's stores of rum) – 'Why, I'm not the man to say a word against another, No, No, but that are little Tyrwhitt did drink, by G-- like Winkin'.[22] His hopes of a vice-consulship in ruins, Tyrwhitt would have given much to accompany the mission as a volunteer – Warrington would not object, and Oudney and Clapperton had offered to make up his salary out of their own pockets. In the end, however, he decided that he could not risk incurring London's disapproval.

Taking advantage of Tyrwhitt's return, Clapperton forwarded to Barrow his rough maps of Fezzan and Ghat, apologising for their quality (they had been executed on a rickety table brought from Tripoli). To fix the mission's positions he had calculated his latitudes by the meridian altitude of the sun and stars and sometimes by eclipses, and estimated longitudes either by the lunar distance method or by Jupiter's satellites; his running positions based on distances and courses marched were rarely off the mark.

Once the dejected John Tyrwhitt had started out for Tripoli, Oudney and Clapperton again began to think in terms of making their own way to Borno. As yet they knew no more about the course of the River Niger than did John Barrow in London – the Arabs travelled on well-beaten tracks and accounts of rivers amounted in many cases only to hearsay. Reliable information on the Sudan, however, was easier to come by, since merchants regularly traded in the great markets at Ngornu and Kano and a number of the mission's acquaintances had been resident there. They spoke of two extensive, stable and militarily-capable states: Borno (ninety days' journey due south of Fezzan in the Lake Chad region) and Hausaland (some twenty days' travel west of Borno).

For four centuries the fief of the Saifawa dynasty of *mais* (kings), the extensive state of Kanem-Borno collapsed in the first decade of the nineteenth century as a result of the Fulani jihad across the central Sudan. Sheikh Mohamed al-Kanemi, 'a wealthy merchant... and a good man'[23], came to power in the following decade and began the process of consolidating a new state centred on Borno. He had been brought up in Fezzan and owned property there, and was well acquainted with the Bu Khulum family. Hausaland, the Arabs explained, formed part of the dominions of the Fulani empire established two decades previously by Uthman dan Fodio whose son, Sultan Mohamed Bello, currently ruled at Sokoto.

From all accounts, both countries enjoyed all the benefits of an Islamic society: working judicial structures, extensive commercial interests and reasonable levels of agricultural production. Produce and manufactures came to their markets from across the Sudan and from other countries to the south and to the west. Merchants in Murzuq also monitored the progress of Al-Kanemi's war with Bagirmi, Borno's powerful neighbour (and former tributary) to the south, where Fezzani armies had twice gone to the Sheikh's assistance in exchange for being allowed to take slaves.

By chance, a number of Fezzani merchants and a party of Al-Kanemi's relations on a trading mission to Murzuq were preparing to travel to Borno. Oudney and Clapperton saw no further need to await an official escort – on their recent expeditions they had after all made little use of *teskeras* and had fared well enough, hiring transport animals and obtaining supplies on the spot in exchange for small payments or presents.[24] They now envisaged proceeding as the mission's advance party, leaving Dixon Denham and any reinforcements (with luck, Tyrwhitt) to catch them up.

While waiting for the merchants to form a caravan, Clapperton was unexpectedly called upon to demonstrate a talent for military organization. Murzuq was thrown into a state of alarm by reports of an imminent attack by a younger son of Muntasir – the former sultan deposed and murdered by Al-Mukni a decade earlier – who was said to be gathering an army in nearby Wadi Etba. Acting-Governor Lizari's problem was that half Murzuq's fighting force (those merchants and renegades who owned muskets and horses) had accompanied Bey Al-Ahmar to Tripoli. Calling the rest to arms, Mohamed Lizari turned to Clapperton who advised concentrating the town's defences within the castle since there were not enough armed men to guard the outer walls and gates. Tuareg riders were sent to spy out the enemy; Hillman set about building a wheeled cradle for Murzuq's old brass cannon, the castle walls were manned and the cavalry (eight horsemen) skirmished flamboyantly before the anxious but admiring womenfolk.

At sundown they were still in want of news, and there was no sleep for anyone that night. Clapperton organized a defensive base in the mission's house and prepared to sell their lives dearly. The following day spies were again sent forth, while the exhausted inhabitants of the town continued to stand nervous watch; the gates remained shut and were visited hourly by Lizari's officers. Clapperton was resigned, 'in the heat of the day the town might have been taken by boys, as all hands went to sleep except in our house'.[25] At last the returning spies brought the glad tidings that the whole affair had been a false alarm – the invading force consisted of Muntasir's son and an old camel driver camped under a date tree and drunk on palm wine, 'In his cups he had thought himself commanding a large army and so sent the formidable and threatening letter to Lizhari which had caused the inhabitants of Morzuk and us so much trouble and Alarm and money'.[26]

Two weeks later Oudney and Clapperton received word from Warrington that Yusuf Pasha had authorized the escort for the mission and that Abu Bakr bu Khulum had been appointed to lead it. And from the same letter they were amazed to learn that, following the unproductive interview with Yusuf Pasha in June, Dixon Denham had taken it upon himself to leave for England, intending to air the matter with the Colonial Department. The harassed Consul further reported that he himself was currently engaged in urgent efforts to bring Denham back to Tripoli.

Clapperton wrote immediately to Warrington and Barrow, and to the new Under-Secretary at the Colonial Office, Robert Wilmot (who added Horton to his surname upon marrying), to remonstrate in the strongest possible terms. Denham's flight to England without a word to his companions, abandoning his so-called assistant in the field without instructions, surely constituted desertion or at the least blatant dereliction of duty; but, he declared loftily, 'His absence will be no loss to the mission, and a saving to his country, for Major Denham could not read his sextant, knew not a star in the heavens, and could not take the altitude of the sun'.[27]

The doctor wrote in similar terms, advising Warrington that he had borne as much from Denham as any man however peaceable could possibly take, 'Had I known the man, I would have refused my appointment'.[28] Even Old Chips registered his disapproval in a letter to Tyrwhitt, concluding, 'I never expect to see him again in Africa'.[29] And Oudney and Clapperton took the opportunity to inform the Consul of their intention to form the advance party to Borno (in the knowledge that a response from Tripoli could not be looked for in much under six weeks).

Dixon Denham's sudden dash for England was in part intended to put pressure on Yusuf Pasha and it had manifestly achieved its object; but the army officer was also working to a hidden personal agenda. In a letter to his brother Charles from the lazaretto in Marseilles he explained that once back in London he intended to lobby for promotion; success (of which he was clearly in no doubt) would not only afford him senior field rank over Clapperton but also secure the unambiguous overall command of the mission. Denham also told his brother that he had no intention of returning to Tripoli before November – in other words, he had already ruled out any idea of making an expedition across the Sahara in the winter of 1822-23. The day before he was due to leave Marseilles for Paris and London, however, he received Warrington's letter recalling him to Tripoli. He took the first available packet back, but not before writing a lengthy private letter of complaint about his colleagues to Earl Bathurst, again carping at Dr Oudney's obstinacy and Clapperton's insubordination; he further submitted that they had put the mission's whole undertaking at risk by setting out on an unnecessary expedition to Ghat.

Circumstances then contrived to set relations between the two Scotsmen and Denham on an irretrievably calamitous footing. On 15 September Denham had left Tripoli for Fezzan with Bu Khulum and at Sockna on 9 October he encountered the courier carrying mail from the mission's temporary base in Murzuq to the Consul-general's office. Following the accepted practice, he opened the mission's dispatches and read his colleagues' indignant letters to Tripoli and the Colonial Department. He immediately fired off to Warrington and to London another volley of criticism, protesting that he had tried very hard to make things work, but that Oudney had harboured rankling ill feelings from the time he was told 'that Clapperton might accompany the Expedition as my assistant, while he was to consider himself as consul of Bornow'.[30] And to his brother Charles he complained similarly, 'Clapperton, my companion and assistant... has been often in open mutiny and told me he had volunteered with the Dr. not with me'.[31] When all the letters reached Warrington, the Consul had to concede that there could no longer be any hope of reconciliation. He wrote forthwith to London with the sensible, if overdue, proposal that another officer be appointed to the mission, to serve as Denham's assistant and thus free Clapperton to travel with Oudney; he suggested John Tyrwhitt, who had just arrived back in Tripoli.

Meanwhile in Murzuq the Fezzani merchants were planning to leave for Borno at the end of September and, having obtained from Mohamed Lizari letters of introduction to the Tubu chiefs on the Saharan road and to Sheikh Al-Kanemi in Borno, Clapperton and Oudney made ready to go with them. There was no knowing when Dixon Denham would return, nor how long it might take Bu Khulum to reach Fezzan and have the escort ready to leave. Moreover, the doctor had found the oppressive heat and humidity of the summer months nigh on intolerable and believed that his physical well-being must be very much improved by moving on.

The departure of the merchant caravan for Borno was delayed yet again – no bad thing given the British mission's general state of health. One by one they had fallen ill. Oudney, Clapperton and Hillman went down with malaria, Oudney suffering also from dysentery and Hillman from inflammation of the eyes. Clapperton himself was bed-ridden for two weeks; and all three kept to their couches until the afternoon to avoid the heat of the day.[32]

Recent news from the desert also made for depressing hearing. Fleeing the persecution of their class by Mohamed Pasha Ali, a group of Mamluks from Upper Egypt had arrived in Murzuq with horrifying accounts of the journey across the Sahara from Wadai, during which half the small caravan's complement had perished at the hands of the Tubu or from thirst in the arid wastes around Tibesti. Clapperton sent them wine and rum to comfort them.

Walter Oudney

At the end of October, Oudney and Clapperton were just four days from departure for the south with the Fezzani merchants when Denham and Bu Khulum and his caravan arrived. Though Oudney's health had shown signs of improvement, Clapperton was still confined to bed with fever, as was Hillman. Even so, Denham later complained to his brother Charles that not one of his colleagues had come out to meet him on arrival; and that when they were all gathered together again at the house, morale seemed rather low. It was hardly to be wondered at.

As to Bu Khulum, the leader of the escort was in fine form and very much in command, having done well for himself in Tripoli; swathed in his newest finery and mounted on a gaily caparisoned horse he cut an impressive figure. Predictably, however, he still needed more time to collect together the remainder of the two hundred strong force and the provisions necessary for the massive expedition; equally true to form, Denham attached himself to Bu Khulum. Walter Oudney and Hugh Clapperton left them to it.

Chapter 9: The Sahara 1822–1823
something like the day of resurrection

Caravan preparations – skeletons in the central Sahara – Wadi Kawar
the Bilma Erg – Tubu country – Lake Chad – military reception in Kukawa

Taking with them Hillman and Deloyice, the mission's servants
and all its baggage, the two friends set off, in company with some
one dozen merchants and their satellites bound for the Sudan and
thirty freed slaves returning home, to Hajj Halil, gathering place
of caravans eight miles south-east of Murzuq. Tradition called for
obeisance at the *marabet* (tomb of the saint) and for alms to be
given to the poor to ensure well-being and safety on the long and
arduous desert journey; and there *fighis* (wandering scholars)
were ready for a small sum to write charms for the amulets of the
anxious or the superstitious. On 19 November 1822, Clapperton
gave a dollar to have the marabut sacrifice an animal and distri-
bute gifts and, with the good wishes and blessings of the many
Murzuqi friends who had come to bid them farewell, the British
advance party headed south into the desert.

The mission's own caravan was of some size. Both officers took
a horse to ride and Hillman a mule, while Deloyice, Absalom and
Madi travelled by camel. Fezzani drivers had been engaged for the
nineteen camels carrying all the baggage, which included food and
firewood and sufficient fodder and water for all the pack animals
on the stages between wells. Arrangements had also been made to
hire manpower from the merchants on an *ad hoc* basis to assist
with camp duties.

The first leg of the journey, round the eastern rim of the Murzuq
sand sea to Al-Qatrun in southern Fezzan, was fairly undemanding,
though poor Hillman was still so weak that on occasion Clapperton
had to hold him upright on the mule and at nightfall carry him
bodily to the tent. For the time being there was no scarcity of well
water, and fresh food in plenty could be bought along the road
from the Fezzani people and Tubu tribesmen tending the date
plantations and small gardens of wheat and vegetables around the
crumbling remains of ancient castles.

At Al-Qatrun, Bu Khulum, Denham and the Arab escort caught
them up. Clapperton took an immediate aversion to the troops

recruited by Bu Khulum, in part because he regarded them as a needless imposition but chiefly because their paramount interest was in raiding for slaves and they openly carried with them irons for securing their prisoners.

The escort consisted of some two hundred Arabs from the nomadic and semi-nomadic tribes which traditionally supplied men for Yusuf Pasha's frontier force. Seventy were of the Megarha tribe from Sirte in the east, but the majority came from Wadi ash-Shati and its outlying regions – among their number were twenty men led by one Abdullah Bougiel, celebrated for never having once surrendered, and another party assembled under Sheikh ben Kaid, whose face had been hideously disfigured by a slash from a Tuareg sword. The tribesmen were no simple herdsmen, but true desert warriors; well-armed, fiery-tempered and ill-disciplined, they made no effort to foster good relations within the caravan and Clapperton distanced himself from them as best he could.

On 6 December, they all set off for Tajarhi, Fezzan's southern-most outpost, to raise provisions for the first stage of the desert crossing, the four-week trek over the central Sahara to Wadi Kawar. The mission had acquired an additional member, and numbered thirteen in all: while in Tripoli, Denham had hired a dragoman and guide, one Adolphus Simpkins, who spoke three European languages well and had fluent Arabic. Simpkins was born of Borno slave stock in St Vincent in the West Indies, and was known as Columbus for having travelled the whole world. He had made his way into the merchant marine and was later captured by corsairs and taken to Tripoli, where he had become one of Qaramanli's personal attendants.

At Tajarhi more merchants joined the caravan to take advantage of an escorted passage to the Sudan, among them their neighbour and friend Old Hadje Mohamed. The seventy-year-old's safe arrival from Murzuq, whence he had been accompanied only by his sons and a few servants, gave Clapperton further reason to regret the collapse of earlier hopes and plans. The continuing growth of the caravan also caused him mounting uneasiness, particularly with regard to provisioning at wells and markets; and theft was rife. Relations on all sides were under increasing strain; the merchants habitually fell out with the escort who were in turn frequently involved in rowdy altercation with the townspeople. But the rich and powerful ruler of Tajarhi, Hadje Mohamed Rashid, a man of mixed Fezzani-Tubu origin, was accustomed to the staging of large caravans in his town and, while successfully exploiting them

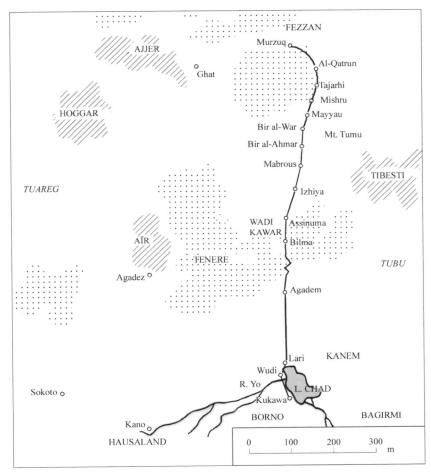

Map 4   Central Sahara 1822–1823

for profit, kept order pretty well – which left no practical role for Bey Al-Ahmar's newly-appointed local administrator, none other than the drunken Neapolitan renegade, Mohamed ben Abd Allah.

The most southerly point reached by George Lyon in 1819, the town of Tajarhi was a pleasant enough spot, with lush oases and palm groves (and to Clapperton's great pleasure, wild duck on the brackish lakes). For all their maps and reference books, however, the sandy track winding southward through the outermost fields and plantations was a step into the unknown for the mission; and the uncertainties ahead were no less daunting to those already familiar with the road.

Before leaving Tajarhi, Bu Khulum ordered a feast and as was customary first time travellers had to provide the fare. The mission contributed two camels to be killed and divided up, and before long 'our camp was all mirth and joy firing guns and feasting ~ and 3 marriges took place with the Arabs – and liberated slave women who marry for the voyage to Bornou only – stipulating that they are to have a camel to ride all the way – and that on her part she will cook and keep her husband warm at night'.[1] The proceedings, Clapperton noted, were attended by a holy man who had followed the caravan to Tajarhi, receiving a present from everyone rich or poor and in return giving them some trifle and a promise to pray for them in their absence. Clapperton was rather dubious, 'I could not help thinking it was something like what used to take place in other countries not many years since when the most villainous actions were all done in the name of god and the church'.[2]

On departure, to relieve pressure on the meagre resources of the wells up ahead, the caravan split into separate groups which started one or two days apart. Oudney and Clapperton left Tajarhi on 13 December and continued to travel independently of Denham as the caravan wound its way up the stony trail towards Tumu, on the plateau forming a saddle between Tibesti and Hoggar.

The same afternoon, at the wells of Oma, they came across a grim reminder of the dangers attaching to a desert crossing. Human skeletal remains lay scattered all around the wells, a scene which Clapperton likened to the site of an ancient city where nothing remained but the bones of its inhabitants. Hillman in particular was very distressed by the white skulls and unhallowed corpses, and needed a good deal of comforting. And at the next well they found the skeletons of more than one hundred human beings, some only partly decayed. 'One poor mabrook [female slave] took the trouble to cover some but the people laughed at her – all around the wells for a dist^{ce} of ¼ Mile each way was covered with skelitons of human beings and other Animals – the former the greater N^o ~ our tents were pitched over these'.[3]

Five days later, the travellers climbed up the long and steep pass to the wells of Al-War. Though Oudney was by then in better health and Clapperton was contentedly immersed in the daily logistics of travel, the rough track, the searing heat and the continual buffeting by wind-blown grit began to take their toll of strength and spirit. Progress was painfully slow. On several occasions only one camel at a time was able to pass between the huge boulders. The exhausted beasts lay down and bellowed, the men grew increasingly short-

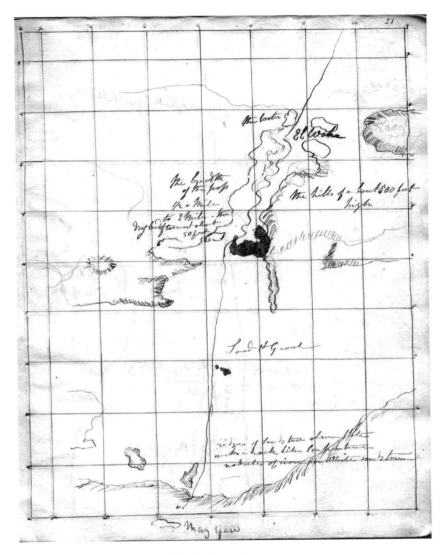

Route map, Mayyau to the Wells of Al-War

tempered and intolerant, 'and the illness of poor Hillman – who today was much worse – added not a little to our miseries'.[4]

At the head of the pass the trail was again littered with the skeletons of humans and animals. And all around the wells at Al-War lay the bodies of those too weak to make the last stage of the north-bound passage; Clapperton was appalled to learn that they

105

were slaves captured in Bey Al-Ahmar's raid across the Sahara the previous year, 'their skins looked like parchment & their bodies & skeletons remained as the life had left them ~ some had their hands at their eyes ~ others were lying with the hand under the head & some with their arms & legs stretched out & lying on their backs – the body of one poor child had the Hands stretched out as if in supplication not to be left to die in such a place'.[5] The shameful reminder of man's inhumanity to man filled Hugh Clapperton with utter revulsion, colouring his dealings with those Arab companions on the journey who traded in slaves and permanently souring his relations with the mission's escort.

With familiarity, however, their sensibilities inevitably became somewhat numbed, 'everywhere you turned we saw the bodies of skeletons of human beings – though we now think not much or feel little concern on passing these – except the thought of their capture is present in our minds and I suppose we will be as bones too in time'.[6] But Clapperton's record continued to bear witness to the deep repugnance he never ceased to feel,

> in the daylight the place had something like a resurrection from intermixture of the dead & living, black & white and speaking a number of languages... the bottom & sides of the pass had a very curious appearance from the long train of camels winding down ~ the groups [of] camels sitting on the black barren rock ~ & the skeletons of Men & animals lying on the path and on each side ~ some of them had fallen in groups or had been thrown together out of the way... near the entrance to the pass we passed the bodies of 2 much mangled ~ they had not an arm lying one way &c-[7]

The indignities visited upon the unburied bodies continued to haunt him throughout the journey; sharpest of all was the sight of crows and kites eating what he had taken for the corpse of a young camel but which turned out to be the body of a slave who had been abandoned there the previous night and died, 'I turned from the scene with horror for though I have seen dead bodies in hundreds at a time killed in all ways yet I never saw beast or bird making a meal from the dead body of my fellow creatures before'.[8]

In the central Sahara, distances between wells increased from four to as many as six days' forced march, but no concession could be made to the weak or frail since any delay would put the whole caravan at risk. The camels were generally able to cope, though they too suffered on the longer arid stages; the horses, however, needed constant watering from *gerbas* (water skins). Everyone was exhausted, '& for myself I have walked these last 2 days owing to the shoe of my horse having lamed his near fore foot – but I have walked thru parts of everyday since we came out'.[9] Worn out by the heat and dust and disheartened by the omnipresent *memento mori*, at night they slept only fitfully, troubled and apprehensive, in fear of marauding Tubu tribesmen and of the jackals which could be heard prowling around the camp beyond the light of the fires. A time of anomy ensued, the disparate groups competing for the best camp site and the first place at a well, and the ensuing uproar regularly ended in physical violence. In such disturbed and disturbing circumstances older beliefs and superstitions were turned to for relief and assistance; magicians were employed to still the winds, and charms were written to ward off evil spirits.

Hugh Clapperton kept himself fully occupied and active. To the irritation of Bu Khulum, who was ultimately responsible for his safety, he would frequently ride away from the caravan to pinpoint landmarks and take bearings for his maps, to establish the positions of mountain ranges, wadis, plateaux and dunes, and to make notes on curious rocks and sand formations. He searched for unusual geological specimens to add to Oudney's collection and kept a sharp look out for desert game for the pot. Back in camp, in dealing with the mission's servants Clapperton trusted to a well-tried formula: hearty encouragement and hard discipline – a hangover from naval service. His reactions were instinctive and his conduct consequently mercurial; he could swiftly turn up rough, knocking a man down for arguing, and even drawing his pistol when he thought it necessary, but he also did whatever he could to care for the infirm. He allowed one ailing camp employee to use his tent while he himself slept in the open air (as was his wont); but another servant, suspected of stealing food, was summarily dismissed without right of appeal.

Two weeks after leaving Tajarhi, the caravan reached the oasis of Izhiya where the various groups were reunited, and Denham once again pitched camp alongside his companions. He called for Clapperton's cartographic records of the journey from Fezzan – as leader of the expedition in the Sahara, he maintained that his right to them was axiomatic. His request was denied. In a terse note, Clapperton declared that although he was ready to oblige with his assistance where appropriate, the present demand was quite out of order. Denham continued to insist, Clapperton to resist,

Tents, 1 January 1823
I thought my previous refusal would have prevented a repetition
of your orders. You take upon yourself a great deal to issue such
orders which could not be more imperative were they from the
Horseguards or the Admiralty. You must not introduce a martial
system into what is civil and scientific; neither must you expect
from me what is your duty to execute[10]

The request was not in itself unreasonable, but if his underlying
intention had been to provoke a quarrel, Denham could hardly
have hit on a rawer nerve. Hugh Clapperton considered his own
navigational skill to be the most significant contribution he could
bring to the Borno Mission and he strongly suspected that the
interloper would later try to take the credit to himself, Denham
who 'could not read his sextant, knew not a star in the heavens...'.
The clash left the two men barely on speaking terms.

Denham copied out their exchange of notes to send to Lord
Bathurst under cover of yet another litany of grievances. Oudney,
he wrote, was totally unfitted by nature or experience to handle
any arrangements for the mission, and was quite impervious to
advice; and he accused Clapperton of an overbearing, 'boasting
and consequential deportment' and of 'extreme intemperance,
irregularity and insubordination', concluding once more that it
was 'a most unfortunate circumstance for me that my assistant
was the friend of Dr. Oudney under whose command as he has
repeatedly told me he volunteered to serve and not mine'.[11] From
then on the feuding factions increasingly went their separate ways.

Three days later they entered Wadi Kawar, at one hundred
miles long the largest *hatiya* (series of oases) in the central Sahara.
Wells were now one day's journey apart, modest provisions were
available from settlements along the road and the leisurely pace of
travel provided a welcome change. An oasis of civilization in the
heart of the Sahara, Wadi Kawar's mixed population of Tubu and
Kanuri peoples had for centuries enjoyed economic success and a
stable social environment. While they made a fair living from provisioning caravans using the central Saharan corridor, their main
business was the production of salt which they sold to Tuareg
traders (arriving at summer's end in huge camel caravans amount-
ing sometimes to thirty thousand head) for transport and resale all
across the Sudan. Occasionally Tuaregs from the west raided the
Wadi to seize cattle and crops and, if their marauding parties were
large enough, also helped themselves to the salt.

Once through the Wadi the caravan entered the immense Bilma Erg – seven days' hard going without wells through six hundred foot-high dunes. A march of a few hours through the shifting sands, in airless hollows, at searing ground-level temperatures and in the full glare of heat reflected from the dunes' south-facing slopes, drained the reserves of man and beast. It was impossible to stay upright, and feet and legs swelled painfully; Clapperton applied henna poultices to relieve the discomfort.[12] Dust storms added to their misery; stifling winds whipped the fine sand from the rocky surface of the southern desert, abrading the skin and turning everyone and everything white. There was no respite.

Propelling the mission's party through the Erg was not unlike sailing a ship in uncharted waters, requiring constant vigilance, assiduous care of precious equipment and the maintenance of accurate logs. Even with the help of guides the best path was not easily made out and Clapperton kept detailed notes of compass courses marched, not only in case they lost their way but also for reference on the return journey.

Conditions were particularly hard on the pack animals. The horses could be watered only from the meagre supplies remaining in the *gerbas* and by journey's end some had not drunk for three days. And even the camels' prodigious staying power began to wane and their loads had to be removed. Merchants sometimes dropped back with their beasts, hoping to see a quick recovery of strength, but in the end the weakest animals were killed for meat and the rest left to follow as best they could or perish on the road. At one point, desperate to arrive first at the halting place, some members of the escort completely lost their heads, descending the sand hills 'like a torrent into the Midst of our camels and only for the exertions of our men we would not only [have] had our things smashed to pieces but our camels killed'.[13] Ten days later Old Hadje Mohamed's party suffered similarly, and left the caravan when Bu Khulum refused to intervene on their behalf.

At length, worn out but intact, the caravan emerged from the Bilma Erg onto the level plains of the lower Ténéré, and the landscape gradually changed. South of the small oasis of Agadem there appeared patches of sparse vegetation and occasionally the tracks of wild animals were seen. The going became easier, with regular marches and daily halts at wells. The camels gorged themselves on the scented *siwak* bush; if they took water too soon afterwards, however, they became drunk – as did one in Clapperton's care, 'though he was a stout camel & walked well on other occasions he fell so often that we had to unload him – the Arabs opened one of the veins of the Nose & took about ½ a gallon of blood from him'.[14]

The moment they encountered the first isolated communities of nomads the escort troops raided them for supplies. Clapperton gave the Tubu tobacco in exchange for their offerings of milk, meat and sauce, 'but the villains of Arabs fell in with a flock of sheep as we were going to the Kaffle and seized 2 ~ I told them if they were hungry that I would buy them a sheep ~ o no says they ~ down there they are infidels, you shall pay for nothing ~ I said their behaviour was not like men and that they ought to be ashamed of themselves after being treated so kindly to rob the people ~ they laughed at me for my pains'.[15] He despaired of the escort, 'slaves of the most abject kind to their superiors & the most unjust & cruel tyrants to those they have it in their power to oppress'.[16] Though often tempted to intervene he had to defer to Bu Khulum, the caravan's bey, who clearly knew exactly how and when to rein in his men and when to allow them some latitude. Such a style of command was familiar to Clapperton and by the end of the Saharan crossing his private opinion of the Bey had altered marginally for the better.

The relief of reaching the northernmost fringes of the Sudan put everyone in a more relaxed frame of mind. Better supplies were at last available along the route, the Gunda Tubu tribesmen offering for sale camels and fresh meat, fat and milk. Clapperton began to ride out again, exploring the land either side of the road, studying shrubs and grasses with Oudney, and hunting antelope, partridge and hare. Shooting competitions were staged; he enjoyed showing off his own prowess and he was very critical of the Arabs' badly manufactured and unreliable flintlocks, as much a danger to themselves as to an enemy.

On 25 January, two couriers appeared from the south, bearing messages of welcome from Sheikh Al-Kanemi – and no doubt also charged with assessing the strength and character of the Fezzani force. They reported that all was well in Borno; the Sheikh's army had just returned from another expedition into Bagirmi, south of Lake Chad, and had brought off a good prize of cattle, camels and slaves.

After eighty days in the desert, the British mission had reached the Sudan (further from Tripoli than Tripoli from London). Five more days took the whole caravan into the savannah region of northern Kanem, and at one o'clock in the afternoon of 4 February 1823, just outside the small settlement of Lari, the British travellers had their first glimpse of Lake Chad,

When we arrived on the Top of the Sandy ridge on which the Town of Lari stands we were astonished at seeing an immense Lake & Marsh on the South side of the ridge extending as far as the eye could reach to the South & to the East Studded with low islets[17]

After the arid wastes of the Sahara such an expanse of water in the heart of Africa seemed an almost miraculous sight. Featuring in many a traveller's account over the ages, its position vaguely depicted on rudimentary maps, and described by Arabs and by Sudanese in confused and conflicting accounts, Lake Chad might well have consisted of a chain of marshes and rivers or wet-season swamps. Clapperton and Oudney were quite unprepared for the reality: the wide scintillating surface of the lake and the lush green vegetation and brilliant flowering plants proliferating along its shores and covering the small islands, and its banks and shallows teeming with bird life – geese, pelicans, herons, several kinds of duck, cranes and countless others they did not recognize. They took it all in, awed and entranced.

The inhabitants of Lari, however, were surprised and shocked by the size and nature of the caravan; some bolted in terror into the reeds at the lake-side while others snatched up their shields and spears and prepared to defend themselves. Calm was restored and before long the villagers had set up a small fair in the travellers' camp, selling millet, fowls and fat in exchange for beads and other small articles of trade.

Once the caravan had left Lari, Oudney and Clapperton set off to explore, convinced that any rivers contributing to so vast an expanse of water must also be of significant breadth. Oudney took samples of the water (for analysis back in Britain), and they boiled kettles beside the lake to establish the height of the land above sea-level. As they journeyed towards the western shores of Lake Chad they wondered at the richness of the increasingly cultivated landscape, the neatly-farmed fields and the abundance of produce in the village markets, and at the stout construction of the walls and buildings of the sizeable towns.

The edge of the lake was bordered by a sandy dyke covered in brushwood; about a mile wide, and evidently inundated during the rains, it was home to a prolific range of wild life. The tracks and dung of elephants were everywhere; Old Chips, who had never before seen an elephant, was amazed and alarmed when he awoke from a rest to discover one looming massively nearby. And a delighted Clapperton happened on a wild pig. He gave chase, cheered by the thought of its rich and fatty meat (a feast which would not have to be shared with all and sundry). Unfortunately, he had no wadding ready for his gun but he scrambled eagerly through the thorn bushes, pistols in hand – only to come face to face with a lion padding quietly out of the scrub; the pig and the disconcerted hunter both came away unscathed.

At Wudi, Borno's frontier town on the north-western corner of Lake Chad, Clapperton bade a fond farewell to an indomitable old black woman, a freed slave returning to her homeland. They had looked after her on the road, often to the disapproval of the Arabs, 'from the Wells of Oma to this place ~ given her food and a ride on the camels when ever our loads would admit… only for us she would never have seen her native country [again] ~ she was between 60 and 70 years of age… and at her age to undertake a journey of 1200 Miles nearly to return to it and that 2/3 of the way on foot was no small undertaking'.[18]

On arrival at the banks of a river (the Yo) they made estimates of the flow and calculated that it was of too meagre a volume to be Mungo Park's great waterway. However, they had a refreshing bathe and in the evening 'the D[r] and I seated ourselves on its banks & enjoyed a beautiful setting sun, the Winding of the river & the lofty trees, gum trees, decking its banks & the vivid red rays of the light reflected from the river formed as beautiful a scene to us as our imaginations could wish'.[19]

When they got to within half a day's ride of Borno's capital, Kukawa, they were in for another surprise. During the course of the journey the mission had heard contradictory accounts of the nature and capability of the Sheikh's armed forces, and thus had no idea what to expect when it was announced that Al-Kanemi would come out with an escort to welcome his visitors.

The following morning each one dressed himself in his finest. Bu Khulum drew up the caravan in martial order, the flags in the centre, the cavalry on the wings and the camel train behind; the British party he kept at his side. As they advanced across the plain, to everyone's amazement and consternation, an army of some twelve thousand men was discovered drawn up before them. Al-Kanemi's horsemen galloped up, skirmishing in time-honoured durbar fashion, making repeated rapid forward dashes, firing over their heads, and spinning round just short of Yusuf Pasha's official representative and the main group of visitors. The Sheikh's foot-soldiers then closed in, encircling Bu Khulum and his bodyguard in a seething, jostling mass. It was a very considerable demonstration of power.

The Bey flew into a rage. He was divided from his flags as were the horse from the foot; the escort had been scattered all over the field, not five men together but in twos and threes. Those Arabs who had remained near Bu Khulum 'began shoving at the Sheikh's horsemen and swearing like their commander ~ the horsemen of the Sheikh retaliated by stealing the red caps off the heads of the Arabs and pricking them with their spears – this made bad worse – sometimes B.k.m. rode one way some times another without knowing what to do – he beat two of the Sheikhs officers and his relations most heartily... I therefore thought it high time as Major D- did not interfere to give B.k.m. a little advice... he had better halt and get his men together before he did any more ~ he followed my advice and this also gave time to the Sheikh's people to think what they were about'.[20]

Once order had been restored the large caravan was led into Kukawa, where the British travellers were permitted to rest and eat before being taken to the palace for the formal reception. To Bu Khulum's indignation he and the mission's officers were made to wait in the full heat of the sun for a good two hours. Yusuf Pasha's envoy was received first, reappearing a little later to discuss the proper mode of salutation for the occasion. The Sheikh's officers had recommended prostration, a suggestion instantly rejected by the British visitors who declared that as personal representatives of His Majesty, the King of England, they would do no more than salute and shake hands. When they eventually gained admittance to the palace itself, they found the stairs barred by two scimitar-bearing guards of enormous stature who permitted them to ascend only one at a time.

Sheikh Mohamed al-Amin ben Mohamed al-Kanemi of Borno had been at some pains to make it clear that the stay in his capital of Bu Khulum, the assorted merchants, the disorderly and potentially dangerous posse of Arab warriors and the singular British mission would be strictly on his own terms.

Chapter 10: Borno 1823
severely put to it

Sheikh Al-Kanemi's Borno – residence in Kukawa
a malicious calumny – the River Shari – a raid in Mandara
expedition to Manga – the rains and fever – Hadje Ali bu Khulum's debt

The son of a Kanembu scholar-priest and his Fezzani wife (the daughter to a wealthy Zawila merchant), Mohamed al-Kanemi had been brought up in Murzuq. Following studies in Tripoli and other northern African cities he settled in Borno, where he began to introduce enlightened religious and social policies in direct competition with those of the corrupt and incompetent traditional dynasty of Saifawa *mais*. Over the next decade he continued to strengthen his position, building on his personal connections in Kanem, the approval of influential Shuwa Arabs in the Lake Chad region, the friendship of leading intellectuals and the support of the merchant community. In 1809, at the Mai's request, he took command of the military campaigns to halt the Fulani invasions from the west and deal with Bagirmi's repeated incursions in the south. He was rewarded with gifts of money and land, eventually building his own independent capital at Kukawa and assuming the title of Sheikh (denoting both tribal and religious leadership).

By 1819 Al-Kanemi held the reins of power in Borno, and on Mai Dunama's death in battle that year he appointed Dunama's suggestible nineteen-year-old brother, Ibrahim, to the succession. When the British mission arrived in Borno in February 1823, the Sheikh was still preoccupied with consolidation of the influential and administratively coherent state he had created.

Al-Kanemi received the mission's officers in a room hung about with dust-covered swords, blunderbusses and muskets. He was plainly dressed and seated on a small Turkish rug, a guard armed with pistols to either side of him. Clapperton judged him to be in his forties; about five foot nine inches tall, he had large eyes, a long Roman nose, projecting teeth, a short grey beard and a strong rather hoarse voice. He spoke excellent Arabic, his demeanour was pleasant and his manner courteous; and after the customary compliments and having read Yusuf Pasha's letter of introduction he assured his British guests that anything he could do to show them his country would give him pleasure.

The formalities over, Clapperton and his companions withdrew to lodgings prepared for them in that part of the town set aside for foreign visitors, an area surrounded by twenty foot-high walls with a single gate. Their compound consisted of half a dozen *kusis* (small circular huts) built of clay, each about five feet six inches high, its simple wooden roof-frame covered with coarse straw matting and supported by a forked stick. Within the walled suburb they were fenced off from quarters housing the Fezzani merchants and other foreign visitors. And a vizier, Mohamed Karaouash, was appointed to see to their needs, to act as intermediary with the Sheikh – and to keep a close eye on their activities.

That evening supplies of food, and fodder for their animals, began to arrive. Though Clapperton did not much care for a ready prepared meal delivered to them – of *bazeen* (corn meal porridge) made up with a great deal of grease and without salt, unleavened pancakes of sour rice and tainted, stinking mutton – he did enjoy the sweet flour-and-honey cakes, traditional gifts to visitors. Over the next few days a huge volume of provisions was brought to their compound: two camel-loads of fresh fish and fifteen loads of wheat, rice, milk, vegetables, fat and honey; four camel-loads of *gussub* (millet) for their horses; and ten bullock-loads of other produce from the market.

Two days later the mission presented the official gifts, which featured the most modern and refined manufactures from Europe including clocks, watches, fine cloth, swords, a double-barrelled gun and pistols. The presents were much admired, and Clapperton was asked to demonstrate the use of the compass and the winding of the watches. Al-Kanemi was very impressed by the Congreve rockets which Clapperton set off and, intrigued by the technology of warfare, he was particularly keen to learn how a walled town could best be attacked by artillery.

In the early days the British travellers received an endless stream of visitors – townspeople, Arab merchants and temporary residents – and the doctor was as usual besieged by requests for medical advice. The pace of visits and activities soon slowed, however, and they were able to take their ease in their cool and airy *kusis*. They wrote lengthy dispatches and letters home; and Clapperton used the opportunity to draw up fair copies of his charts of the route and to take astronomical readings to fix the position of the capital (he set Kukawa some 1.5° east of its true position but his estimates of latitude were accurate). And then, for one hundred Spanish dollars they hired two men with a camel apiece to take all their correspondence to Murzuq, where Bu Khulum's brother Hamadu had agreed to handle communications with Tripoli[†].

Beginning a fresh journal, Clapperton signed it with a flourish on the frontispiece in English and then in Arabic, using his travelling sobriquet, *'Huq Klabatun Abd allah bin Skatland, Town of Kuka'.*[1] And having tended to the mission's horses and pack animals, mended equipment and repaired personal belongings, he turned his mind to travel beyond Borno.

Clapperton's signatures, Kukawa

The immediate aim was to head west and south across the Sudan to find the River Niger at Yawri or at Bussa (the furthest point reached by Mungo Park). But the mission was destined to spend the remainder of 1823 in the Sheikh's dominions, finding itself hostage in turn to local politics, the rains, tropical illness and straitened financial circumstances.

[†] It took roughly twelve months to receive a reply to mail sent by courier from the Sudan to London via Tripoli – for example, the mail dispatched from Kukawa in April 1823 was received in London in October, and replies written in November 1823 reached Borno in May 1824.

According to an agreement reached the previous September between Warrington and Yusuf Pasha, the travellers were required to give Bu Khulum a written release if they proposed to quit the escort or undertake independent travel, 'His head is answerable for your safety unless he is exonerated from the charge by a written document'[2]; and the Pasha's letter to Al-Kanemi similarly underlined the Sheikh's personal liability. All progress was clearly dependent upon the goodwill of Al-Kanemi and Bu Khulum, whose individual intentions had yet to be made known.

In the interim, Clapperton went hunting, accompanied by his servant Madi, an escort officer and two archers. On the shores of Lake Chad, the crisp soil and burnt vegetation made a stealthy approach well nigh impossible and though he saw more game than he shot, he was satisfied with what success he had. The fast-running grey-brown francolin was difficult to hunt down in the arid grasslands and among the scattered trees; and the corigum (Western hartebeest), he avowed, was 'the sweetest and tenderest meat I ever ate'. Camping by the lake, however, was not nearly so agreeable – their nights were disturbed by 'ants and mosquitoes, the growling of jackals and the roaring of lions; the horse and the mule were as uneasy as we were'.[3]

When later that month he and his companions set out to visit Ngorno, the commercial hub of Borno, they were unaware that Al-Kanemi had arranged that en route they and Bu Khulum would pay a formal call on Mai Ibrahim at his residence at Birni Kafela. Upon arrival at the former capital, therefore, they were taken aback when the Pasha's representative, attired in all his finery, produced handsome presents for Ibrahim. They had nothing with them and it was too late to go back; a good deal embarrassed, they promised to send their gifts. The pageantry of the court of the once mighty Saifawa kings, however, struck Clapperton as absurd: the Mai's courtiers teetered around in layers of baggy elegance – one was enveloped in seven *tobes* (voluminous wide-sleeved shirts) of different hues, his turban hung with leather charms and tufts of ostrich feathers, making him 'more like an immense bale of cloth than anything ~ with part of a human face sticking out of it'.[4]

In Birni Kafela, Oudney again went down with the ague and Clapperton, feverish himself, accompanied him back to Kukawa, leaving Denham to travel on to Ngorno with Bu Khulum and the merchants. The doctor's pulmonary consumption had been steadily increasing upon him and, weakened by the hardships endured on the desert crossing, he was particularly hard hit by the resurgence of fever; he was confined to his tent for two weeks in a precarious state of health.

The hardships of the Saharan journey continued to take their toll of the mission's animals. A few days later Clapperton's horse, an affectionate and stalwart companion, gave up the struggle,

> My poor horse died this Morning to my great regret ~ I brought him from Tripoli ~ he was the fleetest the strongest, the highest & most tractable horse that came out in the Kaffle and used to follow me like a dog when I chose to dismount & walk – I could fire off his back as steadily as from the ground ~ he would never wince & often have I levelled the rifle upon his neck and back & shot a Gazelle & when I ran to secure my game he would gallop after me ~ apparently as pleased as I was – but alas poor Dick will gallop after me no more[5]

The British party had arrived with four horses, three mules and several camp dogs brought from Tripoli. By the summer of 1823, however, all save one mule were dead; the camels from Murzuq had also succumbed. The Fezzani merchants were adamant; they would not remain in Kukawa in the wet season (July to October) since the climate of the low-lying Chad basin had all too frequently been fatal for both man and beast.

The mission's officers grew increasingly concerned about how much they could realistically hope to achieve before the onset of the rains. Clapperton and Oudney were bent on travelling west to the cities of Hausaland, some twenty days' journey from Kukawa, and thence to Nupe, to reach the River Niger where they believed it must begin its final course to the sea and the Bight of Benin. Denham's ultimate aim, on the other hand, was to head eastwards towards Darfur and Kordofan where he confidently expected to find the junction of the Niger and the Nile; he would then return home via Egypt. In the meantime, however, all were agreed that they must first establish whether any major rivers other than the Yo flowed into Lake Chad and, if so, where they rose, and attempt to ascertain what outlets there might be. Despite earlier affirmations, however, receipt of the necessary permissions still appeared to be in doubt. At issue were the complex politics of the Sudan.

In 1823, Mohamed al-Kanemi faced rebellion and unrest along all his borders. Since the end of the conflicts which had arisen in the preceding decade as a result of the Fulani *jihad*, the caliphates of Borno and Sokoto had officially co-existed in peace. Relations continued uneasy, however, in the light of competing claims for territory and the doctrinal differences between the two scholarly leaders, Sheikh Al-Kanemi and Sultan Mohamed Bello, over the justification for killing or enslaving Moslems in a holy war.

Between the two caliphates lay the ungovernable non-Moslem country of Bede, stubbornly resistant to influence from either side. To the south, Fulani populations continued to encroach on Borno's traditional preserves in Mandara; in the east, Borno's influence in Kanem had been eroded by an assertive neighbour, Wadai. In the north, pressure from Tuareg marauders had created zones of anarchy where indigenous populations, such as the Manga on the northern rim of the Yo valley, seemed bent on shaking off tributary status. But Al-Kanemi's most troublesome and persistent enemy was Bagirmi; despite having suffered several defeats at the hands of the Sheikh's combined forces during the previous five years, they continued to mount armed incursions into the rich lowlands of south-eastern Borno.

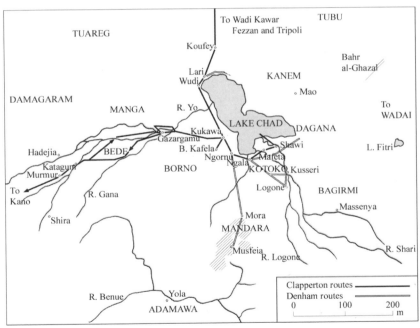

Map 5   Borno and Lake Chad region 1823

The Sheikh's immediate concern, however, was to gauge the Pasha's real objectives and thus determine how best to treat with

119

Bu Khulum, who clearly had his own problems dealing with the large numbers of people for whom he was responsible. The armed and volatile Arab troops were impatient for booty and a speedy return home, while the Fezzani merchants, keen to sell their wares and take in a stock of Sudanic goods before the onset of the rains, continued to chafe at the delay in setting out for Hausaland.

With regard to his British guests, Al-Kanemi was inclined to accept at face value their expressed desire to see his country even though he harboured misgivings about the mission's likely role as the forerunner of a commercial invasion. Whatever their intentions, however, their safety outside his own dominion could not be guaranteed and he could not allow them to travel freely.

When Oudney and Clapperton requested permission to go to Hausaland, the Sheikh regretted that the roads through lawless Bede country were not safe. His ruling was not open to appeal. Hugh Clapperton viewed their situation with mounting anxiety. Al-Kanemi himself seemed less accessible, his aide Karaouash had proved an unreliable go-between, and the travellers found themselves fielding probing questions and prevarication from all sides. During the impasse, Clapperton returned to his hunting expeditions on the shores of Lake Chad, and the frustrated Arab tribesmen of the escort continued to bicker amongst themselves; Old Hadje Mohamed, Al-Abidin (the qadi from Murzuq) and the qadi of Kukawa did what they could but failed to reconcile the quarrelsome factions. And then, at the beginning of April, word reached Kukawa that the Sultan of Bagirmi was mustering a force along the River Shari, intending to invade south-eastern Borno.

Although there was general anxiety among the townspeople when the Sheikh began to make his military dispositions, the Arabs were elated by the prospect of plunder and slave raiding, and stayed up through the night debating how best to convey their likely spoils back across the desert. In the event, however, Al-Kanemi decided not to confront the old enemy; furthermore, he had no desire to unleash Bu Khulum's troops so near his own borders. Their plans and schemes abruptly set at nought, half the Arab force mutinied and decamped, which effectively forced the Sheikh's hand. In an attempt to defuse a potentially explosive situation, Al-Kanemi cast around for another target, finding it in the troublesome Fulani groups which, supported by Sokoto and allied with pagan hill tribes, were currently active on the southern fringes of Mandara. If successful, the sortie would give the Arabs the booty they craved; furthermore, it would serve both to bolster the

Sheikh's ally the Sultan of Mandara and to strike a blow against Sokoto's ambitions to expand its influence in the region.

The prospect pleased all Al-Kanemi's visitors, and when the troops began to assemble the British officers asked to be allowed to accompany the Sheikh's forces in order to visit the country to the south of Lake Chad. While the mission had received explicit orders forbidding it to take part in any activity connected with raiding for slaves, its members were of the opinion that simply travelling alongside an army did not put them in breach of their instructions. Yet again, however, Al-Kanemi refused his permission; they could certainly travel to the River Shari but not to Mandara.

Oudney and Clapperton were content to abide by the ruling but Dixon Denham had other ideas; frustrated by the delays and profoundly irritated by his colleagues, he determined to act unilaterally. He had no intention of losing an opportunity to travel east, and attempted to bribe Karaouash to intercede on his behalf with Al-Kanemi; when that worthy declined, he approached the general commanding the army, Barca Gana, whose favourable opinion he had been assiduously cultivating for some time. Barca Gana encouraged his hopes, and, in self-satisfied and truculent mood, Denham engineered a showdown with Clapperton,

> Saturday 12th Light Airs & Clear – ~~I received a most infamous letter from Major D.~~[6]

The brief entry (subsequently reconsidered and struck through) was the only reference in Clapperton's journals to a rancorous affair originating in a lengthy missive from Dixon Denham,

> I should neglect my duty were I any longer to delay setting before you in the strongest light I am able the continued extreme impropriety of your conduct both public and private, which I regret to say is no less discreditable to the Mission and the country and to yourself as an officer and at the same time injurious in the highest degree to our Interests at the present moment...[7]

Denham's complaints related to alleged insubordination and reprehensible treatment of the mission's employees, and he cited occasions on which he believed Clapperton had brought the entire British undertaking into disrepute with those such as Bu Khulum on whom they were counting for support.

Clapperton immediately took the extraordinary communication to Oudney. The references to disciplinary incidents within the mission were readily explicable; Hillman acknowledged that he had on occasion complained about Clapperton's rough and ready style, and Oudney knew that his companion's severe handling of the indolent and unreliable Deloyice had been justified. As for bringing the whole mission into disrepute, the doctor maintained that Bu Khulum respected Hugh Clapperton at least as much as he did Dixon Denham; but although the loyal Oudney offered his friend a stout defence, the truth was that Clapperton had not tried as hard as he should have to overcome or at least disguise his dislike of Abu Bakr bu Khulum. His surly attitude towards the leader of the unwanted escort during the trials of the desert journey was perhaps understandable; however, his failure to mask his personal antipathy once in Borno, and his public disparagement, his carping remarks and cynical asides had indeed done nothing to enhance the mission's prospects.

Clapperton and Oudney naturally rejected the allegations out of hand but what really mystified them was the reference to *private* impropriety. On the evening of 13 April, in the doctor's presence, Clapperton demanded an immediate and full explanation. In reply, Denham accused him of having engaged in homosexual relations during the desert journey with a camp employee, one Abdullahi. Clapperton exploded in fury, at which point Denham turned on his heel, informing them as he left that he intended to make his own way to Ngorno where he would wait for them; he stole away from Kukawa at midnight, riding to catch up Barca Gana whose army had left earlier in the day.

Blinded by his personal grievances, Dixon Denham had taken several steps too far. Hugh Clapperton was already spoiling for a fight, having just closed a letter to the Under-Secretary concerning the spat at Izhiya over his navigational charts. The following day he wrote to Consul Warrington to register the strongest possible objections to Denham's calumnies, with particular reference to the allegation of homosexuality which, though an obvious fabrication, certainly had the potential to bring his career in the Royal Navy to an abrupt and ignominious end. Walter Oudney set in train his own investigations; although Abdullahi could not be called upon to give evidence, since he had already left Kukawa, others came forward to shed light on the matter.

The mission had frequently employed casual Arab labour to help with daily duties, making and breaking camp, loading and re-loading camels. The charge of homosexuality was a revengeful invention by a man Clapperton had discharged at Assinuma in Wadi Kawar on suspicion of the theft of the carcase of a young camel. The accusation had filtered through to the dismissed man's tribal chief (whom Clapperton had earlier offended by refusing him tobacco) and evolved into a popular camp-fire story, told and re-told in jesting mockery of Abdullahi, an ugly fellow over forty years old who had regularly worked for the mission. Abdullahi hotly denied the charge, threatening to shoot anyone who dared repeat it. A version of the tale eventually reached Denham's ears and he had kept it to himself, for future use.

Oudney wrote to Consul-general Warrington, expressing his personal indignation: the malicious fabrications were the work of 'a mind void of every drop of the milk of human kindness; a mind that hoards its venom to sting when it may find an opportunity – a man that takes memoranda on the conduct of others is one that ought to be expelled from society; he is a nuisance, he is a curse'.[8] No one in the town believed the story and the Sheikh himself had needed no convincing. While Al-Kanemi's understanding was naturally gratifying and Oudney's unswerving support a solace, the infamous allegation left Clapperton profoundly disturbed by his inability to present his immediate refutation of Denham's charges to the relevant authorities in London; the psychological wound festered for months to come.

Two days after the confrontation, accompanied by an escort officer, Sidi Mustafa, and Belal, the Sheikh's slave and personal representative, Oudney and Clapperton started out for the River Shari expecting to find Denham in Ngorno; but the Major had already left for the south with the army. Making no attempt to follow him, the two Scots headed east, beginning with a three-day journey round the south-western corner of Lake Chad, over an interminably flat and dusty terrain of baked red-grey soil where only the thorn scrub afforded occasional shade to the cattle of the nomadic Shuwa Arabs. The scattered settlements were small and the stench of rubbish and rotting carcases, picked over by vultures and kites, was overpowering; but, however poor, the inhabitants were welcoming and very generous.

On their journey, Sidi Mustafa stood interpreter and Belal, a man of considerable authority, saw to it that the local headmen furnished all necessary assistance and supplies. Six feet two inches tall and proportionately strong, Belal stalked about in lofty silence, supplying all their needs 'before we know that we want anything our selves'.[9] Al-Kanemi's rule was law and his officers controlled the frontier district with a firm hand.

The Scots set up camp beside the Shari. Clapperton was in his element, hunting on the banks of the slow-moving river, taking navigational observations and recording the life of the riparian communities. While Oudney collected specimens of water plants, Clapperton studied local techniques for catching eel and bream, and watched the villagers crossing the river on floats made from tied bundles of ambach (balsa-wood) roots, stout sticks serving as paddles; and in the evenings he sat by the river as people arrived to collect water and bathe,

> I could not resist the temptation of taking a swim myself & went in to the water on a clear spot between the men & the women – I did not like to go to a great distance for fear of the Aligators which are very numerous – they say they are quite harmless but I had no inclination to trust them too far not knowing but they might relish a piece of white flesh – and being a Kafir they might intrude without fear but they might consider it dangerous to touch a true believer ~ I found the water warm & pleasant & after swimming across to an Isl$^{\underline{d}}$ two or three times I came out & went home[10]

He went out as often as possible with his rifle and shotguns. There were antelope on the river-banks, and his guides pointed out to him the branches overhanging the track where leopards could lie hidden. The villagers helped him retrieve duck, guinea fowl and monkeys – looking on in astonishment when he attempted to shoot a crocodile or hippopotamus – and enthusiastically joined in the chase when he shot and wounded a buffalo.

The Sheikh of Shawi and his courtiers accompanied the visitors on a boating trip down the river. The canoes were each paddled by at least ten – and sometimes as many as sixteen – men, with one man to steer. Forty-five feet in length, four and a half feet in breadth and three feet deep, their planks lashed together with hemp and caulked inside and out with rushes, the vessels made a good deal of water, requiring to be baled out every five to ten minutes. In all there were thirty-three boats; the crews sang as they paddled, and on board the Sheikh's boat flutes played to the accompaniment of a hand drum. The plaintive air seemed very pleasant to Clapperton, 'the slow soft & clear tune had a fine affect ~ but I am no judge of music ~ it was finer than anything I have heard since I left Malta'.[11]

Oudney and Clapperton were given permission to explore the meandering river down to Lake Chad. It took a full two days to pole and paddle through the tangled rafts of vegetation and reeds to the open waters of the lake, where they slept out on an island; Clapperton kept a note of compass bearings from which he later constructed an accurate chart of the main stream.

Pleased with their discoveries and happy in the thought that they were the first Europeans ever to have sailed that great inland sea, the two explorers retreated to Shawi to collect any additional information from the inhabitants about the source and course of the River Shari. From all accounts, the river was formed by two branches rising to the south and south-east of Lake Chad, and they concluded that it could not therefore be the Niger.

After ten days on the Shari they set off to return to Kukawa, anxious to be back by the time the armed forces returned from Mandara; and two days distant from the capital, they received word that the raid had ended in disaster. Five days later, 'Major Denham arrived from his unsuccessful campaign, unfortunate to both the Arabs & himself'.[12] The entire Borno army, its allies from Mandara and the Arab troops had been completely put to rout by the Fulani; Bu Khulum had been killed and Denham had only just escaped with his life.

Setting to one side his discreditable behaviour towards Hugh Clapperton and the deliberate flouting of Al-Kanemi's express instructions forbidding the British officers to accompany the army into Mandara, Dixon Denham emerged from the debacle with some honour, having displayed considerable personal courage during the affair. The military operation on the other hand had proved an out and out fiasco from the very beginning, as the Scots learnt to their dismay.

When General Barca Gana eventually reached Mandara, the anticipated brief punitive raid upon apparently backward people escalated into a large-scale deployment deep inside rebel country. An army of three thousand Bornoese and Shuwa Arab troops, together with two thousand Mandara cavalry and Bu Khulum's two hundred men, marched three days south into the mountains. At the village of Musfeia, in a circle of high hills, they confronted a sizeable Fulani force well-armed and dug in behind a picket line. The Mandara and Shuwa forces unaccountably hung back but the eager Arabs (half of them mounted) and the disciplined Borno troops advanced, instantly coming under a deadly rain of poisoned arrows. To a man they turned tail and ran.

During the ignominious flight down the valley, with enemy foot soldiers in hot pursuit, Bu Khulum was killed. Dixon Denham himself was surrounded and stripped of his clothing. He received several spear thrusts before managing to escape on foot into the woods, forfeiting his horse and a pack mule with the baggage containing his instruments, journals and the rest of his belongings. He borrowed clothes from Barca Gana and was loaned a horse to ride (his own was later found, luckily unharmed). Forty-five of the Arab tribesmen died and many others were wounded; they lost a number of horses and their possessions were pillaged by both foe and ally. The depleted escort, a sobered Borno military force and a chastened Major Denham had retreated swiftly to the plains.

On the army's return to Kukawa, the remnants of the escort set off home – with precious little booty. The long-suffering merchants from Murzuq and Tripoli were finally allowed to proceed to Kano; and Al-Kanemi sent couriers to Fezzan and Tripoli to give his nominal allies an account of the raid. It was Clapperton's private opinion that Al-Kanemi had in fact tricked Bu Khulum; what was certain, however, was that Yusuf Pasha would be far from pleased.

Relations within the British camp continued strained. Though the three officers were naturally seen about together in public, in private Clapperton and Denham communicated only in writing and Oudney mediated when necessary. But all three were worried about the implications for their expedition of the defeat of the Borno armies and in particular of the death of Bu Khulum, an event which placed the mission in a very awkward position. And their entire financial reserve had been in his hands, invested in trade goods (which arrangement had suited both sides since the British had no wish to be carrying specie across the desert). In September 1822 Consul Warrington had handed to Abu Bakr, against the latter's signed receipt, the two thousand dollars which had been promised to the mission and Oudney had been content that the money should remain with Bu Khulum – but, with hindsight, Dixon Denham had of course blamed the doctor for not having insisted that at least part of the sum be handed over upon arrival in Borno.

Any hope of having their funds restored to them now lay with Abu Bakr bu Khulum's younger brother and executor, Hadje Ali, who was absent in Hausaland; and unfortunately Hadje Ali had just dispatched back to Fezzan a caravan load of Sudanic goods which the mission might have been able to sequester. They consulted Al-Kanemi who said it would be necessary to prove the debt in court; they had perforce to wait until Hadje Ali returned.

The Sheikh, meanwhile, was making ready to launch another military expedition before the onset of the rains. Its purpose was to quell incipient rebellion in Manga on Borno's north-western borders. He invited the British officers to go with him, partly to keep an eye on them, but perhaps also to allow them to see his army in a rather more flattering light. For Clapperton five weeks spent journeying through the heartlands of ancient Borno at least represented the opportunity for further exploration – and there were no other options on offer.

Escorted by one of the Sheikh's chief slaves, Omar Gana, and taking the mule to carry their baggage, Oudney and Clapperton left Kukawa on 21 May. They travelled ahead of the army, keen to maintain a certain degree of independence and to avoid involvement in what might turn into a rather prolonged campaign. Denham proceeded separately, judging it politic to stay close to Al-Kanemi. On the journey through the fertile Yo valley, Clapperton as usual rode out ahead but took a guide with him, partly on account of the formidable pit-traps. Some twelve feet deep and four to five feet wide at the top, each pit contained four solid spikes of sharpened wood projecting upwards from its depths. Disguised with grass and reeds, over which sand was strewn, the traps were primarily used to capture large animals but were also effectively deployed in chain formation against human intruders.

Clapperton admired the country folk he met along the way, 'the finest of the Negro race I have ever seen – particularly the women ~ they are kind and affable and I have good opportunities of judging as I go through the villages & towns unattended – and have ever got what I asked for to eat and drink with the greatst willingness & been often accompanied by them to hunt'.[13] He shot game for the pot whenever and wherever he could and collected specimens of unfamiliar fauna, including several species of falcon and monkey, and the crowned crane. There was a legend attached to the crane which was said to be an enchanted Fulani girl, transformed as punishment for being late for the funeral of the Prophet because she had been having her hair combed by her slaves, the braid of hair worn on the crown of the head and the graceful form of the Fulani women being likened to the distinctive comb and slender neck of the crane.

Ten days later, however, Oudney and Clapperton inadvertently incurred the Sheikh's grave displeasure when, their mule having fallen lame, they turned back for Kukawa. Word of their departure soon reached Al-Kanemi and Omar was sent for, sharply rebuked and dispatched to fetch them back. Clapperton was taken to task for deserting the expedition without the Sheikh's permission and without even having called upon him. They sent their apologies, explaining that indeed they had intended no disrespect, but had been delayed in making the formal call by lack of animals to ride, and turned around to follow disconsolately in the rear of the army. Al-Kanemi considerately sent them a horse.

Shortly afterwards, the army (eight thousand horse and foot) advanced into Manga territory. According to Al-Kanemi, the Mangawa could field twelve thousand foot soldiers armed with bows and poisoned arrows. Patrols were sent forward to skirmish, spies were captured – and executed – and in the evening the troops were paraded in attack formation for review by the Sheikh,

> About 7 PM when the wooden Trumpets were sounded ~ the foot beat their wooden shields with their spears ~ the noise was extraordinary ~ I do not know what noise to compare it to but it has a fine & warlike effect – the galloping of an immense multitude of horses the rushing noise of a thousand torrents – was nothing to the sounds as they rose & fell according to the distance ~ it was more like the falling of a large city from the top of a high rocky hill where the fragments of the houses would rush down its sides in unequal and thundering masses[14]

But battle was not joined. The Sheikh's well-judged show of force combined with generous terms for submission allowed him to win back the Mangawa into the Borno fold and thus secure an important frontier without bloodshed. Affirming his allegiance to Al-Kanemi, Mallam Fanami 'swore on the Koran to behave as a good subject in future – he is to pay 150 horses & 100 slaves for his past misconduct… so that happily for both sides the War is at an end – as it would have been attended with every kind of cruelty on both sides'.[15]

It was Al-Kanemi's show. The principal Arab merchants who resided in Kukawa were in attendance; the Sultan of Bede called to pay his respects and Mai Ibrahim was also present. The Sheikh and the puppet Mai publicly saluted each other but, as Clapperton observed, 'they never visit one another – I suppose it is attended with too much trouble to the Sheikh – & appearing as lessening the dignity of the other'.[16]

While official deliberations continued and the tribute was being collected, Oudney and Clapperton were permitted to ride back to

Kukawa ahead of the Sheikh's army. The rising temperatures and high humidity made life on the march very uncomfortable; those who were observing Ramadan, Clapperton noted, suffered a great deal '& take a great merit for it'.[17] On the way, they experienced their first tropical downpour – an ominous sign.

Back in Kukawa at the end of June, the mission's officers found themselves once again at the mercy of distant political events and manoeuvrings. From Fezzan had come the news that, upon Bu Khulum's departure, Yusuf Pasha had decreed that one of Sheikh Al-Kanemi's wives and two of their children should be detained in Murzuq, to ensure that the Sheikh did not turn on the Pasha's representative. Al-Kanemi was considerably angered by the slight. And then word was received from Tubu country that the returning Arab escort troops had attacked villages and taken slaves, and filled in the wells in the southern Ténéré.

Fearing repercussions once Yusuf Pasha learnt of Bu Khulum's death, Al-Kanemi stationed troops on his northern border at Wudi and banned further trade and communication with Fezzan. The ban effectively spelled the ruin of the mission's current hopes. No movement of couriers meant no communication with Warrington and consequently no supplies, instructions or reinforcements; and there was certainly no prospect of travel outside Kukawa, even to return home. And almost inevitably, the British visitors became tarred with Tripoli's brush. The Sheikh cross-questioned them closely about their connections in Murzuq, in particular with the powerful Lizari clan. The population of the town began to turn against the travellers. Small courtesies were withdrawn, the flow of provisions dried up and Al-Kanemi refused to receive them. Suspicion turned quickly to hostility and soon all contact, unless with appointed persons, was forbidden. (Columbus was several times called upon to apostatize, but he had an ever ready response, 'If it is written, so it will be'.[18])

The British travellers found themselves at a nonplus. They were not permitted to leave but they could barely afford to stay. Their funds nigh exhausted, they had to eke out their meagre resources in an increasingly hostile community; and within their camp the atmosphere had not changed for the better, Denham continuing to snipe at Oudney for poor management of their finances and still only communicating with Clapperton in writing. To add to their miseries, at the beginning of July the rains arrived, with alternating spells of extreme humidity and violent storms. They suffered wretchedly from prickly heat; the huts were never dry, straw-matting roofs leaked, water washed in through the doorways and the baked soil in their compound turned into a quagmire. They were tormented day and night by vicious flies and mosquitoes, and had to light fires of damp straw and weeds in an (unsuccessful) attempt to drive the pests away. In the huts the black ants were more of a problem than the scorpions; and in the compound, the horses and other animals were also afflicted. Supplies of fresh food in the market had run out; pools of stagnant water became polluted and dysentery was rife. There was no relief; and, inevitably, the onset of the rains brought with it an outbreak of tropical sickness.

Hugh Clapperton went down at the beginning of September, 'my complaint, the Dr. said, was a remittent bilious fever'.[19] It was the last entry in his journal for eight weeks. The illness had struck quite suddenly, and the emetics and cures which Oudney had employed the previous summer in Murzuq proved of little use. Clapperton's temperature reached alarming heights and for two whole days he suffered deep delirium. Recurrent bouts of fever and dysentery continued over a further two weeks, and three weeks later he remained dangerously ill and so reduced that the doctor began to despair of his friend's survival. A further four weeks passed before he had recovered sufficiently to leave his tent, though even then he could not walk any distance without a stick; and at the beginning of December, he was still sadly pulled down.

He was not the only victim. Oudney too collapsed, the bouts of sickness further weakening his already consumptive frame. For a month he took nothing but a little sour milk; he treated himself with a daily dose of two ounces of Epsom salts in a pint of water and three grammes of emetic tartar, and tried cupping but to little effect. And the poor doctor was simultaneously suffering from painful inflammation of the eyes. Denham's attacks of ague were shorter and less virulent; but Hillman was struck down with fever and delirium, coming very near the brink of the grave. However, according to Denham, the irrepressible Old Chips had 'such a knack of rallying from Death's door almost that his illness seems to have no danger in it. Drink Grog he will whenever he can get it, tho' it kills him. He told me the other evening that he had made up his mind to learn 'Harribik'. "I can't make no hand of it," said he, "So I get Columbo to teach me a little Hitalian, for I tell you, B__ the Navy Board"'.[20] Columbus and the servants from Tripoli also succumbed, as did the Arab merchants who had remained in

Borno and even Al-Kanemi himself; and there was an outbreak of smallpox among the slaves in the Arab merchants' quarter.

The severity and duration of his illness left Hugh Clapperton mentally as well as physically exhausted. Subsisting on a poor diet in the fœtid atmosphere of the sodden compound, he recovered slowly and incompletely and the unaccustomed incapacitation was unnerving, 'I hope my late fever will prove a lesson to me, should I be obliged to stay another rainy season in the interior of Africa'.[21]

Fresh breezes and cooler weather at last arrived, heralding a new dry season, and life in Kukawa began to return to normal. Clapperton resumed his hunting and collecting excursions – in which Al-Kanemi showed some interest, sending him specimens of rare hornbills. The Borno army was set to musket training and Clapperton saw them improved in their marksmanship as a result; he also observed that the Sheikh's palace had been smartened up.

Sheikh Al-Kanemi was once again in relaxed mood. The threat to Borno from Tripoli seemed to have receded; to the relief of everyone in Kukawa, there had been no reaction from Yusuf Pasha either to the Mandara fiasco or to Bu Khulum's death and no sign of retaliatory action against Borno's people or interests in Fezzan. The northern border remained calm, and communications across the desert had been resumed. The Sheikh's other frontiers also appeared to be under control and he began to consider mounting a campaign to restore his position in Kanem. At last there was cause for hope that Oudney and Clapperton could make an early start for Hausaland.

When Hadje Ali bu Khulum returned from Kano, Oudney took steps to recoup the mission's funds. Unfortunately the affair was not at all straightforward and looked set to drag on for some time. At first Hadje Ali denied the debt; so on the advice of a number of trusted Fezzani merchant friends who were concerned for the mission's interests – the Zy Abidin brothers, Hadje Bu Zaid and Mohamed ebn Taleb of Sockna – Oudney took him to court. Formal proceedings were held before a panel of Al-Kanemi's judges and elders from the city's commercial community. Sympathetic to the mission's position, and less than enamoured of the Bu Khulum family, Al-Kanemi had pointed out the best legal advisers and followed the affair closely.

In the courtroom, Hadje Ali continued to create difficulties. He announced that he had no cash anyway, having reinvested all his money, including the sums owed to the mission, in trade goods to sell in Fezzan. Then he raised a technical issue, questioning the validity of an agreement that had been witnessed in a third country and drawn up not in Arabic but in Italian (common practice in Tripoli). Prolonged negotiations ensued inside and outside the court, both directly with Hadje Ali and through intermediaries.

Warrington was applied to for the notarised translations, and letters were written to Sultan al-Ahmar and to the Lizari brothers in Murzuq requesting their testimony in the mission's favour. At length agreement was reached and, finding himself now under considerable pressure, Hadje Ali undertook to repay the money by means of trade bills, part to be honoured in Kano and part in Tripoli. It was a satisfactory outcome; the Bu Khulum family name was good and their commercial paper could be discounted for cash through any number of Arab or indigenous merchants in the extensive and sophisticated trading network of the central Sudan.

The fortunes of the Borno Mission appeared to be on the mend; and a short while later they received the long-awaited mail from Tripoli – in which by far the most important communications were letters addressed to each of them from Warrington, written at the end of March, informing them that the Colonial Department had agreed that John Tyrwhitt should join the expedition.

In fact London had long since reacted to Warrington's concerns about tension and discord within the mission and, at the urging of Wilmot Horton, Lord Bathurst had approved the appointment of Tyrwhitt as a fourth officer, finding it 'desirable on public grounds that Mr. Clapperton should be placed under the exclusive orders of Dr. Oudney, and that in order to supply Mr. Clapperton's place, Mr Tyrwhitt has been authorised to join the Major'.[22]

Oudney and Clapperton lost no time in making ready for their departure, and obtained the Sheikh's permission to join the next caravan bound for Kano. Deloyice would travel with them while Hillman stayed behind with Columbus in Kukawa where, it was envisaged, Old Chips would build two boats for Al-Kanemi's use on Lake Chad (although he was still too weak to embark on so major a project and in any case was not confident of being able to manage it single-handed). Denham meanwhile would continue to explore to the east of Lake Chad alongside Al-Kanemi's army and await Tyrwhitt's arrival.

In Al-Kanemi's estimation, any perceived threat posed by the British travellers had sensibly diminished. He had been impressed by the correctness of their behaviour through difficult times and in reduced circumstances, and he now held out no objection to their travel to Kano and Sokoto. However he attached to their mission a trusted Arab resident, Mohamed al-Wurdi, to be their official escort officer. *Teskeras* were issued, and letters of recommendation written to the subsidiary chiefs and emirs along the route. When they called on their host on the eve of their departure Clapperton told the Sheikh that they intended to go to Nupe, but that he could not say what they would do thereafter, at least until they had had audience of Sultan Bello. He said he hoped to return to Kukawa before the rains; and he thanked Al-Kanemi most warmly for his friendship and support. It was sincerely meant; despite the ups and downs of the year, he and Oudney were genuinely grateful to the Sheikh who had 'conducted himself as a father to us'.[23]

For his part, Al-Kanemi wrote a courteous letter to Mohamed Bello in Sokoto, entrusting the British visitors to his care. He also took the precaution of allowing secondary, private, messages to go forward to Kano and Sokoto with warnings to be watchful.

Clapperton's francolin (*Francolinus clappertoni*)

Chapter 11: Hausaland 1824
such an enterprising Fellow

Bede country – Katagum – death in Murmur
residence in Kano – maps of central Sudan – journey to Sokoto

On 14th December 1823, seven months after the excursion to the Shari delta, Walter Oudney and Hugh Clapperton set out for Kano and Hausaland. Denham, Al-Kanemi and a number of Kukawa's notables rode with them to the gathering place of caravans where Zy Abidin said prayers for their safety.

In Al-Wurdi's train were twenty-seven Arab merchants, two wandering *shereefs* (descendants of the Prophet) and some fifty Bornoese merchants; Hadje Ali bu Khulum had also joined the group. Oudney and Clapperton took with them their servants, Absalom and Madi, and three of the mission's Fezzani camel men; the Sheikh had put up a camel-load of supplies for the journey and Jacob Deloyice went along as store-keeper. Also with them was a devoted patient who refused to leave the *tabib*, 'The Man is a Hadje & got his throat and several of his fingers wounded by the bursting of his gun ~ and he pitches his tent always close to ours and rides where the Dr- rides'.[1]

Already aware that his fragile constitution might have been irreversibly undermined by recurring illness during the rains, Oudney continued to rest his hopes of recovery in travel and a change of air; but by the time the caravan reached the eastern borders of Borno, the doctor's mounting exhaustion and frailty were plain for all to see. Clapperton accordingly began to take on more responsibility. His own health having steadily improved, he was soon organizing their journey with energy enough for both of them; and a difficult river crossing provided as much private amusement as it did general commotion,

All was noise and Confusion... The female slaves of the Merchants & the camels were worse to get over than all the rest of the things ~ they squealed and cried as if they were going to be slaughtered instantly ~ some of the men were as bad – the Fezzaneers as none of them could swim – and some of the Shouacs jumped overboard 3 or 4 times before they could muster courage to cross ~ the camels were a great deal of trouble ~ one man having to swim ahead and another behind beating him with a stick – the poor animals are very bad swimmers[2]

On the borders of Bede country some five hundred nervous Bornoese (petty merchants, mostly on foot) joined them for safe passage across the plains to Katagum, the first town in Hausaland. But Clapperton, untroubled by the thought of possible encounters with armed robbers, continued to ride out ahead. Returning to the caravan after one such excursion, he was dismayed to discover that two unknown but seemingly harmless Bede travellers whom he had greeted on the road had subsequently been seized, stripped and bound by some of the Bornoese traders who had taken them for bandits come to spy out the caravan. Clapperton insisted upon their clothing being returned to the two men and demanded that they be put into the custody of the proper authorities in Katagum to verify their bona fides; and he charged nearby Arab merchants with ensuring that the Bornoese did not further ill-treat their Bede prisoners. A short while later, however, he found to his fury that one of the two men had been dreadfully cut about under the ear, allegedly while trying to escape, 'which was impossible surrounded as they were by men armed with loaded guns... Notwithstanding the severe wound they had a rope around his neck to lead him by ~ I was much grieved that I had left them so soon as my presence would have prevented it ~ I gave the Bornowee a good beating & made him tye up the wound with his *tobe* & told him if he offered to use him ill again I would put the contents of my gun into his head'.[3]

The two unfortunates were then led quietly on to Katagum where it was soon established that they were respectable persons, and Clapperton was left to reflect upon the rooted prejudices among Islam's converts. The people of Bede had never received the doctrines of Islam and were 'everywhere regarded as a race of outlaws, whom it is incumbent on every good Mussulman, Bornouese, or Felatah, to enslave or murder. This race is said to have no religion; but their common practice of first holding up to heaven the carcass of any animal killed for food belies their being atheists... On the contrary it harmonizes with those universal feelings of reverence and awe for a Supreme Being which have ever existed among all nations and in all ages'.[4]

Unhappily, travel and change of air had yet to work any miracle cure for Walter Oudney; and, to add to his discomfort, for the first time since arriving in Africa he and Clapperton were suffering acutely from freezing early morning temperatures. The doctor grew progressively weaker and one evening owned to his friend that it was undoubtedly all over with him; he began to talk of where he wished his papers to be sent after his death but, 'as this was a painful subject, I did not encourage its renewal'.[5] On arrival in Katagum, Oudney again took to his bed, knocked back by an acute bout of diarrhœa. Clapperton had fresh milk, meat and other provisions brought in for him and, having seen to his friend's comfort, set about investigating their new surroundings.

Its population in the main Hausa and its leaders Fulani, Katagum, the largest town Clapperton had seen since leaving Tripoli, was a significant outpost of the Sokoto Caliphate and the town's defences matched its importance. The walls were twenty feet high, with well-placed steps to a parapet path and breastworks, and surrounded by a double dry ditch twenty feet deep. The Emir's equally impressive palace was built in a large square with a forty foot-high wall; the internal pillars were formed from the tall stems of the fan palm covered with clay and had 'not an inelegant appearance by any means'.[6]

The Emir himself, Mohamed Dan Kauwa, was pleased to show Clapperton everything of interest and in return the traveller entertained the Emir and his household with tales of foreign countries and customs, instructed them in the use of his sextant and telescope, both of which were much admired, and showed off with his rifle. (Asked by Dan Kauwa to fire at a mark, 'at a distance of about ~~300~~ 60 or 70 y^{ds} ~ I fired twice & struck the bulls eye both times – he called out the Lord preserve him from devils'.[7]) Their discussions were lengthy and wide-ranging. Clapperton told the Emir about the Royal Navy's efforts to halt the Atlantic slave trade, and Dan Kauwa was amazed to discover that the British mission desired neither slaves nor horses but had merely come to see the countries of the world and to learn. He asked Clapperton if he prayed, 'I said I should not be a good man if I did not ~ but that we allways prayed alone – at which he was highly diverted'.[8]

Their stay in Katagum was comfortable; Emir Dan Kauwa sent round generous daily supplies of couscous and *daweeda* (a kind of coarse wheaten macaroni, eaten with butter or sauce), and fresh milk for Oudney. On one occasion Clapperton's servant had the misfortune to upset a jar of honey in the palace and the explorer admitted to an anxious moment, 'had the pot been broken the Omen would have been unfortunate – [but] the Sultan was highly elated at the accident and ordered the poor to be called in to lick it up... they came in, rejoiced at the lucky omen for them & [went] down upon their knees & licked it up with their tongues in no time & there was not a little squabbeling about it ~ one man came off with double allowance he having a long beard which he carefully Cleaned into his hand & put in his mouth'.[9]

Clapperton visited the qadi and took presents to the wives of the town's notables, and his new acquaintances cheerfully answered his many questions about the geography of the surrounding region and its trade routes. Hameda, a wealthy Tripolitan, became a particular friend; the leading Arab merchant resident in the town, he owned a great deal of land and five hundred slaves. Clapperton gave him medical advice; and Hameda provided supplies of fish, vegetable sauce and some rather sour-tasting *tiskery* (a paste of ground guinea corn seasoned with pepper dried in the sun and mixed with milk or water).

Within a week some of the merchants began to move on, and it came to Clapperton's ears that Hadje Ali bu Khulum, that 'arrant rogue and much our enemy'[10], had been making critical remarks about the mission in the nearby town of Hadejia, persuading its leaders that the British had been sent as spies. He decided against informing Oudney, however; the poor doctor could barely sit up long enough to write a line to Denham to report their safe arrival in Hausaland, 'My paper is small but it is as much as I can fill... Clapperton is strong and active, I weak and helpless'.[11] For five days Oudney had been unable to take solid food and had drunk only a cup of coffee. He had had himself cupped on the breast by a local doctor, but his cough was no better; and he continued to suffer from diarrhœa. However, though weak and emaciated, he thought himself ready to undertake the next stage of the journey to Kano. Since the doctor was clearly not up to riding a horse, Clapperton had a wooden litter made for him, padded it with bed-clothes and strapped it onto a camel's back, and on 10 January they left Katagum to catch up with the caravan.

Making an early start, they travelled slowly through the acacia scrub and tall reedy grasses along the sandy floor of the valley and at three in the afternoon they halted to make camp, Oudney being too ill to continue the journey that day. On the following morning they set out again, but the doctor's condition swiftly worsened and, believing his friend would not survive the night, Clapperton called a halt at noon at the village of Murmur, a small collection of huts under a few shady trees,

Monday 12ᵗʰ   the Dr. Alive & sensible ~ he drank a cup of coffee at day light & ordered the camels to be loaded ~ I helped him to dress & when assisting him to rise & mount the camel I saw that he had not an hour or 2 to live & got him to return to the tent & lay down[12]

The rest of the page, like the next one, was left blank; at the time Clapperton could not bring himself to set pen to paper and it was much later that he added to the entry in a fair copy of his journal, 'I sat down by his side, and, with unspeakable grief, witnessed his last breath, which was without a struggle or a groan. I now sent to the governor of the town to request his permission to bury the deceased, which he readily granted; and I had a grave made about five yards to the north of an old mimosa tree, a little beyond the southern gate of the town'.[13]

In that journal he also included some more introspective lines, 'Thus died at the age of 32 years Walter Oudney, M.D., a man of unassuming deportment, pleasing manners, steadfast perseverance, and undaunted enterprise; while his mind was fraught at once with knowledge, virtue and religion. At any time, and in any place, to be bereaved of such a friend, had proved a severe trial; but to me, his friend and fellow traveller, labouring also under disease, and now left alone amidst a strange people, and proceeding through a country which had hitherto never been trod by European foot, the loss was severe and afflicting in the extreme'.[14]

Clapperton had the doctor's body washed according to local custom, dressing it in turban shawls originally earmarked for presents. After reading the burial service, he caused a wall of clay and stakes to be built round the grave and a hut constructed over it, to keep off birds and animals; and on returning to the town he had two sheep killed and distributed to the poor.

Dr Walter Oudney's mantle necessarily fell upon his friend's broad and capable shoulders and, as his diaries reveal, Clapperton's whole outlook changed as he became progressively more aware of his isolation and responsibilities. His sights were set on reaching the Niger and solving the geographical conundrum; there would be no turning back. The day after burying his friend, Clapperton left Murmur, still suffering from a fever; but a chance meeting on the road lifted his spirits; a Fulani girl, 'going to market with milk and butter, neat and spruce in her attire as a Cheshire dairy-maid' approached him, taking him to be of her own race; and parried his solicitations to join him on his journey 'with roguish glee... I don't know how it happened, but her presence seemed to dispel the effects of the ague'.[15]

The landscape softened as Clapperton approached the heart of Hausaland, thorn scrub savannah giving way to broad valleys with large shady trees and rich plantations of indigo, cotton, corn and vegetables; houses in the villages were well constructed and the streets tidy. At Tsangeia, a neat walled town picturesquely situated under a rocky mount, he was particularly struck by the volume of produce for sale in the market; but the headman, a eunuch from the Emir of Kano's palace, 'in person fat, coarse and ugly, with a shrill squeaking voice… kept me awake half the night laughing and talking among his people'.[16]

On 25 January 1824 Clapperton reached the outskirts of the ancient city of Kano, the richest and most populous Hausa city-state and the commercial fulcrum of central Sudan, some fifteen hundred miles from the Mediterranean and five hundred from the Guinea Coast. He donned full naval uniform to ride into the city and, though not one head turned to look after him, he was proud to be 'the first that has carried the English Name and Religion into these Regions and the glory of this is no small stimulus to me ~ I have ever done my duty and will not relax for it now'.[17]

Having heard a good deal about Kano from the Arab merchants Clapperton had rather expected to find a grand conurbation on the European scale and was initially disappointed to discover that only part of the area within the city walls was built upon; before reaching the centre of the city he had to travel two or three miles across swampy marshland frequented only by ducks, cranes and the ubiquitous vultures.

On arrival in the centre, however, Clapperton was put up in a large and handsome house owned by Hadje Hat Salah, a Tripolitan merchant and leader of the local Arab community who acted as Al-Kanemi's principal commercial agent in Kano and, effectively, as Borno's ambassador to the Emir of Kano's court. For three days he was too ill and exhausted to stir from his quarters and barely up to receiving Al-Wurdi's Arab friends, all of them eager to meet the British visitor. He did however write to Warrington, Sheikh Al-Kanemi and Denham notifying them of Walter Oudney's death.

Meanwhile, a courier had come from Borno carrying cheering news from Denham: another officer had arrived in Borno to join the mission. But it was not John Tyrwhitt, who had fallen sick on his return to Tripoli. The new volunteer, Ernest Toole, had been hastily recruited at Warrington's request from the British Headquarters in Malta. The twenty-three year-old brother-in-law of the Assistant Chief Secretary at Valletta, Ensign Toole had been in line to be appointed adjutant but was intrigued by the prospect of joining the Borno Mission. A likeable and very able fellow, he had jauntily crossed the desert from Murzuq accompanied only by a guide, arriving in Kukawa on 23 December 1823 – just nine days after Clapperton's departure. Denham wrote that he and Toole were about to set off for the River Shari to learn more about its source and tributaries; after that they hoped to travel with a Borno force which was preparing an expedition round the southern shores of Lake Chad to campaign against the Sheikh's enemies in Kanem.

The mail was accompanied by some very welcome parcels of supplies that included gunpowder, coffee, sugar and tea, three bottles of port, three silver watches, Arab clothes from Tripoli to use as presents, and Peruvian bark to be taken as a palliative for fever.[18] Denham had also forwarded the *teskera* from Yusuf Pasha Qaramanli on Hadje Ali, for the money owed to the mission, which Warrington had prudently sought immediately upon hearing of Bu Khulum's death. From the newspapers (brought out by Toole), however, Clapperton discovered that the well-known traveller, engineer and Egyptologist Giovanni Belzoni had embarked on an expedition to the Niger via Morocco and Timbuktu. Belzoni had left Paris for Tangier in February 1823 and in May was reported to have reached Fez, seeking the Emperor of Morocco's permission to cross the Sahara with a caravan starting from Tafilelt. Although he himself had a head start, Clapperton found the news unsettling.

Once on his feet again, he called on the Emir, Ibrahim Dabo, at his fortified settlement five miles outside the city from which he was prosecuting a long-standing war against rebels in the north. In the name of his master Sultan Bello, Emir Dabo offered all possible assistance; he also made it plain that the explorer's next step must be to present himself in Sokoto. That suited Clapperton well enough; the Sultan's permission and support were necessary to his progress and Bello's capital, fifteen to twenty days' journey to the west, was not far from the traveller's intended route to the River Niger. The Emir undertook to provide an escort as soon as his own troops returned from campaigning.

In the meantime, Clapperton had begun to refine his under-standing of the geography of the central Sudan. From a nephew of Sultan Bello, an intelligent young man who spoke elegant Arabic, he obtained details of the caravan route to Timbuktu. The most significant information about roads to the south and to the Niger, however, came from Mohamed ben Dahman, a Fezzani merchant residing in Katagum, who for many years had lived and travelled widely in the Sudan. In 1801 he had journeyed from Murzuq to Nupe with Friedrich Hornemann, a German explorer sponsored by the African Association, and had been with him at his death (he reported that Hornemann's papers, left in the hands of the local imam, had unfortunately been destroyed in a fire). He drew Clapperton a map of the old caravan route from Kano through the province of Yawri and western Nupe across the River Niger (in Hausa, the *Kwara*) to the sea. And Hadje Hat Salah, long immersed in Sudanic trade and familiar with the complicated politics of the region, had his secretary construct a detailed chart of the current main route from Kano direct to central Nupe and the Niger by way of Zaria, the capital of the ancient Hausa state of Zazzau.

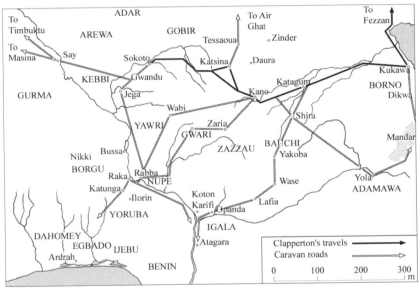

Map 6   Trade routes in the Caliphate of Sokoto 1824

The two maps[19] indicated the location of hills, forests, rivers, ferries and provincial borders, the size of settlements and where Arabic speakers were to be found; and the recommended routes led through the southern provinces of the Caliphate to the so-called seaport of Rabba in Nupe and thence to the sea. By the direct road, Rabba was distant twelve days' hard (twenty days' slow) travelling from Kano. Clapperton had heard that it was possible to reach the sea by water but his merchant interlocutors (none of whom ever ventured beyond Nupe) recommended proceeding overland from Rabba through Yoruba country to the coast.

Ben Dahman also produced a general chart of the principal trade routes through the eastern emirates of the Caliphate. This sketch-map, centred on the town of Shira (three days' journey south of Katagum), showed a caravan road leading south, eight days' travel, to Bauchi whence it continued south a further twenty days' journey to the town of Funda (Opanda) and the sea. Another road led south-east from Shira to Adamawa – a journey of fifteen days – and from there a return to Borno could be accomplished on a twenty-day route through Mandara in the east.

Armed with these maps, it was possible to construct an outline of the whole country, even if it was not yet clear to Clapperton exactly how and where the River Niger reached the sea. A caravan journey of twelve to twenty days from Kano south and west to Rabba implied a distance of some three hundred miles, and would still leave the sea-port about two hundred miles from the coast. The final course of the river and the position and characteristics of the delta hypothesized by M'Queen remained to be determined, but for the first time Clapperton felt confident that he would be able to resolve those important questions.

Without going into further detail, he wrote to inform Denham that he might have to stay throughout the rains. But his enthusiastic reporting of the possibilities to Warrington encouraged the ever-optimistic Consul, who received the letter that August, to suggest to London that the traveller was most likely by then already on his way home from the coast, '[He] is such an Enterprising Fellow that I should not be surprised if he has given you the whole news in person'.[20] Clapperton may well also have written from Kano to James Kay and other friends of Oudney's, but he was not the most assiduous of correspondents.

Hat Salah arranged for Clapperton to exchange Hadje Ali bu Khulum's commercial bills for Spanish dollars, and he and other merchants were also prepared to provide supplies against bills drawn on the Consulate-general in Tripoli. Clapperton converted enough dollars for his immediate needs into cowries, the general trading currency of the Sudan, and raised further funds by selling the mission's coveted Borno horses. His finances once restored, he bought camels and provisions, hired additional servants for the onward journey and appointed Hat Salah his agent, 'I could do no better – though I knew he was cheating me'.[21]

If on occasion he found himself at the wrong end of their commercial dealings, it was very much in Clapperton's interest to get along with the Arab merchant class. Their efficient financial network and their ability and willingness to fund his travel were crucial to his own purposes and their mercantile power permitted them a certain amount of influence, even if they were constrained to operate within the limits and laws set down by local princes and governors. And indeed they had become useful allies and, for the most part, staunch supporters of the British mission, 'they look upon us as their own – & though we are Kafirs we are English and next to themselves – as I believe they would risk their lives in our defence'.[22] They were also a source of shrewd counsel concerning the affairs of the Sudan, alerting him to its political leaders' deeply ingrained suspicions of foreign powers, 'for it is commonly believed among them that strangers would come and take their country from them if they knew the course of the Quarra'.[23]

Unhappily, however, several incidents involving a number of individual merchants, such as Hadje Ali bu Khulum, had given Clapperton cause to mistrust the motivation of a number of his Arab acquaintances, and he was frequently driven to distraction by their unreliability. Relations continued ambivalent, fluctuating between gratitude and out-and-out suspicion.

While waiting for the Emir's promised escort, Clapperton had more time to get to know the great city of Kano and its renowned markets.[24] As well as a large and regular slave market, there were thriving individual markets exhibiting goods and produce from all over Africa: spices from the south, luxury goods and delicacies from the east; sizeable stores of natron and salt from the desert; kola nuts from the west; iron and brass-work from Nupe, and manufactured cloth and leatherwork from various parts of the Sudan. Separate markets sold meat, fruit and vegetables and all manner of locally-produced household goods. Also available were imported Manchester cottons, china and pewter ware received in trade from the Guinea Coast, paper from France, swords from Germany and glass beads from Italy; and Clapperton bought 'for three Spanish dollars, an English green cotton umbrella, an article I little expected to meet with, yet by no means uncommon'.[25] In addition, the city offered all the fun of the fair – musical entertainment, tumbling, boxing matches, and horse racing in the large square in front of Emir Dabo's palace.

When the Emir's escort officer, a young military captain named Mohamed Jolli, finally made his appearance Clapperton gave into his agent's care Jacob Deloyice, who was ill and who had become rather bad-tempered and disruptive, and those of his belongings for which he had no immediate use. According to custom, he had two bullocks slaughtered and given to the poor and then, on 23 February, set off with Al-Wurdi and a handful of merchants for Sokoto.

The journey got off to a slow start. Throughout his stay in Kano Clapperton had been plagued by intermittent bouts of fever (for which he had treated himself with calomel) and shortly after his departure he again succumbed, finding it impossible to walk any distance without assistance and frequently needing to rest. By the time they reached the western fringes of Hausaland, however, his health had improved and he could once more take pleasure in the journey and his surroundings.

There was an enforced stopover at the troubled town of Zurmi on the fringe of a lawless region, the haunt of rebels and thieves, outside Caliphate dominion. Caravans sought the protection of armed escorts when undertaking the final stage of the journey to Sokoto across the Gundumi wilderness, and Captain Mohamed Jolli had to wait for troops to come out from the city to collect his party. Impatient to get on, however, Clapperton endeavoured to make a start without the official escort; when other members of the caravan talked him out of that, he proposed a quick visit to nearby Katsina instead. The merchants and a *shereef* from Hon in Tripolitania who had joined their party, a cheerful rogue full of stories of his younger days before he had lost his eyesight, all refused to accompany him there either – it was Hugh Clapperton's belief that the holy man was not so much frightened as reluctant to give up the splendid time he was having in Zurmi, given 'the number of pious females who sought edification from the lips of a true descendant of the Prophet: besides the chance such visits afforded for transmitting to their offspring the honour of so holy a descent'.[26]

In Zurmi, Clapperton found himself the focus of attention, and was somewhat bemused to be regarded as a *fighi*, 'pestered at all hours of the day' to provide charms; his washerwoman insisted on being paid with a written charm 'to make people buy her pots quickly at the market'[27] in spite of every effort by Clapperton to persuade her that such influence was beyond human power and induce her to take money instead. And a visit from three cheerful wives of the headman of the neighbouring town of Kwari made him smile,

In the cool of the afternoon, I was visited by three of the governor's wives, who, after examining my skin with much attention, remarked, compassionately, it was a thousand pities I was not black, for I had then been tolerably good-looking. I asked one of them, a buxom young girl of fifteen, if she would accept of me for a husband, provided I could obtain the permission of her master the governor. She immediately began to whimper; and on urging her to explain the cause, she frankly avowed she did not know how to dispose of my white legs. I gave them each a snuff box, with a string of white beads in addition, to the coy maiden. They were attended by an old woman, and two female slaves, and during their stay made very merry, but I fear their gaiety soon fled on returning to the close custody of their old gaoler.[28]

A party of Sokoto foot soldiers returning from campaigning also joined the caravan at Zurmi, led by a fine-looking Fulani officer accompanied by his pretty young wife, who 'politely joined her husband in requesting me to delay my journey by another day, in which case they kindly proposed we should travel together. Of course it was impossible to refuse so agreeable an invitation... The figure of the lady was small but finely formed and her complexion of a clear copper colour; while, unlike most beautiful women, she was mild and unobtrusive in her manners'.[29] Clapperton was back on form.

The escort from Sokoto finally appeared, one hundred and fifty men led by trumpets and drums. They accompanied the caravan around the swamps and lakes to halt at a small *ribat* (fortified settlement) before starting on a forced march of some sixty miles in two days across the dangerous wilderness of Gundumi. Hugh Clapperton's terrified fellow travellers set off at breakneck pace through the thorn scrub, expecting armed attack at every moment.

The route took them through thick woods, to the considerable discomfort of those riding camels, before at length it emerged into more open country whereupon several groups of bullocks, asses and camels broke out in dangerous stampedes. Parties of men, women and children scurried breathlessly along the path, fearful of being left behind, and all the while reconnaissance units raced past at full stretch from the front to the rear of the caravan and back again, raising clouds of suffocating dust. Every ten minutes during the day and every two to three minutes at night drums were beaten at the rear and answered by trumpets in the van.

At two in the morning a halt was called to permit the watering of pack-animals. Clapperton took a nap and was three or four times nearly trodden underfoot by bullocks, 'I slept so sound [that only] the care of Absalom my servant saved me from this unchristian like death, and I arose quite refreshed'.[30] The motley company then set off again on another fourteen-hour march, finally reaching safety at eight in the evening at the wells of Dan Kamu in the Rima river valley ten miles north-west of Sokoto, 'all extremely fatigued. I ordered a little kouskousoo for supper, but fell asleep before it was ready. When I awoke at midnight I found it by my side; never in my whole life did I make a more delicious repast'.[31]

Chapter 12: Sokoto 1824
Ra'is `Abd Allah, a very intelligent and wise man

*The Sokoto Caliphate – failure to reach the Niger at Yawri –
successful negotiations for a second mission – Gidado, the beloved
Oudney's grave desecrated – return to Borno in the rains*

I arrayed myself in my lieutenant's coat, trimmed with gold lace,
white trowsers and silk stockings, and, to complete my finery, I
wore Turkish slippers and a turban. Although my limbs pained
me extremely, in consequence of our recent forced march, I
constrained myself to assume the utmost serenity of countenance,
in order to meet with befitting dignity the honours they lavished
on me, the humble representative of my country.[1]

On 16 March 1824 the humble representative of his country entered
Sokoto and was conducted to the apartments which had been
made ready for him and his servants in the palace of the Waziri;
Uthman ben Abubakr dan Laima returned at around midnight
and immediately called on his British visitor. Hugh Clapperton
took an instant liking to the Waziri, 'an elderly man who spoke
Arabic well… polite and kind as any man could possibly be'.[2]

Dan Laima was a powerful figure in the Caliphate. Heading his
own cabinet of deputies and counsellors, he administered the state's
foreign relations and external trade and had charge of the treasury
and buildings and works; and he directly oversaw relations with
Kano, Sokoto's most economically vibrant emirate. Uthman dan
Laima was Sultan Mohamed Bello's principal adviser, his closest
friend from the earliest days of the *jihad*, and the husband of Bello's
sister Nana Asma'au. His most important personal responsibility
was for the well-being of the Moslem community, and the Waziri
was known by one and all simply as Gidado (the beloved).

The following day Clapperton, accompanied by Gidado, went
to the palace to make a formal presentation of his credentials and
the gifts from King George IV. The Sultan of the Fulani received
his visitor in a small reception room painted blue and white in the
Moorish fashion. Five foot ten and portly, with a fine forehead
and a short curling beard, Mohamed Bello appeared younger than
his forty-four years. He was dressed in a light blue cotton *tobe* and
wore a white turban wrapped around his nose and mouth.

The *Amir Musulmin* (Commander of the Faithful) controlled an empire, founded by his father Uthman dan Fodio, whose dominions stretched across the central Sudan from Gao in the ancient state of Songhai on the Niger Bend to the Cameroun mountains in the east, from the borders of Aïr in the Sahara to the confluence of the Niger and Benue rivers. Mohamed Bello had been his father's principal adviser and a field commander during the campaigns of Dan Fodio's *jihad* (1804–1808) and subsequently played an active role in the administration and political formation of the Caliphate. In 1809 he had a new capital built for his father at Sokoto on the junction of the Rima and Sokoto rivers, and when Dan Fodio died eight years later Bello succeeded him. More secular in outlook than his father, Bello was a man of the world who understood the politics of power, and in 1824 he was engaged in consolidating the empire following a wide-spread uprising of non-Fulani peoples against central authority.

Hugh Clapperton was Mohamed Bello's first European visitor, and the Sultan was curious about the messages from Al-Kanemi; a single traveller posed no obvious threat but the appearance of a British mission in the Sudan at that particular time gave him cause for reflection. Clapperton, for his part, had two major concerns. The first and most important involved reaching the Niger, fulfilling both his geographical brief and his personal ambition. The second covered the establishment of official relations with Sultan Bello. The mission was required to secure the future cooperation of any ruler able substantively to further British aims in the interior, such aid being deemed to include assistance with geographical and commercial reconnaissance and agreement to the establishment of British consular representation as and where London judged it to be necessary. During the complicated and protracted negotiations which ensued Clapperton conducted himself admirably, but Bello proved a formidable interlocutor.

At their first meeting, the Sultan asked a great many questions about England. The conversation turned to distinctions between different branches of the Christian religion. Were the English Nestorians or Socinians? Having declared them to be Protestants, Clapperton tried to fend off further interrogation on the subject but was at length 'obliged to confess myself not sufficiently versed in religious subtleties to resolve these knotty points, having always left the task to others more learned than myself'.[3] Changing tactics, Bello produced English books and journals belonging to Dixon Denham (taken from him in Mandara) and complained bitterly about

Bu Khulum's predatory raids into his territory, 'I am sure the bashaw of Tripoli never meant to strike me with one hand, while he offers a present with the other: at least it is a strange way for friends to act. But what was your friend doing there?'[4] Cornered, Clapperton replied that Denham had merely wished to see the country – 'A strange way of doing it, says he'.[5]

In a further conversation later that afternoon Sultan Bello asked what he might give the King of England in return for the official visit of the Borno Mission and His Majesty's handsome presents. Clapperton declared the most acceptable gift to be the Sultan's co-operation in inhibiting the slave trade on the Guinea Coast; and he spoke at some length on the abolition of slavery in England, the work of the Africa squadron and his country's efforts to rehabili-tate slaves who had been rescued. Bello's encouraging response formed the basis for subsequent discussions on the establishment of diplomatic relations.

Clapperton then asked for permission to visit Yawri and Nupe and the Sultan assured him that he should see all that there was to be seen in the Caliphate. Diplomatic courtesy prohibited an initial outright refusal of the visitor's request but the next time Clapperton enquired Bello cautioned that it would be difficult to get to Yawri because the road was unsafe on account of the wars in the region, and that in any event the imminent onset of the rains would not allow sufficient time for such a journey. And ultimately, at first through intermediaries and then in person, Sultan Bello completely ruled out such travel. Unfortunately Hugh Clapperton misread the various signals, in part because he had meanwhile received encouragement from another quarter.

With a letter of introduction from Hadje Hat Salah, Clapperton had called on Sokoto's senior resident Arab merchant, Mohamed ben Ghamzu, who had lived for some years in Yawri and was a personal friend of that province's elderly waziri (a native of Sockna in Fezzan). It also transpired that ben Ghamzu had been in Yawri at the time of Mungo Park's demise (of which event he gave an account which matched that delivered to the British by Park's first guide, Isaaco). He had visited Funda and Rabba, the Caliphate's ports on the Niger and, having been a prisoner in Oyo for three years, he appeared to be familiar with the entire southern region. According to ben Ghamzu, Yawri was distant only five days from Sokoto, though at that time the journey took twelve days on acc-ount of the wars. Clapperton was delighted with all the information and the merchant afforded him a letter of introduction to the

Waziri of Yawri. But he also sounded a warning note concerning the mission's connections with Fezzan and Borno, associations which could well prove a stumbling-block. Bello and Al-Kanemi had fallen out; furthermore, the Bu Khulum family name was in bad odour in Sokoto. Hadje Ali bu Khulum had doctored a list of presents he had brought from Al-Kanemi to give to the Sultan, keeping aside some for himself; the deceit was uncovered and Hadje Ali had been summarily dismissed from Bello's court.

Clapperton's determination to get to Yawri by any possible means rendered him oblivious to the realities of his situation. Al-Wurdi and the other merchants attempted to put him off, terrifying his servants with grim accounts of the wars and bombarding Clapperton himself with warnings of the inevitable delays and risks to life and limb to be expected following the onset of the rains. But, paying no heed to anyone, Clapperton continued his researches, mapped out a route from Yawri to Nupe and looked around for a guide. He did not have much luck. One contact refused to help in any way; another possible candidate, tempted by Clapperton's offer of a fee of forty thousand cowries (twenty dollars), insisted on a quick journey there and back because of the insurrection, with the proviso that Bello should not be informed. The man's proposal was utterly impracticable, and Clapperton would anyway have had trouble raising the cowries in Sokoto.

Any lingering hopes were irrevocably dashed when Mohamed Sidi Sheikh, a scholar from Tuat who was both Bello's private secretary and his doctor, told Clapperton point blank that it was impossible to travel safely without an armed force, and that there was no one who could or would go with him, 'I remained silent; for had I once begun to give vent to my feelings, I might have committed myself. I thank God that I had never once lost my temper amid all these crosses and vexations and in spite even of this deathblow to all my hopes of reaching Youri'.[6]

On the other hand, discussions with Bello about future relations with Britain were progressing satisfactorily; and Clapperton's initiative to persuade the Sultan to put a stop to the Caliphate's trade in slaves with the Mediterranean and Atlantic coasts also appeared to be bearing fruit. The mission had no abolitionist brief – indeed official instructions required all its members to act with circumspection and avoid offending local authorities in any way – but after two years in Africa Clapperton could draw a clear distinction between the inhumane traffic in slaves across the Sahara and local domestic servitude, 'it is quite certain that domestic slavery is so interwoven with their laws, their religion, & state of Society that it never will, nor can, be dispensed with; but we are not to estimate the condition of such Slaves with that of those who are transported to the European Colonies; they are, in Africa, considered as Members of the Family in which they live, and, from their manners and appearance are a happy People'.[7]

Mohamed Bello for his part was ahead of his time, having given a great deal of thought to the ethical principles involved in the treatment of captives and the trade in slaves, Moslem and non-Moslem, and in particular to the export of slaves to dealers on the coast who 'sell them to the Christians so we are told. I mention this to stop people selling Moslem slaves to them, because of those who buy them. Harm will result from this'.[8] Clapperton's proposals therefore received a sympathetic hearing, and he was inclined to take Bello's agreement to curb slave trading in the Caliphate at face value, though noting in his journal, 'How far he will keep this promise, I cannot pretend to say'.[9] If henceforth the Sultan could not be held personally responsible for slave caravans passing through his dominions, Clapperton clearly suspected that Sokoto was likely to continue to exact dues and taxes from transiting slavers. The key point, however, was that it should in future be known to be against Caliphate law to sell slaves to Christians.

In exchange for thus restricting the trade in slaves between his dominions and the coast the Sultan required aid and commercial advantage, asking for a modest amount of technological and military assistance (two field guns, a supply of personal firearms and ammunition) and for access to European markets. He also requested a selection of modern western products, and books for himself. Concerning future trade, he invited Clapperton to suggest which goods would sell well in Britain. Clapperton cited senna, gum arabic, bees' wax, untanned hides, indigo and ivory; and when Bello mentioned the gold and silver to be obtained in the hills of Yakoba and Adamawa, he was given the rather grandiloquent assurance 'that we were less anxious about gold mines than the establishment of commerce, and the extension of science'.[10]

Clapperton recommended a commercial exchange by river and sea as the simplest and quickest route to the European markets, and suggested that the British, with their maritime traditions, could help with ships and train people in shipbuilding. When Bello proposed that the field guns be sent across the Sahara, the half-pay naval lieutenant was insistent that if they did not come by sea they would not come at all. Regarding access to markets in the interior,

Bello said that he was ready to cede the King of England a place on the coast to build a town; and if vessels were unable to navigate the river he would have a road cut to Raka (the river port to which European goods were customarily delivered from the coast).

Having heard much of Walter Oudney's medical reputation, Bello also asked for a physician to be sent to Sokoto, and he hoped that the British would establish a consul to help with trade at Funda where the River Niger entered the sea in the rainy season. In explanation he drew a map in the sand, naming the emirates and principal towns in his dominions, and the Caliphate's so-called sea-ports where the Christians' people came to trade.[11] And he invited Hugh Clapperton to appoint the date on which he could bring a new British mission to the coast; on arrival they should forward letters to him and he would send down an escort to conduct them to Sokoto.

A deal was struck, which Bello subsequently formalised in a letter to King George IV,

> ...Your Majesty's servant, who acknowledges your favours and services, Ra'is `Abd Allah, came to us, and we found him a very intelligent [man] and saying right things; representing in every respect your courage and greatness and wisdom and power and comprehension and diplomacy.
>
> When the time of his departure came, he requested us to form a friendly relation, and correspond with you, and to prohibit the exportation of slaves by our merchants to Ataghira, Dahumi, and Asanti. We agreed with him upon this, on account of the good which will result from it, both to you and to us; and that a vessel of yours is to come to the harbour of Raka with two cannons, and the quantities of powder they require and shot, &c, which they require; as also, a number of shells. We will then send our officer to arrange and settle with your consul custom taxes for every thing, and fix a certain period for the arrival of your merchant ships; and when they come, they may traffic and deal with our merchants.[12]

In his eagerness to close a diplomatic arrangement which he was convinced would be attractive to his superiors in London, Clapperton unhesitatingly committed himself to a return with a new British mission the following summer, naming Whydah (half-way between Cape Coast and Benin) as the port where he would land. He said he would confirm the details once he had rejoined

Denham in Borno; but his promise to Bello effectively ruled out any possibility of remaining in the Sudan until the following dry season, and at best allowed no time for anything other than a very hurried visit to the River Niger itself.

Throughout their discussions Sultan Bello continued adamant that immediate travel to Yawri and Nupe was out of the question, though he did offer to send the mission there after the rains. But time was of the essence and Clapperton could not afford to sit out the wet season in Sokoto. Dejectedly he contemplated the prospect of a return to England having failed in his quest, so near and yet so far from the Niger. In his disappointment he laid the greater part of the responsibility for the frustration of his current hopes squarely at the feet of the Arab merchants. He was convinced that regional wars and rebellion were being used as pretexts for holding him back and believed that, conceiving their wide-ranging and lucrative commercial opportunities in the central Sudan to be under threat, the merchants had persuaded the Sultan to 'embrace this disingenuous expedient to disengage himself from his promise'.[13] And he regretted having spoken with such enthusiasm about the possibilities for moving trade and pilgrims by sea more quickly and cheaply than was possible across the desert.

Clapperton's fears were in fact largely misplaced; the Arab community had no influence with Sultan Bello, upon whose good will it was dependent for its very livelihood, but he came to believe that his erstwhile friends had betrayed him, and began to avoid them. And his insistence on getting to Nupe might have led Bello to regard the journey as one of strategic reconnaissance rather than of geographical enquiry. Searching questions about the Royal Navy's defeat of an Algerian force in 1816 and on the subject of British activities in India had amply demonstrated the Sultan's concerns about Britain's long-term imperialist ambitions and the likely implications for Moslem Africa.

Although confined to his quarters on a number of occasions (with fever and internal disorders, and in constant pain from sore and swollen legs), Clapperton absorbed a great deal of information about Sokoto, its political history, its social structures and its customs. He wrote notes in his journal upon every subject from slavery and trade to marriage and burial rites, from farming to religious practices and superstitions; and the Sultan had copies made for him of two extracts from *Infaq'ul Maisuri* – Bello's own account of the Fulani *jihad* and the founding of the Caliphate, a seminal document in the written history of the central Sudan.

Clapperton also had dealings with members of the court. He negotiated with Bello's austere and powerful brother Atiku a price for the return of some of Denham's possessions. But Gidado cautioned him against too close a contact with Atiku or any of the Sultan's rivals; such association was open to misinterpretation and might be seen as some part of a conspiracy against the throne.

Gidado's brother Mallam Mohamed Mudi was responsible for the day to day welfare of the British traveller and his satellites. Two gallons of fresh milk were delivered each morning for Clapperton himself, and sour milk and *tiskery* for his servants at noon; three roast fowls with Indian corn sauce were brought in the afternoon, and after sunset two bowls of *bazeen*. He never failed to tip Mudi's servants, and the girls from Gidado's household were allowed to visit his compound; inside the house they sat very primly, but outside in his courtyard they giggled and played.

Clapperton also made his own regular rounds of the markets to buy supplies, water and firewood, chickens, onions, macadamia nuts for oil for his lamp, fodder and ropes for his horse and camels, and kept a record of his disbursements. On most days he would allow himself one or two kola nuts, and he unfailingly gave a few cowries to the poor. He made a number of small personal purchases (pipes and pipe stems, a pair of sandals, a bridle, a straw hat and a sling for his gun) and for thirteen hundred cowries he had a pair of trousers made. He also bought a carpet from the Sultan.

He was comfortably at home in the capital. If the infidel was sometimes heckled by the crowds attending the Friday mosque, he bore them no resentment; and when inquisitive country folk crowded into his compound to stand and gape at the kafir he was amused rather than put out. And he took great care to show the necessary deference to the great men of Sokoto, be they political leaders, marabuts or the town executioner – but the person with whom Clapperton spent by far the greater part of his time was his host, Gidado dan Laima. They became fast friends, turning to each other for advice and discoursing upon every imaginable subject.

Once Gidado, who had been reading about the interpretation of dreams, asked Clapperton whether he believed in them; the reply was typically down-to-earth, 'No, my lord Gadado; I consider books of dreams to be full of idle conceits. God gives a man wisdom to guide his conduct, while dreams are occasioned by the accidental circumstances of sleeping with the head low, excess of food, or uneasiness of mind'.[14] When smallpox broke out in the town, several children in Gidado's household died, among them his favourite son (by Bello's sister Nana Asma'au). Clapperton went to the Waziri's house to offer his personal condolences and comfort him, sitting with him nearly an hour in silence.

Concerned for Clapperton's health, Gidado suggested that he should take his customary early morning ride on higher ground rather than down on the swampy valley floor. And he took his visitor with him on some of his business excursions around the town. Gidado was having a new mosque built at his own expense and was determined to see it completed before Ramadan, 'Some workmen were employed in ornamenting the pillars, others in completing the roof; and all appeared particularly busy, if from the circumstances of the gadado being here to receive me'.[15] The master builder was a shrewd-looking little man from Zaria, whose father who had been to Egypt and acquired there a smattering of Moorish architecture; he owned himself in need of a Gunter's scale and Clapperton obligingly sent one round to him.

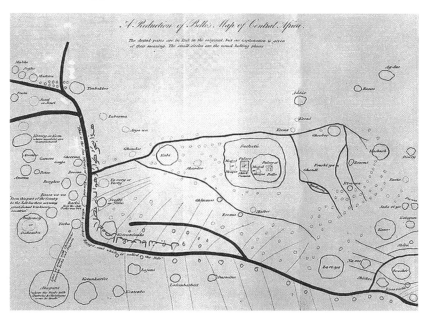

A Reduction of Bello's Map of Central Africa

The onset of the rains was imminent, and there was no prospect of even a quick excursion to the River Niger. Clapperton was keen to return as soon as possible to Kukawa, but the Waziri warned him that if he attempted to set off suddenly and without express permission such action would certainly be misconstrued. When the Sultan was absent, particularly accompanying his army, no one might come or go freely, on pain of death.

As to the River Niger, the Sultan had given him a copy of the map of the Caliphate previously only drawn on the sand; unlike that simple sketch, which had depicted the Niger flowing south towards the sea, the paper version showed the course of the river running east and parallel to the coast; and an inscription had been added to the effect that the line represented 'the river of Kowara which reaches Egypt, and which is called the Nile'.[16] Clapperton knew that to be incorrect; during their most recent conversation, Bello had reaffirmed that the Niger entered the sea at Funda during the rainy season and that Atagara was a town 'on the sea coast' where a number of influential Fulanis resided. Distances upstream of the sea-ports, however, remained unclear; and there was no way of judging where the river could be entered by ship.

Once the Sultan was back in his capital official arrangements were made for Clapperton's immediate return to Borno; it was settled that Mallam Mudi would take the traveller back across the Gundumi wilderness to Zamfara, and one of Gidado's officers, Dan Boji, would accompany him as his personal escort through Kano to Katagum.

On 4 May 1824 Clapperton bade farewell to Sultan Mohamed Bello, who repeated the Fatiha and prayed for his safe return; he then took an affecting leave of 'my good old friend the gadado, for whom I felt the same regard as if he had been one of my oldest friends in England, and I am sure it was equally sincere on his side'.[17] Accompanied by Al-Wurdi and a small group of merchants, among them Hadje Ali bu Khulum, he left for the gathering place of caravans at Dan Kamu where Mudi's troop of soldiers and other travellers awaited them. Because of recent troubles in Zamfara, Mudi turned off the usual track to take a more northerly route across Gundumi. They rode through the night and lost their way for a while, straying uncomfortably close to the outposts of the Gobirawa; panic gripped the caravan and terrified slaves ran from it, screaming. Mudi urged Clapperton to prepare his guns but the latter, having with him his own detailed course records from the outward journey, was able confidently to persuade him to head south-east.

Calm restored, they continued through tangled woods where Clapperton 'got all my trowsers torn & my legs were blood from the knees to the ancles'.[18] The men were exhausted, and several camels died. Nor could the travellers feel safe on arrival in Zurmi where attacks by rebels and freebooters could be expected at any moment. Clapperton was warned not to go out at night and the merchants locked up their belongings and their slaves – three of Hadje Ali's female slaves took the opportunity to escape, however, 'preferring, naturally enough, liberty and a husband, to slavery and a bad master'.[19]

In Katsina, the terminus of caravan roads from Aïr, Clapperton discovered a cosmopolitan community of Arab merchants from Ghadamis and Ghat. The senior resident merchant thought the traveller needed extra domestic help and invited him to choose someone to manage his house, do the cooking and minister to his needs when he was sick. Clapperton chose an old female slave with two young girls to assist her and was pleased with their work. But not all servants were easy to manage and on the road there were incidents of theft. Al-Wurdi's gold was stolen from his saddle bag; since it was obviously an inside affair, all his slaves were put to a trial, being required to blow up an empty water-skin; the guilty party, it was maintained, would be incapable of doing so and indeed the culprit owned up before the trial began.

On arrival in Kano on 22 May, Clapperton called on Hadje Hat Salah, hopeful of word from Borno and further communications from Tripoli or London, perhaps even an official response to the letters he had sent the previous April about Denham's infamous allegations. Together with a welcome box of supplies, including gunpowder and three bottles of port wine, he found a letter from Denham, bringing the sad news of the death of Ernest Toole; on 26 January, only six weeks after arriving in the Sudan, Toole had died on the return journey from the River Shari. Denham also reported that in February a Bagirmi force had advanced into Borno territory and that he had himself witnessed the battle on the plains south-east of Ngala. With the assistance of the field guns, for which Hillman had made solid working carriages, the enemy had been routed and Borno had won a rich booty of slaves. But Denham had been unable to make any progress in exploring the eastern shores of Lake Chad. And there was a letter from Al-Kanemi, expressing sympathy over the death of Walter Oudney, 'a wise and excellent man he was'[20], and asking Clapperton to forward a pair of pistols which the doctor had promised the Sheikh.

Hat Salah and former Arab companions from Kukawa residing in the city helped Clapperton prepare his onward journey. Jacob Deloyice, who was still unwell, and rather fretful at having been left in Kano on his own, was glad to be able to return to Borno. And when Clapperton tried to pay off his temporary servants they begged to be allowed to stay with him – so he relented, re-hiring them on half their former pay, with which they were well satisfied.

He left the city on 3 June, again accompanied by Dan Boji; Al-Wurdi remained in Kano, and Mudi retuned to Sokoto. The month of Ramadan had just ended and all along the road the villagers were decked out in their finery, celebrating the *Id al-Kabir*. But Clapperton hurried on, having picked up a rumour in Kano that a party of Arabs from Awjila had destroyed Oudney's grave. He rode in to Murmur late in the evening, ahead of the escort, and found the report 'but too true ~ the wall I had had made round the grave was thrown down & bust to pieces and a fire made on the grave – of the wood that covered it'.[21]

Oudney's grave destroyed

He could hardly have suffered a greater personal injury. At sunrise the following morning he sent for the headman 'to inquire who had committed the outrage, when he protested it was the Arabs and not the people of the town. I felt so indignant at this wanton act of barbarity, I could not refrain from applying my horsewhip across the governor's shoulders, and threatened to report him to his superior, the governor of Katagum, and also to dispatch a letter on the subject to the sultan, unless the wall was immediately rebuilt'.[22] (Denham, when he had first learnt of the desecration of the doctor's grave, criticised Clapperton's insistence on the full rites of a Christian burial as a gesture which risked inciting Moslem hostility towards the mission – well-motivated perhaps, 'but yet it was imprudent and ill judged'.[23])

The weather had suddenly turned oppressive, with lightning and distant thunder, and, having settled his affairs in Murmur, Clapperton was keen to move on. Dan Boji attempted several times to persuade him to accept an escort across Bede country – Gidado's lieutenant had done rather well out of the journey; at every halt on the route he had been given a slave by the local emir or chief, as a mark of respect to him as Bello's representative, thus acquiring a considerable retinue. Clapperton resisted all blandishments; he spent a relaxed last evening with Hameda, the Traboleze merchant, during which he tried to persuade his old friend to accompany him on the return journey to Tripoli for proper medical treatment, but Hameda was unwilling to leave his business interests, family and slaves for so long. After a last leave-taking at the ferry (where Dan Boji was finally outwitted by the declaration that it was bad luck to cross a river with a friend), the traveller rode on to Borno confident that Joseph, his young camel driver, knew the route. A Fezzani hired by Walter Oudney in Kukawa, Joseph had earlier been captured and sold into slavery in Bede; and because he was rather simple, he was regarded as a *fighi*. They had travelled only as far as the old frontier town of Sansan, however, when they met a courier from Kukawa carrying a letter from Denham and with it a fine sabre, sent from England as a present for Bello. There were letters, too, from Warrington and Wilmot Horton.

The sword and the mail from England had been brought to Borno by John Tyrwhitt, who had arrived in Kukawa on 20 May 1824 to join the mission.[24] And the cheerful young midshipman had been the bearer of heartening tidings: Yusuf Pasha had given up his ambitions in the Sudan and traffic had resumed along the caravan corridor between Fezzan and Lake Chad. Following his return from London to Tripoli, Tyrwhitt's departure for Borno had been somewhat delayed; the delay, however, proved fortuitous. Warrington had played an important role in the negotiations which had secured the release of Al-Kanemi's wife and children from house arrest, and Tyrwhitt was detailed to escort them home from Murzuq. Their safe arrival was a source of immense relief to the Sheikh and everyone in Kukawa, being taken for a sign that the Pasha's designs on Borno had indeed diminished; the mission received a fair share of the credit for the hostages' return.

Regarding further work of exploration, it appeared that Denham had not made any discoveries of geographical significance, but he and Tyrwhitt were about to set off with Barca Gana's army into Kanem. Clapperton therefore hastened back to Katagum to make arrangements for the sabre to be forwarded to Bello. In a letter to accompany the gift he also confirmed the date when he planned to arrive on the coast at Whydah with a new mission – July of the following year, an ambitious aim but a firm commitment – and a courier was hurriedly dispatched to catch up with Dan Boji who was already on his way back to Sokoto.

By the time Hugh Clapperton was able to set out again across Bede territory on the last leg of his return journey to Kukawa, the rains had fully broken; all the low-lying country was inundated and tracks were waterlogged. He began to suffer violent attacks of dysentery, biliousness and fever. Thunderstorms raged nightly, and the further they travelled the worse the conditions became. The ground was saturated – they could neither cook nor camp in any comfort; the tents were always damp, their baggage drenched. On the way, Clapperton had been joined by a petty merchant, a seller of fish. The two of them set up camp in the driving rain, lighting fires in an attempt to keep warm (both were ill) while poor Joseph sat outside huddled in his sodden blankets among the camels. There was no escaping the wet and, it being the end of the growing season, supplies of food and fodder from the villages en route were woefully inadequate.

Clapperton made fewer and fewer entries in his remark-book; he was already familiar with the road, and there was precious little but misery to report. The only good cheer came from the sighting of antelope and buffalo in the Yo valley, and from the satisfaction of shooting hare and guinea fowl around the camp for the pot. There was a brief encounter with Al-Fanami, the Manga chief, who was returning from a visit to the Sheikh; the erstwhile leader of rebellion cut a sorry figure, 'a dirty looking old Man & had one drum beating before him & a N° of ragged followers armed with bows & Spears'.[25]

On 8 July 1824, Clapperton arrived back in Kukawa, where he was welcomed by Hillman; Denham and Tyrwhitt were away on their eastern expedition. The only entry in his remark-book that day concerned the altered accommodation arrangements,

My old house occupied by Mr Tyrwhitt's things ~ Mr Hillman occupying the D^r's house & Hillman's house occupied by the

Maraboots female slaves ~ so not wishing to disturb the ladies I pitched my tent in the square until I could have a coozie built – in the evening I moved my things into an old coozee of Hadje Moh'ms[26]

A Coozee (Kanuri, *kusi*)

Chapter 13: Return to England 1824–1825
it proved a princely feast

End of the Borno Mission – Clapperton's dilemma
Tyrwhitt remains in Kukawa – a slave caravan – winter in the desert
celebrations in Tripoli – Gordon Laing

The day after his return to Kukawa, Clapperton paid a call on Al-Kanemi, who, concerned for his guest's health, later sent round very welcome luxuries, by hand of Karaouash, 'a Burnouse 3 pair of Soc[k]s 2 loaves Sugar, and a bag of Coffee… [and] a present of a sheep, 2 bags of Wheat, & a jar of honey'.[1] The ailing traveller then withdrew and did not leave his tent for seven days. The rains continued. Karaouash brought further presents of food from the Sheikh, and Arab acquaintances attempted to call on him but he could not cope with visitors and had a new palisade of straw built around his hut to keep them all at bay. He needed solitude, a quiet time apart to think and, above all, to regain his strength.

Hugh Clapperton had never really recovered from the severe bouts of malaria and dysentery which had afflicted him during the rains in the October of 1823; and since leaving Kukawa with Oudney in the December of the same year his progress had been hampered by recurring illness. He had several times been laid low by fever on the road to Kano and, once there, the ague had returned every two weeks or so, each time lasting two or three days; and in Sokoto he had endured similar and increasingly frequent bouts of fever, headache and bilious vomiting.

While the mission's medicinal supplies held out, Clapperton relieved the symptoms of fever with a few grams of cinchona bark mixed in water. He used tinctures of powdered jalap root, aloes of colocynth and calomel as purgatives, and swallowed copious draughts of tamarind water. For bilious disorders he regularly took Epsom salts (magnesium sulphate) and sodium bicarbonate and, on occasion, strong emetics – tartar (acid tartrate of potassium) and ipecacuanha. Powdered preparations – Dover's (ipecac and opium) and James's (antimony and phosphate), familiar to all in the Royal Navy – helped bring on sudation, and at times he employed cathartics – croton oil and an arsenical solution. Chalk and antacid powders were of some help when diarrhœa struck. Suspensions of opium in various forms were all to be found in

162

Oudney's medical chest, but Clapperton did not make use of them in any significant way; and unlike Oudney, he had never had himself cupped nor had he had much if any truck with local medicines.

His constitution was generally robust. During naval service Clapperton learnt that illness had simply to be endured, recovery appearing to him to depend more on mental strength and good luck than anything else. On his African travels, however, he had come to believe that if he stayed in the same place for two days and more he would inevitably suffer (but any coincidence was, of course, just that). The occasional chill seemed to generate internal complications, and the diet available was often poor; there was little he could do about dirty water or the insanitary conditions found in houses, villages and markets. His mission colleagues – and most travellers in Africa at that time – suffered similarly. And unfortunately many medicines then in use were improperly understood; some were highly toxic and, taken in the wrong dosage or too often, may well have complicated rather than ameliorated health problems.

Nervous exhaustion and a great hurry of spirits contributed to Hugh Clapperton's failure fully to regain his strength; and when Denham eventually returned from the expedition to the east of Lake Chad and first clapped eyes on the man in his tent he did not recognize him, 'so satisfied was I that the sun-burnt sickly person that lay extended on the floor, rolled in a dark blue shirt, was not my companion, that I was about to leave the place'.[2] Sympathetic to their colleague's plight, Denham and Tyrwhitt did what they could to relieve it, urging continued rest. But once his companions had returned Clapperton was unable to relax; he described the agreement he had reached with Bello and the undertaking he had given the Sultan to land a new official mission on the Guinea Coast the following July and, without expanding upon exactly what he had learnt on his journey to Hausaland and Sokoto, impressed upon them his need to return to London as soon as possible.

Dixon Denham too was ready to return to England, having been frustrated in his efforts to complete a survey of the eastern shores of Lake Chad. Al-Kanemi's generals had been on campaign on the southern fringes of Kanem but when Denham and Tyrwhitt joined them they had found the army in baulk and so, the rains threatening, they had elected to return to Kukawa having been unable either to establish whether any watercourses other than the Shari and the Yo flowed into the lake or to rule out the presence of outflows. Apart from a last possible foray round the north-eastern corner of the lake, Denham considered that the Mission to Borno should forthwith be closed down. They had spent three years in the field, lives had been forfeited and the mission's expenses had well overshot the mark; it now seemed sensible to take the first available opportunity to travel back across the Sahara.

A number of Arab merchants in Kukawa were waiting for others to join them from Kano as soon as the weather improved, and a sizeable caravan was expected to leave for Fezzan within a few weeks. Denham proposed that he and Clapperton should travel with them, and that John Tyrwhitt, were he willing, should remain in the city as vice-consul, to support the intended follow-up mission to the Sudan the next year and to assist any other British travellers sent from Tripoli to Borno. The scheme was acceptable to Al-Kanemi and Tyrwhitt agreed to stay on.

Initially in entire agreement with Denham, Clapperton then began to waver. Tyrwhitt's readiness to stay in Kukawa presented him with further food for thought. If he were now to postpone his return home and sit out the rains in Kukawa, he could set off for Nupe with Tyrwhitt either in company or in support. In the light of his own extensive geographical knowledge of central Sudan and the distances involved, and with the ready support of resident Arab merchant communities, he was confident of being able to accomplish the journey. Lightly burdened, carrying a supply of Spanish dollars and a few presents, he could quickly settle the Niger question. It was a tempting option. Though he had travelled hard and far, at the last he had failed to reach the great river, and he was haunted by the fear that his lack of success might be seen in London as dereliction of duty. Recounting to his colleagues the events which had conspired against him had been painful enough; the prospect of returning to report his failure to his commander-in-chief, John Barrow, filled the prostrated traveller with mounting apprehension.

Unable to cope with the additional mental stress, he fell into a depression, his anguish and confusion obvious even to Al-Kanemi, as Denham recorded, 'Mr. Clapperton, on his first arrival, said he should return forthwith to Tripoli – after a few days however he said that he had determined on returning to Soudan, provided he could have sixteen hundred Dollars advanced to him. I wrote to say such a Sum was at his disposal, but in two days after I received an application from him for Four hundred Dollars, to enable him to return to Tripoli. He changed his mind so often, that the Sheikh sent to me for information, as to what he meant to do'.[3] Hugh Clapperton could not bring himself to discuss his quandary with Dixon Denham, nor did he wish to put pressure on John Tyrwhitt. Sheikh Al-Kanemi, no doubt out of kindly concern for his health, strongly advised him to return to England.

And another cloud loomed on the horizon. Through Al-Wurdi, Al-Kanemi had been alerted to the nature and detail of Clapperton's dealings with Bello, and the Sheikh had indicated to Denham his surprise that the British should wish to open up a communication with the Sudan without passing through Borno. Embarrassed, Denham had replied that he thought, and hoped, that that was not the case; privately, however, he feared that Clapperton's impulsive initiatives, in particular with respect to the slave trade, might compromise future British interests in Borno and possibly throughout the whole Sudan, 'Indeed these proceedings appeared to me to be carried on with the most dangerous kind of haste... How fully was I convinced that an imprudent zeal is more to be dreaded even than apathy and Indolence'[4]; grounds for discord within the mission had surfaced once more.

Weighing up the real possibility of reaching the Niger at Rabba or Funda and heading for the sea well before Denham could be back in England against the equally pressing reasons for getting home as quickly as possible (indeed for arriving at the same time as his colleague), Clapperton continued wracked with indecision. The fulfilment of his personal pledge to Sultan Bello would require the earliest possible attendance in London to lobby for Admiralty and Colonial Department approval for a second expedition; the issue of Denham's malicious conduct had to be officially dealt with and, if Clapperton were not on hand to rein in him, the Englishman would no doubt attempt to secure for himself the credit for all the mission's achievements.

Essentially a practical man, in the end he had to accept that a sudden dash to Nupe, the Niger and the sea was no longer feasible. Leaving aside the issue of the crucial permissions to be secured from Al-Kanemi and Bello, he would have been dependent upon on their support, timings and controls. Furthermore, having once reached the coast he could not be sure of quickly finding a ship for his return passage. Time was not on his side; the merchants were readying themselves for the desert crossing, and Hugh Clapperton resolved to go home with them. He so informed his colleagues.

The mission's affairs in Borno were quickly wound up. Equipment was handed over to Tyrwhitt. Al-Kanemi and his viziers sent round presents for King George and personal gifts for the travellers: a Borno horse and a suit of quilted armour, a camel, a set of spears, twelve *tobes* and a box of civet for the King; and for the members of the mission, a rare giraffe skin from the south, two leopard skins, leather carrier bags and water skins, elephant tusks and antelope horns. And a list was drawn up of items the Sheikh would like from England: minting equipment (a suitable design for coins was agreed upon), the latest pistols, a patent folding bedstead and a medicine cabinet. Barca Gana asked for a suit of armour; and by way of military equipment Al-Kanemi hoped to be given two 2-pounder brass guns and three hundred hand grenades. Hillman and Columbus set about preparing boxes and cages for the menagerie of live animals the mission had accumulated: a monkey, five ostriches, three Borno dogs, civets, four parrots, an ichneumon (river rat), a horse of Mandara breed and one Borno sheep. And Denham obtained permission from Al-Kanemi to take with him a Mandara boy and give him his freedom.[5]

Tyrwhitt wrote to Denham formally accepting the post of vice-consul in Kukawa, assuming what he felt to be his patriotic duty with courage and quite some unease, as he told his father,

> Kouka, Kingdom of
> Bornou N. Africa
> August 19th 1824
>
> My dearest Father,
>
> Major Denham and the rest of my countrymen being about to return to England, I avail myself of that opportunity. It is fixed that I remain here as resident until the pleasure of his M. Government are [sic] known, in compliance with the wishes of the Sultan of this Kingdom.
>
> The situation god knows is far from an enviable one and attended with some danger and many many disagreeables, putting out of the question the unhealthiness of the climate – but it was my duty to remain and therefore I must not complain. I have as yet thank God enjoyed good health and performed the journey here – a distance of 1600 miles – in 85 days from Tripoli.
>
> I calculate that before answers reach me from England it will be a twelvemonth. Should they order my return I should be in England in 18 or 20 months from this time – when I hope Lord Bathurst will do something for me – for God knows those who come to such a country as this deserve it.

I am suffering much at this moment from ophthalmea and am hardly able to write, but beg you to give my best and kindest love and duty to my dear mother - I send love to James, Sophia, William and accept the same yourself from your truly
   dutiful and affect- Son
   J Tyrwhitt Jn.[6]

Delayed by unusually heavy rains, the long-awaited caravan from Kano eventually appeared, and farewells were made to the mission's many friends in Kukawa. Clapperton took affectionate leave of his host and Al-Kanemi handed over a letter thanking King George IV for sending his trusted servants to Borno, and welcoming further commercial travellers from Britain – but on certain conditions; 'our country', he wrote, 'does not suit any traveller with heavy loads, who may possess great wealth. But if a few light persons, as four or five only, with little merchandize, would come, there will be no harm. This is the utmost that we can give him permission for; and more than this number must not come'.[7] Suspicions of British motivation had not been entirely allayed.

   There was no let-up in the rains. Clapperton continued to suffer from dysentery and painfully swollen legs, and his fever returned. But finally, on 22 August, in company with Tyrwhitt and Hillman, he left Kukawa with the caravan for the border town of Wudi. Denham joined them there one week later; he had ridden ahead to make a last excursion round the north and east of Lake Chad but found northern Kanem in ruins and its population extremely hostile following months of sustained civil war; and at the lake itself he had discovered no sign of any major inlet or outlet.

   At Wudi, Clapperton toured the encampment to introduce himself to the merchants and establish the number of camels and slaves being transported by each trader. By any standards the count of those journeying to Fezzan represented a very significant commercial enterprise: thirty-five merchants, six hundred and thirty-seven slaves and ninety-four camels. Including servants, guides and camel drivers, the caravan accounted for some seven hundred persons. Several of the merchants were already well known to Clapperton from his year and a half in the Sudan; and among them was Barca, Denham's former servant, now a free man and apparently successfully setting himself up in trade.

   On 14 September they moved up towards the desert. Tyrwhitt accompanied them as far as Lari where, after bidding farewell to his friends, the newly appointed Vice-Consul turned back to take up a lonely vigil in Kukawa.

Heading for the Ténéré, the caravan split into small parties, leaving at intervals of one or more days – Denham and Deloyice joined one group of merchants, leaving Hillman and Columbus to attend Clapperton with another – but the sheer number of men and animals made for endless complications. At the final watering-place before the desert, Clapperton had to have his men fill up their *gerbas* and water the camels in the middle of the night. And there he bought a camel from Denham, given that there was no prospect of hiring or buying any more beyond that point.

The hundred mile journey through the sand dunes of the Bilma Erg once again severely tested both endurance and organization. Clapperton's continuing bouts of fever and bilious vomiting so weakened him that he could barely keep his seat on the camel; and the second day out the guide was accused by frantic merchants of having taken the wrong path. The old man halted and said not a word. From reciprocal readings from his notes on the southbound journey, Clapperton knew there had been no mistake and quietly encouraged the guide to continue; the two of them set off at a measured pace and the merchants soon fell in behind. The alarm was raised again the following day when a party which had been travelling by night in order to catch up failed to reappear. Men were sent to scour the horizon from the dune summits and signal gunshots were fired. It was not until the evening, just as Clapperton was forming his own men into a search party and loading up extra water and food, that one of the missing traders stumbled into the camp, sun-burnt, parched and exhausted; the others were soon located.

The punishing trek through the dunes was particularly hard on those slaves forced to take up the loads removed from dead or moribund camels and by the time Bilma was sighted the threat of mutiny was clearly in the air. The passage through Wadi Kawar, however, allowed everyone a short rest, and frayed tempers and spirits were generally soothed. The local people supplied fresh provisions and, crucially, offered camels for sale or hire and them-selves as guides and carriers. The merchants then hurried on north again, perturbed by reports of Tuareg attacks on salt caravans on the outskirts of the Wadi. On the arduous passage to Tumu, dates could be bought and camels hired (for extortionate prices) from other Tubu merchants travelling the route, and messages could be forwarded to Fezzan by courier for anyone who required extra camels to be sent down to help bring in his goods. Those who could afford assistance took it; the majority struggled on in slow and ragged procession.

November nights in mid-Sahara were bitter and the wind chill; as the distances between wells increased, supplies of water began to run short. Merchants drove their slaves ever harder; for the latter, the choice was simple: keep up or be left behind to die. Clapperton was dismayed to come upon the body of a young male slave by the roadside; the man had belonged to Gadum, a black-smith from Murzuq, 'a cruel hard-hearted wretch who drives his slaves along like beasts more than like human beings.'[8] A few days later, 'That monster Gadum left a poor female slave to perish on the road today ~ her head was terribly swelled & [she was] unable to walk & insensible ~ when I fell in with her one of his male serv'ts was waiting by her untill she died ~ not to bury her but to bring away the few rags she had on – I stopped ~ intending to have carried her on my camels but she could not hold on being quite insensible and we would likely have shared the same fates had [I] waited to bring her to – which was apparently hopeless'.[9]

The skeleton-strewn pass at Tumu seemed even more desolate and vile than on the southbound journey; and there Clapperton lost a favourite camel, one 'that had travled with me from Bornou to Sackatoo to this place carrying still the heaviest load ~ I felt a little at loosing this old friend as I had intended to have given him to the consul at Tripoli which would have been like giving him his liberty – but poor fellow he could not even come up the hill even without his load'.[10] At the wells of Mishru they encountered a party of Arabs from Fezzan who had come to meet Clapperton's friend Mohamed Ebn Taleb, their camels laden with wheat, dates and other provisions. Denham hired some of the camels, and sent a bowl of camel's milk to Clapperton, 'a real blessing as we have had no tea or coffee for this some weeks past – and I am unable to eat any thing we have'.[11] Clapperton appreciated the gesture; the perils of the road had reinforced a slight improvement in relations between the two officers following his return from Sokoto.

On 9 November, amid general rejoicing, the caravan finally sighted the palm groves of Oma and arrived that same evening at Tajarhi, Fezzan's border post, where the Bey's administrators counted the camels and inspected their loads. Amazingly, with the exception of one of the grey parrots, the mission's little collection of live animals had survived the journey well – destined for King George, the Borno horse may have received special care, but the aged sheep had been left to plod gamely along by itself at the tail-end of the caravan. Those merchants who had abandoned loads along the road, leaving small groups of servants on guard, made haste to send newly-provisioned camel trains to fetch them. For the mission's officers it was a time for farewells and gratuities, and Clapperton's old guide requested a leather bucket.

In Tajarhi, luxuries such as coffee and tobacco were available, and merchandise from the Sudan could be exchanged for wheat and other supplies. Refreshed and re-equipped, groups began to move off north round the Murzuq sand sea. Clapperton travelled at a restful pace, even making time to visit one or two ancient castles that he had missed on the way south. On 21 November 1824, three years and a day since their departure, Clapperton and his party arrived back at Hajj Halil. Great were the celebrations and many the prayers of thanksgiving offered at the *marabet*, where he bought a sheep to give his men a well-earned feast.

In Murzuq, a new Bey, Sidi Hussein, had arrived only a few days before to replace Mustafa al-Ahmar, who had died earlier that year. The appointment of the gentle, cosmopolitan official confirmed the effective abandonment by Yusuf Pasha of the costly and ultimately profitless scheme to extend his influence into the Sudan. Neither Clapperton nor Denham wished to take advantage of Sidi Hussein's invitation to prolong their stay in his capital, however; they were content just to take a short break among old friends and in familiar surroundings before starting on the forty-day journey to Tripoli. For Clapperton, some awkward interviews lay ahead. In a note sent forward to Warrington he outlined the undertaking he had made to Bello to be on the coast in July 1825, but his failure to reach the Niger was still preying upon his mind,

I have had a most successful journey to Soudan and only for the severe illness under which I laboured and the still more miserable state of mind I should not have returned this year.[12]

Two weeks later the British mission left for Tripoli, accompanied by a handful of merchants who had also made the desert crossing and a few other travellers from Murzuq. Hugh Clapperton was in a more positive frame of mind than he had been for some months, and relations with Denham had improved to the extent that on Christmas Day 1824 the two men shared a festive meal and a bottle of wine. Clapperton made drawings of rock formations in the Jabal as-Sawda and in Sockna stood doctor, constructing a splint for the broken arm of an Arab traveller. And there he called on Ebn Taleb's family, and was struck by the unhappy plight of the wife of one of Ebn Taleb's brothers (Michah, who had stayed on in Kano), 'she is young and has been married 3 years, 2 of which her husband has been in Soudan – she said why did I not bring him with me ~ why did he stay and a no- of complaints of his absence ~ it is too bad of these fellows ~ they marry a young handsome wife ~ leave her at home for years – if she goes astray they cut her throat ~ while they live openly with concubines & have some children who are entitled to the same right[s] as those born in wedlock'.[13]

A woman of Sockna

In early January their main enemy was the cold weather; temperatures dropped sharply at night and the travellers awoke in the morning to hoar frost. Clapperton felt very sorry for the slaves, particularly the women (who sang and made music in an attempt to keep themselves cheerful) and he had no hesitation in taking matters into his own hands, insisting that fires be lit for them at night, and threatening merchants with his gun if insufficient water was handed out. One cold and rainy night he gave shelter and food to one of the female slaves named Lafia, 'who had been the life and joy of the whole of the others by her wit and mimickry – particularly of the owner of the house she stopped at in Sockna, a blind man who used to keep rather too strict a guard over his dates and female slaves in Lafia's opinion – I have not escaped myself sometimes from her – but this night she gave up ~ she was cold wet and hungry and began singing in a mournful tone what had she done in her lifetime to cause her to be taken from father mother and husband to be made a slave'.[14] On another occasion Lafia got into a fierce argument with a female slave from Wudi about the relative merits of their home towns, 'They fought and tore the cloths off one another ~ when the Master of the Wodie girl coming up was going to beat Lafia this I prevented by telling him if he laid hands on her I should certainly beat him'.[15]

From the oases of Al-Jufra, Denham made a detour to view the Roman remains at Ghirza; but Clapperton travelled on at a steady pace on the main route across the great wadis of the Misurata lowlands. The two met up again at Bani Walid for the final stage of the journey to Tripoli and on 24 January 1825 they halted at a well one day's ride from the capital,

> The consul's broker met us on the road ~ They had been out 2 days with the Consul who had rode home last night and left orders for a messenger to be dispatched when we arrived ~ When we arrived at the Well we found a carpet spread ~ toast Sandwiches and Coffee ~ it proved to us a princely feast[16]

Consul Warrington was extremely proud of the Borno Mission's achievements, to which he himself had made a significant contribution, robustly promoting their cause in London and supporting them unstintingly in the field. He planned great celebrations. But Clapperton had other things on his mind and he brooked no delay in attending to his two most pressing concerns.

In a private interview with Warrington, he demanded a formal enquiry by the Consul into the complaints and allegations made by Denham in Kukawa in April 1823. Warrington assured him that Denham's charges had already been dismissed by both the Admiralty and the Colonial Department as malicious concoctions. Clapperton's name had long since been cleared; Lord Bathurst was 'entirely of the opinion that no suspicion whatever attaches to Lieutenant Clapperton's character' and had ordered Denham to substantiate his allegations on return, 'or if he cannot, to bury the whole discussion in oblivion.'[17]

When Clapperton continued to insist, and put his request in writing, Warrington gave further reassurances; and, while there is no firm evidence, he may have passed on an affirmation in Dixon Denham's letter to him of May 1824 that 'he had ever believed the

Arabs' story about Clapperton to be a very malicious and wicked falsehood'[18] (something Denham never brought himself to admit to his colleague face to face). The Consul-general also reassured Clapperton that Denham had been reprimanded for dereliction of duty on account of his attempt to return to England in 1822 and for his ill-judged participation in the failed raid on Mandara. As to the quarrel at Izhiya over Clapperton's charts, the Under-Secretary at the Colonial Department had considered both officers to be equally at fault. Mightily relieved on all scores, and deriving at least some consolation from official criticism of his colleague, Clapperton took no further formal action.

His personal concerns disposed of, Clapperton next solicited Warrington's help with the proposal for a new mission. The Consul reacted positively and engaged to inform London immediately of his support for the project; he believed the arrangements with the Sultan to be admirable. This response was encouraging and so Clapperton sent another confirmatory note to Sokoto by way of Ghadamis; but he was aware that Warrington's enthusiasm for British initiatives in the Sahara and the Sudan might not count for a great deal when London came to weigh up the pros and cons of sending out a second expedition. Meanwhile it had also been something of a relief to learn that nothing had come of Giovanni Belzoni's efforts to reach the Niger; turned back in Morocco, Belzoni had attempted an approach from the Guinea Coast but died of dysentery near Benin in December 1823, shortly after arrival. On the other hand, the news that yet another expedition into Africa was already under way came as a considerable shock.

Hanmer Warrington, proud impresario of Saharan exploration, reported that London had sanctioned a new mission to Timbuktu and that Major Gordon Laing, an able young officer in the Royal African Colonial Corps who had already travelled widely in the interior of Sierra Leone, was presently en route to Malta, bound for Tripoli.[19] Accompanied only by personal servants and guides, he intended to travel from Fezzan (escorted by Hatita) through Tuareg country to Aïr, to reach the River Niger at Timbuktu for an onward journey downstream. Warrington was convinced that his two protégés would meet on the river at Yawri and had already written to Laing recommending Clapperton, 'He is an honest, good fellow, and you will find him so'.[20]

Hugh Clapperton was extremely put out. His old anxieties and self-recrimination over the delays in departure from Sokoto the previous year returned to haunt him – personal competition aside,

Gordon Laing's expedition could undermine the likelihood of the British government gratifying Clapperton, who had signally failed to reach the River Niger, with approval to mount another full-scale mission to Sokoto.

The irony was that Laing's plan was based on the enthusiastic reports which Oudney and Clapperton had sent to Warrington some three years earlier from Fezzan, highlighting a route to the Sudan through Aïr and recommending Hatita as a knowledgeable guide; they had also repeatedly remarked on the ease and practicability of travel by small parties in the desert and commended the extent of existing communications in the Sudan. Warrington's rosy vision of his two protégés raising the British flag together on the banks of the Niger added insult to apparent injury; had he only remained in Kukawa with John Tyrwhitt, Clapperton could already have reached the river in Nupe, way ahead of any competitor. Thus, when the Consul asked him to write a note of advice for Laing on methods of travel in the Sahara and Sudan, he failed to respond. Anxious to be on his way back to England as soon as possible, Clapperton was in no mind to assist a rival.

The Consul was not to be done out of his proposed celebrations to mark the Borno Mission's achievements, however, and there was a good deal of wining and dining; the returned travellers were fêted at many a party in consular circles and the Pasha himself held a glittering reception in their honour at the Castle.

A passage for Italy was quickly arranged; farewells were made and souvenirs exchanged. Clapperton left with Warrington a horse he had bought in Murzuq for one hundred and fifty dollars; and Hillman presented the Consul with a lion's skin as a token of his esteem. Denham obtained Yusuf Pasha's formal signature to the Mandara boy's freedom, and arranged to take the youth with him to England for a spell of education.[21] Jacob Deloyice planned to return to his community in Tripoli and despite their major-domo's shortcomings Clapperton paid him a gratuity of one hundred and twenty dollars on top of his pay, for loyal service.

For Hugh Clapperton, departure was an exhilarating moment. The junior naval lieutenant who had bowled into Tripoli with Walter Oudney on board a Maltese *spirano* in October 1821 had long since proved himself an accomplished explorer. There was a last warm leave-taking of the Consul-general and his amiable family; Clapperton's letter of appreciation was heartfelt, 'As a member of this Mission I cannot leave Tripoli without offering you my sincere thanks for the prompt Aid and great assistance we have on every occasion received from you… I cannot therefore too strongly express my obligations to you for the cordial execution you have unremittingly employed for our welfare and success'.[22]

Clapperton and Denham sailed from Tripoli on 21 February 1825, bound for Italy. In strong northerly gales the ship had to be re-routed via Elba, and their passage lasted twenty-eight days, adding considerably to the inevitable delay in returning home necessitated by the prescribed twenty-five days of quarantine at Livorno. They stood the confinement in the lazaretto better than most inmates, enjoying the Tuscan breezes, the little taverna in the grounds and comfortable beds with a real roof over their heads, and used the time to write letters and prepare reports. And at last, in mid-May, they were able to set out on the overland journey home, by way of Florence and the Alps to Paris. Having charge of the mission's baggage, the gifts from Borno, the specimen plants and minerals and the exotic menagerie from the Sudan, Hillman and Columbus travelled to England separately, on board the brig *Britannia*.

Word of the mission's return preceded them, relayed from newspapers in France to England. In London a hero's welcome awaited them; and on 30 May 1825, straight from disembarkation, and in company with Denham, Lieutenant Hugh Clapperton RN presented himself at the doors of the Admiralty, a somewhat apprehensive but undeniably proud 'Abdullah, Barrow's pioneer'.[23]

Chapter 14: London 1825
infinite trouble and anxiety

Return to London – a new expedition proposed
acclaim for the Mission to Borno – appointments and preparations
bureaucratic wranglings – departure for Africa on HMS Brazen

At the Admiralty, John Barrow pronounced himself delighted with his pioneers. He wrote that afternoon to the publisher John Murray of his immense satisfaction, 'as you may suppose, when I state that I have had Denham and Clapperton with me for more than an hour – and all their papers are in London and I have told them [are] yours'.[1] To Clapperton's great relief, his own report of the circumstances surrounding his failure to reach the Niger at Yawri was entirely accepted; and his proposal for launching a new mission to the Sudan from the Guinea Coast was received with enthusiasm. When manning the Timbuktu initiative, though not particularly taken with Gordon Laing (who had not been his first choice), Barrow had had to move quickly to counter growing French ambitions in the Sahara. In Hugh Clapperton, however, a naval officer of proven aptitude and experience, he had a recruit who had already been to the central Sudan; and he seized upon the importance of an immediate start in the light of Clapperton's promise to Bello to be at Whydah on the Guinea Coast in July.

In Downing Street, however, the Colonial Department was not so easily placated. Under-Secretary Robert Wilmot Horton required Clapperton and Denham to present their final dispatches without delay; and annoyed by Clapperton's failure to provide guidance for Laing he issued written instructions for immediate compliance. Clapperton naturally fell into line, but his memorandum, though containing perfectly sensible advice, was couched in such general terms that Laing subsequently dismissed it as patronizing and valueless.

In the main impressed by Clapperton's reasons for mounting a second expedition, Wilmot Horton required further particulars. Although military and foreign overtures were currently out of favour in parliament, the abolitionist dimension of the proposals struck the right note. But the government had only the traveller's word for the state of affairs in Sokoto, and relations with a power which remained largely an unknown quantity could not be lightly embarked upon. Clapperton was therefore asked to prepare a full report on the Caliphate, its influence, its geography and the nature of its communications with the coast; this he did within days.

One week later Hillman arrived in London with the mission's baggage and, to the dismay of port officials and the amusement of bystanders, the menagerie of live birds and animals, gifts from Al-Kanemi to His Majesty, was off-loaded at the Tower of London pier and prepared for removal to Windsor (the parrots went to the royal apartments, but the ichneumon ate the two small crocodiles from the Shari while in the Tower). The four surviving ostriches proved a great favourite with the public; and an exchange of notes between government offices indicated that the horse and the sheep from Borno were to be given special consideration. A thoughtful Colonial Department official pointed out to Sir William King (of the Royal Household) that the decrepit sheep had become too attached to the horse to survive a separation, and warned that the horse was naturally savage.

Arrangements for assessing the product of the Borno Mission's work were put in hand. Specimens of natural history were passed to the zoologist J.G. Children.[2] Robert Brown at Kew, a leading member of the Linnæan Society, received the botanical specimens[3] and Charles Keving at the British Museum the geological material. Some seventy-five specimens of minerals were sent to Professor Jameson in Edinburgh. Samples of trade goods such as civet, hides and ostrich feathers were dispatched to the relevant commercial enterprises for evaluation, but the cotton, samsuk (tamarind) and the indigo plants were found to be 'so dirty and full of insects and the quantity so very small… we would strongly recommend that a few hundredweights should be collected and be sent home from Africa in order that further experiments be made with it'.[4]

Meanwhile, the press was hungry for news about the Niger and Mungo Park. Editors were disappointed that Hugh Clapperton had not succeeded in reaching the river, and initial reports that the mission had brought back important new details about Park's fate had had to be denied. The presence of European goods in the interior of Africa, however, caught the public's imagination, as did the travellers' depiction of previously unknown peoples and their accounts of the horrors of the Saharan slave trade. Clapperton himself was applauded for having established the geographical positions of Lake Chad and the city of Kano, and there was also considerable speculation about the rivers flowing into the lake and on the geography of the surrounding region.

While there were few new facts to report, the mission's officers' conjectures regarding the termination of the mighty river excited considerable attention. Denham remained openly sceptical of Clapperton's assumptions, 'He carries the Niger of Park into the Atlantic by means of the different branches of the River Formosa. I never met anyone who agreed'.[5] But a body of opinion, notably in Scotland, quickly picked up on Clapperton's findings, linking them to James M'Queen's hypothesis. The positive feedback from natural scientists, men of letters, politicians and general public interest encouraged the Colonial Department in their consideration of a second mission. Meanwhile Barrow put Clapperton and Denham in touch with John Murray, to discuss publication of their material.

Murray showed great goodwill and enthusiasm for the Borno Mission's 'most brilliant and astonishing discoveries'.[6] He soon introduced the travellers to a distinguished circle of his personal acquaintances interested in the latest universal findings, among whom were George Lyon (just back from the Arctic), Marsden the geographer and linguist, and the cartographer Thomas Murdoch; and arranged a reception at which several well-known travellers, publishers and authors, including Barrow and Robert Hay from the Admiralty (both contributors to Murray's *Quarterly Review*), gathered to meet the returned explorers from Africa.

Unfortunately there is no record of Clapperton's reactions to such leading figures of the British Enlightenment movement, nor any indication as to what they in turn made of him, but the predilection of those scientists and scholars for facts over theories chimed exactly with Clapperton's own methodology. His maritime training, his exposure to Oudney's systematic approach and, most significantly, his own experiences in Africa, all reinforced his natural tendency to rely on visual evidence rather than on the word of others.

John Barrow also arranged a meeting with a personal friend, Colonel Edward Sabine; of an age with Clapperton, Sabine was a former artillery officer who had served in Canada in 1812-13 and been present at the siege of Fort Erie. He had since undertaken research in biology, ornithology and terrestrial magnetism, made himself an expert on African geography and had taken part in expeditions in the Arctic. There was clearly no meeting of minds, however – indeed Clapperton appears to have been at his most petulant and difficult. Edward Sabine was a close friend both of Gordon Laing (whose book of travels in West Africa he was seeing through the press at the time) and of Dixon Denham, and Hugh Clapperton was most unlikely to have taken kindly to any cross-questioning about Sokoto and the River Niger by someone whom he instinctively mistrusted. Indeed, he remained very touchy when it came to the subject of Laing, and the aversion was mutual; before departure for Malta, Laing had publicly declared that any return to Africa by Clapperton would be wasted effort since he, Laing, was certain to have solved the riddle of the Niger within a few months.

Laing subsequently wrote to Sabine, acknowledging receipt of his friend's account of the meeting with Clapperton, 'I smile at the idea of his reaching Timbuctoo before me – how can he expect it? Has he not thrown away the chance? I cannot think what were his ideas – a man to be within two days of the Niger, and to come back without ever seeing it – and I feel certain that to me the honour of the solution is left'.[7] And Sabine's impression that Clapperton was 'not exactly cut out for a drawing room'[8] drew forth scornful tittle-tattle from Laing, 'How is it that the Turks speak so constantly of the quantities which Abdullah (his country name) used to drink – Four bottles of Port wine before dinner whenever he could get it?'[9]

Two weeks after return to England Clapperton was received by the Secretary of State, Lord Bathurst, who gave his approval for a second expedition into the interior under the Scot's personal command; Clapperton was cock-a-hoop, and his determination redoubled, 'It will be necessary to start again without delay to avail myself of the most favourable season for prosecuting my inland journey ~ nor is this to me a hardship for I have only this wish on earth – to complete what yet remains undone'.[10]

And the high point of his career as naval officer and explorer was attained ten days later when on 22 June 1825, responding to a commendation from Lord Bathurst with respect to Clapperton's services on the Borno Mission, the Lords Commissioners of the Admiralty promoted him commander for rank. The following week he was granted an audience with King George IV – he was accompanied by Bathurst (whose Private Secretary reminded Clapperton to report to the Colonial Department first, at 1 p.m., and to be sure to be punctual). For Hugh Clapperton, loyal subject and sentimental patriot, promoted commander after twenty years' service in His Majesty's Royal Navy, and with an important new mission preparing under his command, the occasion was a source of immense personal pride and pleasure. He had indeed come a long way since the Liverpool Rendezvous.

From his lodgings at 13 Duke Street, Adelphi, off the Strand, Clapperton embarked on eight crowded weeks of preparations for the new expedition. He continued to suffer the after-effects of illness and prostration from his exertions on the return journey across the Sahara and tired easily. And, as he told James Kay, he had been so busily employed in making out reports to government that he had 'not a moment's leisure to attend either to pleasure or friendship'.[11] But he did eventually find time to contact family and connections living in the south. He visited his brother Charles, now a lieutenant in the Royal Marines serving at Chatham, and he also saw something of his uncle Samuel, a lieutenant-colonel in charge of recruitment there. However, though he soon became a public figure in Scotland, given his commitments in London he was unable to travel to Edinburgh to visit his sister, or indeed to Dumfriesshire to see his son Duncan. Martha Bell had died and the child was being brought up by her sister Elizabeth and Elizabeth's husband, William Gibson, a slater in Lochmaben, where they lived in a tenement with several other members of the Bell and Gibson families.

In London Clapperton renewed a number of old acquaintances, among them several friends of Oudney's, with whom he could discuss his geographical findings and theories quite freely. He got on particularly well with Captain W. H. Smyth RN, the man who had first identified the opening to the Sudan by way of Tripoli, and who had followed the Borno Mission's progress closely. He also re-established contact with his boyhood companion Edward Irving, then at the height of his fame as a preacher and a leading figure in missionary and abolitionist circles. A charismatic minister, whose fiery sermons, lamentations and tirades drew crowds of adulators to London's Caledonian Church every Sunday[12], Irving was a man of great intellectual energy and eager to learn at first hand of Clapperton's experiences in Africa. Irving's enthusiasm increased the traveller's determination to bring off the unique arrangement he had negotiated with Sultan Mohamed Bello, as did the gratifying interest of the Lord Provost of Edinburgh, an active campaigner against slavery who was also much impressed by Clapperton's representations in Sokoto.

Among Clapperton's Scottish correspondents was Bryce Downie who was delighted with the achievements of his former pupil. But not everyone in Scotland held Clapperton in such high esteem. There were those who considered him to be both tactless and arrogant about his exploits – a Dr Thom of Annan published a lampoon in a Carlisle broadsheet, apparently putting himself at risk of a horse-whipping from the explorer.

In London, Irving put Clapperton back in touch with a mutual friend from Annan days, Dr Thomas Dickson (whose brother Robert was married to Irving's sister). After many years of living abroad, Dickson was at a loose end. He had been a house surgeon at the Royal Infirmary in Edinburgh and served a term as Senior Annual President of the Royal Medical Society there. Following a three-year period working in France and the United States he had practiced for six years as a surgeon in Demerara before returning to Paris; he then moved to London. Dickson and Clapperton had friends and acquaintances in common in Edinburgh's medical and university circles, among them Professor Jameson and members of the Linnæan Society. A lively man who possessed great stores of energy, Dickson was intrigued by the explorer's recent exploits and quick to signal his interest in the adventure in prospect.

Charged with selecting officers for the new mission, Barrow saw no objection to the well-qualified Dr Dickson accompanying it and appreciated Clapperton's determination, after the unfortunate experience with Denham, to take with him at least one person of his own choosing. Like Clapperton in 1821, Dickson accepted the invitation out of a sense of adventure; he wrote a short curriculum vitæ, 'a dish of egotism'[13] which he hoped would do, to be sent to the authorities, and told his friend that while he was not particular about a salary, he insisted on being taken on as an explorer rather than being attached to the mission in a purely medical capacity.

Barrow had quickly found his recruits from the Royal Navy. To act as Clapperton's deputy he chose Commander Robert Pearce, a hydrographer and skilled draughtsman, whose career somewhat mirrored Clapperton's own. After serving in the West Indies and in the Mediterranean as midshipman from 1806 and as master's mate in the Mediterranean and at the Cape of Good Hope from 1810, Pearce had been promoted lieutenant in 1812. He was posted to the North American station and then back to the West Indies, before returning to home waters in 1817; he continued on active service and was promoted commander in July 1824. Barrow next recruited Dr Robert Morison, a naval surgeon 'well versed in various branches of natural history'[14]; he envisaged that Morison would serve in Sokoto as vice-consul, freeing the others to travel to Borno or Timbuktu.

While it was not thought necessary to send a naval carpenter with the expedition, assistants were needed to act as interpreters, guides and overseers of transport and supplies. The first to be enrolled was Adolphus Simpkins (Columbus) whose loyalty and efficiency during the Borno Mission, together with his languages and experience of the Sudan, fitted him well for the new venture.

The Victualling Board had put forward another similarly well-qualified candidate, William Pasco, who had attended Giovanni Belzoni to Benin. Aged about forty, Pasco (whose Moslem name was Abubakr) claimed descent from a chiefly family in Gobir. Captured in war and sold into slavery, he was bought first by a Gonja trader and then by a Portuguese merchant in Ashanti. Following his rescue by a British sloop from a slave ship bound for Bahia, he had joined the Royal Navy. After Belzoni's death, Pasco was re-enlisted, on HM Sloop *Bann*; and he was still on board when she returned to her home port in June 1825. Barrow had him released for special duties, to act as interpreter and guide for the expedition and as servant to Robert Pearce.

It had been agreed that the officers should each take a personal servant, and Hugh Clapperton was in receptive mood when a volunteer presented himself at Duke Street. A stocky twenty-one year-old Cornishman, Richard Lander was one of five children of a Truro innkeeper and had left home aged nine on the death of his father. He secured a post as personal servant to a businessman with whom he went to the West Indies; then, in 1823, he was employed by a member of a commission enquiring into the state of British colonies in South Africa. The following year he had returned home and was taken on by a relative of the Duke of Northumberland. But Lander was restless and unfulfilled in London, and when he heard of the planned expedition, he made haste to apply, 'the very sound of the word 'Africa' makes my heart flutter'[15]; Clapperton was happy to hire the bright and enthusiastic young fellow who exhibited such an admirable taste for adventure.

By mid-July all appointments had been made, but much remained to be done and Clapperton continued hard pressed, 'I have got no sinecure in this new appointment. I have to see the whole of the presents sent off without anyone to assist me. My Journal will scarce be complete before I go and the necessary attendance at the public offices is truly harassing'.[16] There were formal letters to be written to Sultan Bello and also to Al-Kanemi in Borno. In late June, Dixon Denham had taken it upon himself to write to the Colonial Department urging that the new mission go to Borno first and that it should undertake no exploration without Al-Kanemi's agreement because the Sheikh's writ in the Sudan was absolute; Wilmot Horton minuted that this intervention was 'nothing but jealousy of Clapperton and should not alter the plan intended'.[17] It was nevertheless important to write to the Sheikh and to send gifts; and John Tyrwhitt had also to be kept in the picture.

Orders had already been placed with the Royal Ordnance for two brass mountain-guns, muskets and ammunition to be made ready for transport with the expedition. It was left to Clapperton, however, to organize the purchase of all other official stores, and the necessary presents – the personal arms to be delivered to Al-Kanemi, his family and viziers in Kukawa, and the latest fine manufactured goods requested by Bello and his court. There was considerable debate over suitable gifts for the various kings and chiefs, both on the coast and inland, whose help would be vital to the mission's advancement. Supplies of trade goods with which to barter their way were also required, among them rolls of silk and Manchester cottons, scissors, pins, thimbles and mirrors. Dickson helped Clapperton choose their considerable stock of beads and bandanas, pictures, umbrellas and ornamented glasses – and three silver-mounted message-carriers (cleft sticks). Advice from old West Africa hands often served only to confuse, but coral beads were generally reckoned a safe universal currency.

In addition, the explorer was besieged by officials, merchants, geographers and scientists eager for further particulars relating to the previous mission; and he stayed in close touch with Abraham Salamé, the government's Arabic interpreter, who was working on all the documents brought back from the Sudan. The Treasury had endless enquiries regarding the mission's finances. Calculations were complicated by the separate journeys, Oudney's death, the loss of funds with Bu Khulum and the non-receipt of dollars for-warded by Warrington, and it was only on 25 July that a Treasury official was able to confirm that Clapperton could properly be relieved from presenting further accounts. The total cost of the expedition had been estimated by Warrington at £3,260.17s.7d., excluding the sum of £5,000 paid to Yusuf Pasha.

In a private initiative, Clapperton helped James Kay claim the moneys due to Walter Oudney's estate for the benefit of his two dependent sisters (their mother was dying and they were all living in Edinburgh in miserable circumstances). The submission, which was supported by Jameson and other distinguished professors in the Scottish capital, was successful; £500 was granted in full and final settlement of pay and pension due and an additional ex-gratia payment of £100 was allowed from the Royal Bounty.

The settlements for his friend Walter Oudney reminded Hugh Clapperton to draw up his own will, and he appointed his uncle

Samuel, together with a friend in the Royal Marines also serving at Chatham, Major Robert Boys, as his executors. He bequeathed to Samuel the only named possession, a sword presented to him by Yusuf Pasha; the money in his accounts and any future sums owing to him he directed to be invested in a fund, the income from which was to be distributed thus: five pounds per annum to his son Duncan in Lochmaben, and the balance to be shared equally between Hugh's brother Charles, or his family and heirs, and his sister Margaret or her heirs if any. The document was duly drawn up and witnessed on 17 August 1825 by William Hamilton, Walter Oudney's solicitor, and H.W. Kay, clerk in the Royal Navy (in all probability a relative of James Kay).[18]

At the end of July, in a (long overdue) reorganization of the structure and work of the Colonial Office, Wilmot Horton handed over responsibility for the new expedition to Robert W. Hay MP. Formerly a senior secretary at the Admiralty and on good terms with John Barrow, Hay was appointed to be an additional under-secretary; his remit was the Mediterranean and Africa, the East Indies and the new antipodean colonies. Inevitably, the changes led to further delays – both in minor issues (such as obtaining Treasury permission to buy supplies of tea from Twinings duty-free on the basis that they were to be re-exported) and in matters of major consequence to the mission – and resulted in further prolonged correspondence.

Close to the officers' hearts were the questions of pay and allow-ances, since each was expected to pay the subsistence of personal servants out of his salary. Clapperton was awarded the full rate of pay due a commander in the Royal Navy, twenty shillings per day, with effect from 1 August 1825; Commander Pearce received an equal amount, and Dickson and Morison were paid at the rate of ten shillings per day. In addition, a subsistence allowance was granted to each officer of twenty shillings per day. Columbus, in his capacity of Head Servant, was paid at the rate of eighty pounds per annum and Pasco was seconded to the expedition on his able seaman's pay; however, rated as servants for purposes of living expenses, neither man received a subsistence allowance.

The expedition's own equipment had also to be readied. While Doctor Morison got in a stock of medical supplies, Dickson drew up a list of medicines to present to Al-Kanemi, 'those that produce immediate and obvious effects and that may be administered with a certain degree of impunity'.[19] They bought in supplies of writing paper and notebooks, scientific equipment and personal arms –

guns and pistols, and an air gun which Dickson thought would be useful for hunting game and procuring specimens.

Clapperton's tendency to act first and enquire later got him into a certain amount of trouble with the authorities. He was rebuked for ordering excessive supplies of writing paper, in spite of pointing out that the amount was in fact reasonable, given the envisaged duration of the mission and the intention to split it into different parties upon reaching Sokoto. When purchase lists were referred by the Colonial Department to Barrow for approval, the Second Secretary took exception to the volume of navigational equipment procured (on his own travels in South Africa, Barrow maintained, he had made his way with little more than a pocket compass) and he took the suppliers themselves to task – they should have known better than to accept such orders without first checking with him. Clapperton's purchase of a silver pocket watch, personally engraved, for each officer of the mission was thus the final straw and Barrow docked their individual pay accordingly. He advised Robert Hay to issue a severe reprimand, 'give all your travellers one of those strong doses which we at the Admiralty know so well how to administer and which after all are sometimes called for to keep men in order when armed with a little brief authority'.[20]

Pearce offered to write in support but Clapperton, thoroughly irritated by officialdom's referrals and parsimonious quibbling, could see that it would be pointless – as he wrote in quite some exasperation to Kay, 'You cannot have any idea of the infinite trouble and anxiety I have had since I have been in London. If I receive honour and praise they are assuredly earned with labour and pain; the whole of the arrangements of the new mission have fallen on me'.[21]

Though querulously vigilant regarding expenditure from the official purse, Barrow nevertheless did everything he could to get the mission on its way with the utmost dispatch. A passage was arranged on board HMS *Brazen* (Captain George Willes), a ship-rigged sloop completing preparations to join the Africa squadron on anti-slavery patrols. Stores were put aboard, and at the end of July Barrow travelled to Portsmouth to check that everything was proceeding expeditiously.

Clapperton meanwhile continued working on a fair copy of the journal of his mission to Sokoto in 1824. Early in June he had been anticipating leaving his papers 'in the hands of one or two of my friends for immediate publication or allow them to await my return'[22]; the following month, however, realizing that he risked leaving the field wide open to Denham, he thankfully took up Barrow's offer to see his contribution through to publication. Committed as he was to an early departure for Africa, he was in no position to object to Denham overseeing the project, but he trusted Barrow to prevent his erstwhile colleague from claiming all the credit – and Dixon Denham had by then been superseded by Gordon Laing in the role of Clapperton's bête noir.

Interest in the achievements of the Borno Mission meanwhile continued high, and debate about the final course and termination of the River Niger in particular threatened to turn acrimonious.[23] Writing to friends in Scotland, Hugh Clapperton confided his near certainty that the river entered the sea in the Bight of Benin, but kept his own counsel in London – no doubt wary of too open a contradiction of Barrow's own published opinion that the Niger flowed east to join the Nile; and he remained extremely sensitive to any reminder of his failure to reach his goal.

As news of the Borno Mission's achievements filtered out into the public domain, the consensus of popular opinion that the Arabs embodied an unattractive combination of warrior, peddler and thief served to support Clapperton's belief in conspiracies against him in Sokoto. General reactions to the mission's evidence concerning the African slave trade overwhelmingly endorsed his initiative in Sokoto; and it was no doubt gratifying to hear others argue for new efforts to establish communications and trade with the Sudan. Of particular importance to him, however, were the congratulations of friends and acquaintances who unstintingly acknowledged the courage and resolution shown by the mission's officers and men. Such acclamation (and some personal vanity) heightened his determination to succeed; supremely confident of his own ability to pioneer a route into the central Sudan and settle the Niger controversy, he was on fire to prove himself to others.

Clapperton also felt the moment was right to ask for a favour on behalf of his brother Charles who wished to be considered for the important, and no doubt lucrative, position of quartermaster which had recently become vacant at the divisional headquarters of the Royal Marines. Clapperton's fulsome letter petitioning Lord Bathurst to intervene with the First Sea Lord did the trick – Lord Melville, a Scot who had surrounded himself in office with an out-and-out Scottish coterie, found the application 'very creditable... and by no means unreasonable'[24] and in due course Hugh's brother landed the job.

John Barrow and Robert Hay between them framed the formal instructions to the mission. Based essentially on Clapperton's own recommendations, the orders were couched in terms of a response from His Majesty King George to Sultan Bello's expressed wish to establish relations; there remained, however, a number of grey areas, 'from our present imperfect knowledge of this part of Africa beyond the line of the coast, much must be left to your discretion'.[25] Confusion had arisen because no one had previously heard of Bello's sea-ports of Funda or Raka; and it was not clear whether the mission should remain on the coast until communication had been established with Bello, or whether it could proceed inland immediately upon arrival. But when the brief was eventually issued, Clapperton was quite content.

In sum, he was required to travel to Whydah on the Guinea Coast and get a message through to Sultan Bello, who would then arrange to escort the mission to Raka. If unable to communicate with Bello, or if such a course of action looked unpromising, Clapperton was to seek out one John Houtson (a local merchant to whom Belzoni had also turned) at Benin or Lagos and proceed north as advised by him. The primary objectives were: to establish relations with the Sultan; to open up new trade routes by way of the coast and the River Niger; to obtain Bello's agreement to halt the trade in slaves from or through his dominions to the sea; to procure detailed information on the slave trade in the interior and to make recommendations on how it might best be stopped.

Clapperton was also commanded to obtain particulars of those articles suitable for, and required from, European markets. He was directed to report on the major geographical features of the country and on the course of the River Niger, and in particular to ascertain whether or not the river flowed into the Bight of Benin and, if it did, how far up stream it was navigable; and he should explore all rivers flowing into the Bights of Benin and Biafra. Any leisure time was to be used to collect samples of local products and raw materials, and rare or curious objects of natural history. Then, if they had not already heard that Laing had been success-ful, the mission should proceed to Timbuktu.

On first arrival in Sokoto, Clapperton should send Pearce to Kukawa, to link up with John Tyrwhitt and pay the necessary compliments to Sheikh Al-Kanemi before exploring eastward of Lake Chad, the River Shari and Adamawa; Morison would travel with Pearce. Dickson was officially attached to Clapperton (since no one in authority wished to see a repeat of the disastrously flawed arrangements for the Borno Mission). When Clapperton considered his tasks complete, he was to leave a consul in either Sokoto or Raka to promote Britain's trade and abolitionist interests, and return to England by way of Tripoli or Benin as he saw fit.

Parallel orders were issued to *Brazen*'s commander, Captain Willes; and Robert Hay interviewed the mission's officers before their departure. Arrangements were almost complete and in the middle of August, Pearce, Morison and Columbus went on board *Brazen* at Portsmouth, while Clapperton completed his remaining tasks in London, not least with respect to the *Narrative of Travels and Discoveries* of the Borno Mission.

John Murray had decided that the major part of the book should be formed from Denham's fluent account. Two additional chapters, however, would be incorporated, one formed from Oudney's account of the journey with Clapperton through western Fezzan to Ghat in June and July 1822, and the other from Clapperton's record of his journey from Kukawa to Sokoto and back in 1824. Barrow evidently resolved against inclusion of any other extracts from Clapperton's journals, and in so determining he rendered Clapperton less than justice, since the rejected material contained new information as well as entertaining accounts of travel; but there was a fair amount of duplication, and Clapperton's manuscripts were admittedly still in very raw form. In fact Barrow later told Murray that he had made the selected chapter acceptable only 'by dishing and trimming him as much as I dare'.[26]

On the other hand, Barrow and Murray did Clapperton proud with respect to the overall balance of the *Narrative*. They resisted Denham's persistent efforts to omit references to any achievements other than his own – although in his Preface to the *Narrative* he had the effrontery to declare that his colleagues' journals contained 'very little beyond what will be found in my own journals'[27] – and they also took care to expunge from the text a number of Denham's gratuitous criticisms of his fellow explorers.

John Murray's generous contract reflected continuing public interest and excitement. He paid one thousand two hundred pounds for the rights to the mission's papers, a sum which Barrow and Hay agreed should be distributed as seven hundred pounds to Denham, four hundred to Clapperton and one hundred pounds to Oudney's estate. Those were large sums – for Clapperton the equivalent of more than a naval commander's annual pay.

Murray had also decided to include illustrations, engraved from the explorers' own sketches.[28] And he wanted portraits. In

August he commissioned a well-known society portraitist, Gildon Manton, and sent him round to 15 Duke Street, Adelphi, to take Clapperton's likeness; two portraits were to be made, one for Murray and one for Clapperton. The explorer expressed some bemusement,

> 15 Duke Street Adelphi, Friday evening
>
> My dear Sir
>
> As I was only a Sub in the late African pioneers allow me to see my Colonel and Protector Mr. Barrows phiz before mine – God knows I have the pride of a loyal Scot and when I come back I hope I may deserve such a distinction for sweet and dear to me is the praise of honorable men, but allow me to send the portrait to my enthusiastic Country Woman M<u>rs</u> Murray – under no other considerations can I submit to the purgatory of sitting as Still as a Church mouse to have my phiz critically examined
>
> With the kindest regards to M<u>rs</u> Murray and tell her there is none who loves his country better ~ every rock every tree I look on as my brother ~ and the sole ambition of my life has been and will be to have it said by my country-women ~ he came from Scotland ~ when I die I want no other Epitaph
>
> I remain
> Dear Sir
> yours Truly
> Hugh Clapperton
> Alias Abdullah the African or Barrows – Pioneer[29]

Finally, on 25 August 1825, accompanied by Thomas Dickson and Richard Lander, Clapperton set off for Portsmouth and HMS *Brazen*; but even on board ship he continued to receive niggling missives from government officials concerning over-expenditure on equipment. In part to convey his pleasure on learning that Robert Brown of the Linnæan Society had named a plant after their mutual friend Dr Walter Oudney, Clapperton wrote to James Kay from *Brazen*, 'We leave England this morning and as far as I am concerned, I have experienced nothing but misery and trouble since my arrival, and look forward to our voyage for peace and rest'.[30]

Brazen sailed from Spithead for Cowes on the Isle of Wight, to embark a party of troops for the Royal African Colonial Corps in Sierra Leone; the following afternoon, in company with a convoy of transports, she rounded the Needles into the English Channel to head for the open sea in thick hazy weather. When the fog cleared next morning there was no sign of the transports, and *Brazen* sailed on alone, bound for the west coast of Africa. Hugh Clapperton settled down to life on board in the genial company of like-minded travelling companions, delighted to be at sea again.

Extract of letter from Hugh Clapperton to John Murray, August 1825

Chapter 15: The Guinea Coast 1825
a great deal of palavering and drinking

The west coast of Africa – a duel – anti-slavery patrols
ports, forts and merchants – John Houtson – negotiations in Badagry

Captain Willes shaped a course for Sierra Leone by way of the Canaries and Cape Verde Islands. HMS *Brazen* was carrying one hundred and thirty-four men; in addition to the mission, she had on board a surgeon newly appointed to the Africa station and a number of other persons on official passage to the British head-quarters on the west coast.

The sloop's captain proved most agreeable company and the voyage afforded Hugh Clapperton both a very welcome breathing space and a happy return, albeit as a supernumerary, to a vessel on active duty. Heading south, the great guns were exercised, the marines were drilled at small arms and a party of seamen at the cutlass – possibly under Clapperton's direction but certainly under his interested eye. Having called at Porto Santo in the Madeira Islands, *Brazen* arrived at Santa Cruz on Tenerife on 13 September to take on fresh supplies; and on the following day Clapperton's companions, accompanied by some of the ship's officers, climbed the peak to ascertain its height above sea level – Clapperton had set up the barometer on shore and walked to the start of the climb, 'but finding it too much, I returned to Capt[n] Willes'[1]; he was not yet fully recovered. Ten days later they called at St Vincent in the Cape Verde Islands, and 21 October 1825 saw *Brazen* anchored in the roads off Freetown, Sierra Leone.

Founded by philanthropists in 1787 as a home for loyalist black refugees from North America, rebels from Jamaica and destitute blacks from London, the British establishment at Sierra Leone had been taken over by the government as a base for wartime naval deployments in the southern Atlantic. In 1810 it was redeveloped to form a centre for the collection and rehabilitation of liberated slaves and to serve as a headquarters for operations, naval for the most part, to suppress human trafficking.

In February 1826 Major-General Charles Turner had arrived from London to take up the post of commander-in-chief of the British establishments in West Africa (following the tragic demise in Ashanti of his predecessor, Sir Charles McCarthy). A fiery, frugal Scottish veteran who had lost an arm in the Peninsular War, Turner regarded McCarthy's enlightened programme of works at Sierra Leone as feckless extravagance; and, frustrated by the squadron's failure to achieve results, he took pride in having mounted and led a series of minor military expeditions of his own to attempt to halt the slave trade on the nearby coast. He was enthusiastic about Clapperton's expedition and produced further stores – bell tents, caulking tar, gunpowder and shot, two quarts of spirits of wine and two bugles – and also provided canoes and canoe-men for landing personnel and baggage onto the hazardous shores.

While Clapperton oversaw the mission's arrangements, and mulled over the geography of the Bights of Benin and Biafra and the possible termination of the River Niger with the editor of the Sierra Leone *Gazette*, Robert Pearce used the time to interrogate a *shereef* of Segu for information about the interior and the upper Niger. Thomas Dickson, however, caused a considerable stir, with potentially disastrous consequences for the whole mission, when his hot temper led him into an altercation with Captain William Ross, the General's aide-de-camp and personal friend. A challenge was issued and in the duel which took place the following morning Clapperton acted as Dickson's second. Duelling was a serious offence in the armed services, and Turner issued a reprimand,

Sierra Leone, 23rd October 1825
It having been represented to me that Captain Ross my A D Camp as Principal and Lieut. Robertson Acting Brigade Major as his Friend fought a duel this morning with one of the gentlemen employed on the Mission as Principal, and yourself as his Friend – the cause of the [dispute] having originated at my Table and the transaction being so much at Variance with those feelings of goodwill and kindness which I entertain towards yourself and your associates, I have considered it my duty to place these officers (Capt. Ross and Lieut. Robertson) in arrest, and to demand from them for the information of His Royal Highness the Commander in chief an explanation of the circumstances which led to so extraordinary a transaction.

Should you or your friend feel disposed to favour me with any explanation it will be forwarded by the same opportunity.

I have, etc.,

Cha. Turner, Govr [2]

The unfortunate affair was evidently satisfactorily resolved since there is nothing further on record.

Preparations for their departure were soon completed and on 27 October, with an additional complement of eighteen Kru-men to assist in landings on the coast (one registered as Ben Clapperton, another as Bob Pearce), *Brazen* set sail through squally weather, bound for Cape Palmas and the Guinea Coast.

For two centuries the Windward and Leeward coasts of Guinea had been profitable trading grounds for merchant adventurers from many European nations, and a focal point for the triangular Atlantic slave trade. So-called factories were established, and forts built and manned to protect them, from which manufactured goods, guns, tobacco and rum were sold in exchange for slaves, gold, ivory and palm oil. At the turn of the nineteenth century the British establishments were administered by the Company of Merchants Trading to West Africa, successors to the Royal African Company. Following the abolition of the slave trade in Britain and in British vessels in 1807, however, patterns of trade changed and merchants, unable themselves to penetrate inland (and the middlemen were famously unreliable) were hard put to it to run profitable enterprises. Investment fell off, and in 1821 the government at Sierra Leone took over control of the establishments along the coast.

Having rounded the Cape for the Windward Coast, *Brazen* took up her duties on anti-slavery patrol with the Africa squadron. The Royal Navy offered few more exacting tours of duty at that time. Britain had reinforced the squadron with new vessels designed for speed and ease of handling and having improved cargo capacity; efficiently manned and well-equipped, they dominated the seas and the coastal settlements, a gratifying expression of British naval power, but the squadron had its work cut out to counter the complex traffic in slaves along the three thousand mile shoreline.

Day-to-day operations included everything Hugh Clapperton had most relished during his naval career: lively pursuit and cutting out actions, the transport of captured ships, boat work and shore parties. If conditions were trying, the potential financial rewards were not inconsiderable – naval captains received prize money for captured vessels delivered to the Commission at Sierra Leone, where courts and due legal processes had been established specifically to deal with detained craft belonging to other nations.

Clapperton knew a number of the officers on the squadron from his time on the Canadian Great Lakes. His former patron, Captain William Owen, was on station, and he was accompanied by the hydrographer Emerich Vidal (since promoted captain) with whom Clapperton had served at Kingston during the winter of 1816-17. Having completed his four-year survey of the coasts of Africa including Madagascar, Owen had arrived with two brigs to oversee progress on the construction of a new naval establishment and shore base at Clarence Cove on Fernando Po (later Bioko).

Clapperton chafed at the delays incurred through *Brazen*'s patrol activities, but he was both fascinated and sickened to observe at first hand the coastal end of the grim trade he had encountered in the interior. On the passage to Cape Coast Castle, four slavers were chased and boarded. The French brigantine *Eclaire de Nantes*, with only a three-foot height between decks, was carrying one hundred and sixty-nine slaves (having lost many more in shipping them through the surf). The schooner *La Modeste*, bound for Martinique, had two hundred and sixty-nine slaves on board, with only two feet eight inches between decks and without a surgeon. The ships were seized and sent back to Sierra Leone for the captives to be released. Willes also took over a small Spanish schooner carrying fifty-six people in heavy irons and captured another fitted out to receive a human cargo.

When *Brazen* arrived at Cape Coast Castle the commodore of the squadron was away at sea; and following the recent defeat of a British military expedition into the interior, the chief concerns of the commander of the fort revolved around the threat of attack by the Ashanti. The Castle, the principal British fort on the coast and deputy headquarters of the West Africa establishments, was a very unhealthy spot for Europeans; from two companies of white soldiers who arrived in 1823, not one remained alive at the end of eighteen months, and of the one hundred and one men landed from HMS *Thesis* in 1824, forty-five were dead within the week.

At Cape Coast, Clapperton got on particularly well with one of the fort's deputy commanders, P.J. Fraser. While Fraser had no detailed knowledge of the ports and hinterland further east, he was able to confirm that John Houtson was indeed on the coast and not sailing overseas. Before departure, Clapperton appointed Fraser official agent to the mission, to facilitate communication and supply; and as Columbus (suffering from venereal disease) was clearly not able to undertake strenuous travel, Dr Morison personally engaged a new servant, George Dawson, a thirty-three year-old able seaman from Canterbury in Kent.

On the passage to the Leeward Coast, HM Sloop *Brazen* was once again in action. Approaching the Accra roads, she seized a large Spanish slaver which had received thirty slaves from the Dutch fort and was preparing to collect another two hundred at Little Popo. After calling at Accra, Willes anchored off Little Popo, where he gave the thirty captives their freedom and, by dint of threatening to bombard the factory, quickly obtained the release of the two hundred held on shore. Following a tip-off, *Brazen's* officers then intervened in an exchange of slaves taking place between two trading ships.

But at the British forts Clapperton could glean few facts about the countries of the immediate interior, nor was there any word of Houtson's whereabouts; however the commander of the garrison recommended to the explorer's attention a merchant based at Whydah, Frederick James, formerly of the Royal African Company. Four months had already elapsed since the date by which Hugh Clapperton had engaged to present himself on the coast, and it now appeared increasingly unlikely that he would be able to make contact with Bello's representatives there (if indeed there were any). He was thus deliberating upon the best way to proceed on his own – whether to make his way inland to Nupe and Hausaland or to begin a search for Bello's sea-ports – when at last fortune smiled on him. While they were anchored off Little Popo, John Houtson sailed into the roads to have a new bowsprit fitted to his brig, the *Albert*; and it was very soon clear to Clapperton that the enterprising Liverpool merchant was just the man he needed.

Houtson had set up his own trading operation on the coast seven years earlier, at Gwato on the River Benin, and had recently opened a new factory at Badagry. He knew the coast well; he had paid intelligent attention to the politics of those regimes having influence, and from his arrival in the country had systematically collected information about the interior. He advised Clapperton against a start from Benin because the Oba had turned against the British on account of their interference in his lucrative commerce in slaves. As to the geography of the region, Houtson knew that the lagoons, creeks and rivers from Ardrah in the west to Benin in the east formed one single water system, although he could not say how, if at all, they interlinked with the River Niger or any lakes at Nupe – nor did he know whether the rivers entering the sea near Benin and in the Bight of Biafra formed a single delta.

John Houtson had not heard of the presence on the coast of any emissaries from Sultan Bello, but he confirmed that merchants from the central Sudan travelling overland through the countries of Oyo and Dahomey did occasionally appear at the ports. And

Badagry itself, with extensive commercial links along the coast and creeks between Porto Novo and Lagos, was turning into an important centre for trade, and enjoyed reasonable communications with countries of the interior through Oyo. He therefore recommended that Clapperton should proceed to Badagry, where there was a good prospect of obtaining from King Adele a safe passage to Oyo, the southern boundaries of which lay only a few days' journey inland[†]. Clapperton accepted the advice and invited the trader to join the mission. But Houtson was reluctant to leave his factories and his ship as he was in the process of making up a shipment of hippopotamus teeth and other local goods for export; however he engaged to provide all the support he could from his base at Badagry.

On the way there, HMS *Brazen* made a halt off Whydah, where Clapperton looked up Frederick James. James had rare first-hand knowledge of the hinterland and useful information about trade routes. Formerly Commandant of Accra and a member of the Council of the Committee on West Africa, in 1818 James had participated in an official mission to Kumasi, the capital of Ashanti, to negotiate trade relations with the coastal forts; while in Kumasi he had engaged in personal financial speculation and attempted to further his own interests by bringing the trade down to Accra. The leader of the mission, Thomas Bowdich, had filed a complaint with the Governor (Bowdich's uncle) and the case was examined before the Committee. Rather than be removed from the Council James had resigned; he had returned to the Guinea Coast the following year and successfully set up in business on his own in Whydah.

Most significantly, James maintained good relations with the wealthy Brazilian merchant and slave-trader Francisco de Souza, who had long since ingratiated himself with the King of Dahomey, becoming Gezo's personal trading representative, and effectively viceroy, on the coast. James believed that an approach supported by de Souza would secure from King Gezo a safe passage through north-west Dahomey to Nupe or Yawri.

[†] The state of Oyo was founded by Yoruba tribes in the fourteenth century. By the mid-eighteenth century, successive *alafins* (kings) had consolidated Oyo's position as the most powerful empire in the interior of the Bight of Benin. Incorporating parts of Borgu to the north-west and Nupe to the north-east, and with Dahomey tributary after 1730, Oyo controlled the routes to the coast and became the main slave-trading state in the region.

Journal signature and sketch, and medical notes by Thomas Dickson

Armed at last with sufficient information and the necessary contacts, Clapperton considered his options. He had already discounted any possibility of meeting up with Bello's men on the coast, and the likelihood of further significant delay argued against sending a message to Sokoto and waiting for an official escort. He decided to hedge his bets. Having first dispatched a small group to explore the possibility of an approach to the Niger and the Sudan through Dahomey, he would land his main party at Badagry to proceed by way of Oyo.

Thomas Dickson volunteered to travel to Abomey (capital of Dahomey), accompanied by Frederick James and de Souza. John Houtson agreed to provide a base for the main party at Badagry and, if Dickson recommended an advance by way of Dahomey, James could furnish similar support at Whydah. Clapperton then appointed Houtson and James official agents to the expedition; he issued instructions to Captain Willes for maintaining contact and communications between the mission's agents at the ports and with London, and put Dickson ashore into Frederick James's care. Before they parted company, Clapperton got the doctor to jot down some notes on medicines and their use on the front page of his diary; and when saying their farewells on board, he counselled his old friend to set a guard against his temper, recommending to him two basic rules of thumb for a successful progress through the countries of the interior, 'respect the institutions of the native peoples and be kind to them on all occasions'.[3]

HMS *Brazen* put to sea again and Hugh Clapperton set aside his cares in the cheerful company of John Houtson and James Fawckner, a captain in the merchant marine and familiar with the coast, who was travelling with the trader while seeking a new employment. And by the time they anchored off Badagry four days later Clapperton had persuaded Houtson to accompany the expedition inland; for a fee of six hundred pounds, he agreed to make himself available for up to three months, the maximum time he felt he could spare away from his business, and undertook to attend the mission to Oyo's capital, some thirty days' journey from the coast.[4]

Given the uncertainties about their likely rate of progress, and warned of the scarcity of pack animals on the coast, Clapperton elected to leave the bulky field pieces and the large boxes filled with muskets on board *Brazen*. Houtson went ashore first, to see about the mission's arrival in the town, and the following morning the stores were landed. It was a dangerous business. Hearts in mouths, the members of the mission looked on as the huge canoes made for the shore, each paddled by some twenty stout men, a fetish-man garlanded in leather amulets chanting prayers in the bow and calling out the exact moment to catch the breakers and surf onto the sands. One of the canoes was swamped and much of the equipment damaged, including Clapperton's telescope and other navigational instruments, but nothing was lost – though later that morning Houtson was lucky to escape with his life when his canoe capsized on the outer breakers as he was returning to the ship. In the afternoon, last-minute instructions were given to Captain Willes and the mission took its leave: Lander played patriotic tunes on his bugle, the men cheered, and Clapperton, Pearce, Morison and their servants were landed by canoe on the Badagry bar.

That same evening HMS *Brazen* weighed anchor, bound for Prince's Island to take on fresh supplies of food and water before returning to Whydah to stand ready to provide any necessary assistance to Dr Dickson's expedition and to put ashore Columbus, who seemed to be on the road to recovery, to join the doctor.[5]

On the Badagry bar, Clapperton and his party slept out in the open and 'had no disturbances during the night except from the Musquitoes'[6] – it was the end of the season of little rains, and there had been exceptional downpours in Badagry that year, leaving the normally dry sandy bank strewn with pools of stagnant water. The following morning, with a long line of carriers bearing the stores, the whole party set off across the bar to the shore of the lagoon where they were met by Houtson and one of King Adele's representatives. From there they were taken by canoe to Badagry, the King's men firing muskets the while, and carried into the town in hammocks. The officers dined and lodged at Houtson's house, and prepared to begin negotiations with Adele.

A full week of palaver, well lubricated with rum, was required to obtain Adele's agreement to forward the mission up country into Oyo. The King had begun by driving a very hard bargain for the provision of assistance to the expedition but, encouraged by handsome gifts for himself and his principal advisers, in hope of a supply of weapons to aid him in local wars and border conflicts, and stimulated by the possibility of future British protection, he was eventually persuaded to co-operate. In due course, some sixty carriers were hired and riding horses were loaned to the officers. Houtson's invoice to Clapperton for payments made in trade gold to Adele, his counsellors and generals came to over two hundred pounds (with a separate bill for forty gallons of rum). Additional supplies were purchased from the factory for use as presents or trade goods on the journey, together with more equipment for the expedition itself – extra tents, suitable clothing, china and pewter ware; and, finally, the stores were broken down into more portable bundles and the chests and packages counted and recounted by the carriers' supervisors.

During the day, Clapperton walked about Badagry, visiting the markets and taking in the town's commercial and social life. In the slave market he bought the freedom of Mohamed Ali, a Shuwa Arab from Borno, rescuing him from sale to a Brazilian slaver, and took him on as a personal servant. He also made contact with the handful of Moslem traders arrived from the north, to learn what he could about the roads inland. And every evening saw a great deal of boisterous merry-making and the consumption of yet more pints of rum.

Eventually, late in the afternoon of Wednesday 7th December 1825, Clapperton succeeded in getting all his men and the stores aboard the heavy canoes at the Badagry waterfront. From there the British party, their escorts and numerous assistants made their way into the Yewa river where they disembarked for the night on its western bank, preparatory to making an early start on the following day's march inland through the low-lying forests and swamps behind the coast.

Chapter 16: Journey inland 1825–1826
live or die I must go

*Fever takes its toll – the Mountains of Kong – turbulent Oyo
arrival in Katunga – frustrated attempts to reach Nupe
Houtson returns to the coast – Clapperton strikes northward*

Clapperton had intended taking the canoes further up the river, said to be easily navigable for some twenty miles, but their guides strongly advised against it because of the fetish – a fair if double-edged warning. Coastal chiefs sought to frighten off European traders (thus discouraging them from dealing directly in the inland markets for slaves and trade goods), and the mosquito-infested river valley was a decidedly unwholesome place for unacclimatized white travellers.

Houtson and Clapperton went ahead, taking it turn and turn about to ride the shared horse along the winding trail through the thorny scrub; on horseback they suffered painful abrasions to their legs, and on foot soon wore out the soles of their shoes. And after three days Clapperton succumbed to fever and had to travel in a hammock.

The escort proved competent and the mission's hosts helpful and generous; the sixty carriers, however, required constant supervision and encouragement and progress was slow, virtually grinding to a halt when it was necessary to get themselves, their baggage and all the men across the River Yewa by canoe.[1] Eventually they emerged onto higher ground and seven days out from Badagry, by the light of the moon and hand-held torches, they took to narrow tracks past small fetish huts sheltering strange clay figures lit by flickering lamps, and so reached Ilaro, a principal towns in Egbadoland, on the outer rim of Oyo's influence. They had begun to make progress, and Clapperton was pleased to discover that one of the chief of Ilaro's concubines (a girl of extra-ordinary beauty) came from Nupe, so long his ultimate goal.

All was not well within the mission, however. In Ilaro, Robert Pearce fell ill, and was bled to relieve his delirium. Richard Lander also went down with fever; and Dr Morison, who had suffered grievously from the ague during the previous two days, was only recovering slowly. After a day's rest, Clapperton led his party a few miles further north to Ijanna, the southernmost outpost of

Oyo's empire, where the town's influential chief, the *onisare*, was a senior and trusted official personally appointed by the alafin (king) as viceroy of the south-western provinces and tributary states. From Abako, one of the Alafin's officers visiting the region, Clapperton obtained an account of the route to be followed on the thirty-day journey north to Katunga (the Hausa name used by Clapperton), the capital of Oyo; Abako offered to escort the expedition to his master, and the *onisare* agreed to provide assistance and carriers.

Ijanna was an active and noisy little town. Having heard that a Brazilian brig had arrived at Badagry to buy slaves, the townsmen were hurriedly preparing a *razzia* into the country bordering Dahomey; and the *onisare*, whose establishment was graced by a female choir, doled out rum by the gallon to one and all. In the daytime Clapperton and Houtson wandered around the town, admiring the intricate carved door posts, the ceremonial masks and fetish objects and the numerous woven and dyed articles set out for sale; and in the evenings they sampled the hospitality of the chief and his court, joining in the festivities and the communal dancing. At night a guard was set over the mission's baggage and the constabulary made their rounds swinging whistling-sticks on string. Clapperton found the people honest and the government to be competent, 'Humanity, however, is the same in every land – Government may restrain the vicious principles of our nature but it is beyond the power, even of African despotism, to silence a woman's tongue – in sickness and in health and at every stage we have been obliged to endure their eternal loquacity and noise'.[2]

After yet another day of celebration and revelry, Clapperton sent to the *onisare* to enquire when the horses would be ready; the messenger 'returned with an answer that the King was drunk to-night – but would see us on tomorrow'.[3] But it was not the rum which abruptly ruled out an early departure from Ijanna.

Malarial fever struck so suddenly that the mission's records contain few personal accounts of the progress and severity of the attacks; and the travellers did not know exactly what they were dealing with. Contracted on the coast (probably during the first night they spent ashore), the disease declared itself in cycles of burning temperatures and sweats interspersed with severe chills. As it took hold, its victims experienced crushing headaches, racked and aching limbs and, as the body's resistance crumbled, spells of dizziness and disorientation turning to delirium. Purgatives and emetics carried by the mission were of little use, often serving only to further debilitate the sufferer, and draughts of calomel, suspensions of opium, a higher intake of liquid and rest brought only marginal relief. In between bouts there were moments of calm and apparent recuperation; but when the sequence began again it was with renewed and mounting intensity. The travellers' impaired immune systems grew increasingly vulnerable to other invading disorders and diseases, typically diarrhœa, typhus and yellow fever.

While Morison appeared to get stronger, Richard Lander grew visibly weaker, and the outgoing, personable Robert Pearce was patently ailing, no longer at all his old self; Clapperton too began to experience intermittent bouts of ague accompanied by violent headaches. And their sufferings had to be endured in an open compound in full view of noisy crowds of inquisitive townsfolk.

On 22 December, Dr Morison asked to be allowed to return to the coast, convinced that the fresh sea breezes would assist in his recuperation, and Houtson volunteered to accompany him. Clapperton agreed; he decided to push on with the others, even though the sick showed no signs of improvement, and at 7.30 a.m. the next day the hammocks set off through undulating country watered by bright streams and partly cleared of forest. They had not been long on the road when, without warning, Houtson's men suddenly turned tail and fled, overcome by the fear of war and the possibility of capture and slavery. The expedition had to return to Ijanna to hire new carriers.

The roads dreadful bad in places...

On the morning of 24 December, they managed only a few miles along sodden tracks, 'the road dreadful bad in places over the horses belley in places – George Dawson's horse lay down in the midst of the water and he rolled off ~~there~~ as he was weak and ill with ague'.[4] That evening fever claimed its first victim. Able Seaman Dawson collapsed and died. Clapperton was distressed by his death, the more so for having been unaware that the man had formally joined his expedition. On Christmas Day they proceeded a short distance, the sick wrapped up in blankets. Clapperton himself was still not well, and very susceptible to the cold wind of the harmattan; the following day he too had to be carried on the short journey to Aibo, an impoverished place where they were housed in a miserable ant-infested hovel, but 'the village could not afford a better'.[5]

On 27 December they attempted a fresh start, but Robert Pearce was failing fast and they had only travelled three miles when they were compelled to halt at the village of Engwa. And there at nine o'clock in the evening Pearce died. He was buried in a vacant lot in their assigned compound, with a tree at the head of the grave; the mound itself was set around with stakes and a shed built over it. In Clapperton's daybook, a barely legible note composed over two days and containing confused deletions, records that he was too ill to sit up and had to ask Lander to inscribe the headboard, 'here lies Captn Pearce R.N. who died Decr 27th 1825 much regretted by the remain^r of the Mission ~ Captn H. Clapperton – R.L – W. Ps^{co} – this was afterwards cut in the board & the ink filled for which I paid a bottle of rum'.[6] Hugh Clapperton felt the loss keenly; the two had hit it off famously from their very first meeting in London. Memories of Murmur returned to haunt him; feverish and dejected, with Lander also unwell and Dickson, Houtson and Morison out of touch, he pondered unhappily the implications for the mission of Robert Pearce's death.

Having arranged for Pearce's belongings to be packed up and sent back to the coast, Clapperton retreated to his hut. Four days later he was recovered enough to write letters to Hay, W.H. Smyth and Willes, 'It is my misfortune that I have nothing to communicate but the worst of news'.[7] As there was still no word from Houtson and Morison, he decided to remain where he was until he was a little stronger or until he should hear from them. And that very evening Houtson returned with the disastrous news that Morison had died at Ijanna on 27 December – the same day as Pearce; from Houtson's description, the doctor had succumbed to yellow fever.

Clapperton's journal for the following day was left blank, save for a scribbled note of the latitude of Engwa. Although close to despair, physically exhausted and with his plans apparently in ruins around him, no thought of aborting the expedition crossed his mind; he would go on to the Niger and Sokoto or, like Mungo Park, perish in the attempt. With Houtson's help he could get to Katunga, some two hundred miles distant, but the trader would then have to return to his business on the coast. Achieving the mission's wider objectives required at least two officers, and the enterprising and reliable Thomas Dickson, well accustomed to a tropical climate, was his one remaining hope. But though Ijanna was only five days by courier from the coast, Houtson had heard no word of Dickson's progress, and they had no idea when news might be expected.

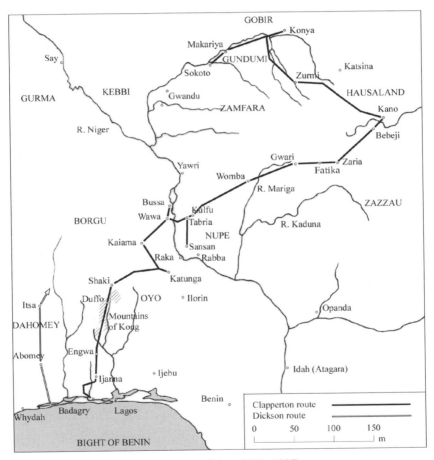

Map 7 Clapperton's second expedition 1825–1827

Fortunately, Richard Lander had shown splendid resilience. At one point he had been so ill that Dr Morison, who had had him shaved and bled to ease his symptoms, had almost despaired of him; but the young man had refused his master's entreaties that he too should return to the coast. And so Clapperton had watched over him, ministering to all his wants – a powerful claim on his servant's loyalty which Lander found only natural to repay with 'the most inviolable attachment and devoted zeal'[8]; and once having pulled through, he had no intention of deserting the man who had treated him so kindly, more like a son than a servant.

Three days later, Clapperton was ready to move on. At 7 o'clock on the morning of 3 January 1826, the diminished and melancholy party started out from Engwa on the road to Katunga, led by Abako and followed by a large team of carriers. Having crossed the rocky bed of the River Oyan, they left the dense vegetation of the valley floor for higher ground. The landscape opened out into a rolling, well-watered countryside with broad tracks running over flat tables of sparkling granite, and in the valleys below there were plantations of oil palms and coconut tree; the air was cooler, 'the Atmosphere was much changed for the better'.[9]

After four days' journey, the road began to wind its way past 'gigantic blocks of granite, which in some places rise to the height of 500 or 600 feet above the valley'.[10] Clapperton assumed that he had reached the foothills of the Mountains of Kong, so-called by European geographers who believed them to be a single unbroken range running behind the coast from the snow-capped mountains of East Africa to the highlands of Sierra Leone. Abako said that the hills before them were some fifty miles in depth from north to south, and ran south-east from Borgu behind Ashanti to Benin. The description gave Clapperton hope that the range could be crossed easily enough, although the question of how the River Niger flowed through or round it to the sea had yet to be settled.

A little recovered and in more positive mood, Hugh Clapperton again began to take note of his surroundings. He recorded the enthusiastic welcome they received from large crowds in the more densely populated villages, the generous and friendly hospitality of the chiefs, the changing patterns of agriculture as the mission travelled north and the cheerful mid-day halts on the road to drink *oti* (mountain beer). The landscape was very picturesque. Villages sat perched atop massive granite outcrops and women ground corn on the flat boulders below; the narrow passes were lush with deep green vegetation, rich with birdsong and myriads of butterflies, and here and there were small open spaces closely planted with crops of corn, vegetables and fruit. But Clapperton was still weak and at Duffo had to be supported by two men when climbing the hill to take a look at the view.

At Shaki, the heavily populated capital of the western provinces of Oyo, Clapperton was able to get his bearings; he calculated its latitude to be 9° North, and his hosts confirmed that Katunga lay to the east, that the River Niger was only two days' travel beyond it and did indeed flow past Benin, albeit over rocks, to enter the sea. To the north of Shaki lay the Kingdom of Borgu, its dominions stretching to the borders of Dahomey and Gonja. Clapperton's hopes of being on the Niger in short order, and of a reunion with Dickson, were immediately rekindled.

He was rather taken with the chief of Shaki, a good-looking man about fifty years of age (always surrounded by his ladies and musicians), who had tidied up his own house in order that his British visitors might have space to stay and rest, 'a true mountain King and the friend of strangers'[11]; the chief's description of the state of affairs in Oyo, however, sounded a warning note. He said that he had hoped that the British officers were messengers of peace bringing blessings to his king and country, for the country was indeed in turmoil and surrounded by enemies. There was civil war in neighbouring Nupe, a war of succession in which the Fulani jihadists had supported one of two contenders for the throne; and in Oyo itself Hausa slaves backed by Sokoto had risen up against the Alafin and seized control of Ilorin, Oyo's second city, two days' journey from Katunga. Bands of Fulani and their allies were attempting to seize territory in the region surrounding the capital, and people went in fear of their lives.[12]

Clapperton was disturbed by the account. Local hostilities had prevented him reaching the Niger once before, and war between Oyo and Sokoto threatened safe passage from the dominions of one to the other. His best hope seemed to be somehow to reach Sokoto's forces in Nupe and seek an escort direct to Bello. He would have a better idea of his prospects once he reached Katunga.

Travelling east from Shaki across the open savannah of northern Oyo, Clapperton soon had evidence of the unrest described by the chief. All along the road to Katunga villages lay in ruins, burnt and laid waste, some still in the process of being abandoned as the inhabitants scattered before the marauding Fulani and their allies from eastern Oyo. Law and order had broken down, and rural communities in their disarray had become prey to bandits from southern Borgu seeking rich pickings on the fertile plains; the terrified people hid themselves away in settlements surrounded by dense thorn bushes and a creeping briar impenetrable to every living thing but snakes.

Clapperton remained in a very poor way, continuing sensitive to the cold, suffering from persistent diarrhœa and, increasingly, from pains in his sides. Feeling 'worse than I have been since I left Badagry'[13], he reverted on a number of occasions to travelling by hammock. He treated himself with strong purgatives from the medical chest, tried out a local remedy of lime juice and pepper, and got some relief from having his side pasted with malaguetta pepper (known to sailors as Grains of Paradise, or Guinea Grains) and rubbed with a piece of cord.

They hurried on to Katunga. At the gathering place of caravans to the north-west of the capital, one of the Alafin's officers arrived with an armed troop to escort the new arrivals into the city. All was 'bustle and hubbub with the great men and their attendants, their large grooms and their little horses'[14]; and a crowd of villagers joined them seeking protection from thieves along the road.

The following day Clapperton and his party rode on to the capital, accompanied by horns and drums, their escort clumsily mounted on makeshift saddles and a posse of bowmen running lightly alongside them sporting 'natty little hats with feathers'[15] and bearing leather pouches at their sides. Attentive as always to matters military, the traveller owned himself impressed by their fleetness of foot, the best infantry he had seen in Africa; but he was rather contemptuous of the ill-mounted cavalry on their small Oyo horses – they would have presented easy targets.

At noon on 23 January 1826, Clapperton arrived at the north gate of Katunga and stopped to rest in one of the houses just inside the walls; but his rest was disturbed by a family row, 'Abuca's wife was cooking a little country soup for us but the pot broke on the fire just as it was ready ~ the pot broke and the house was in an uproar in an instant – only for my interference they would have come to blows ~ Abuca was at one time ready to set fire to the house – at another likely to cry – that he had disappointed us'.[16]

The capital of Oyo's empire was of impressive size. It was an hour's ride from the walls to the centre of the city, along a dusty track and surrounded by a milling, suffocating throng of men, women and children, the musicians playing for all they were worth. Clapperton and Houtson rode past clusters of houses and shady trees, rocks and large open patches of cultivated ground to arrive at the palace where, before a crowd of thousands, they presented themselves to Alafin Majotu who was seated under a verandah formed by two blue and red umbrellas of cloth supported on large poles held up by slaves. After a brief exchange of salutations the chief eunuch took the visitors to their appointed quarters to enable them to organize their affairs and rest. In the evening Majotu came alone to their house for a brief private visit; he said that he and his people had never met a white man before and he could not rest until he had seen them again.

The following day Clapperton presented the mission's gifts: bales of silk and muslin, fine stockings and gloves, powder, shot and flints, and plenty of rum. And for the Alafin himself there was an assortment of special presents: an umbrella, a brass-mounted fowling piece, a sabre, a telescope and a silver-headed walking cane – for the remainder of Clapperton's stay in the capital, Majotu was never without his Newquay cane.

When eventually they sat down to talk business, Alafin Majotu offered to assist the mission in any way he could, expressing at the same time his hopes for a military alliance with the British against his enemies. For his part, Clapperton thanked his host for all the help and courtesies he and his companions had received from Majotu's officers on the way to Katunga and, carefully avoiding mention of Sokoto, said that what he himself desired was a safe passage through the Alafin's dominions to Nupe and thence to Borno, where an English officer had been residing since their previous visit. Majotu appeared to hesitate, but after consulting with his confidants said that the civil war in Nupe made him concerned for Clapperton's safety. However kindly the concern, Clapperton was not to be denied,

> I told him I was a servant of the King of England and must go where he sent me ~ live or die I must go ~ that I had nothing to do with wars and had nothing to do with either side – That all I wanted was a passage over the Quarra as they call the Niger into Nupe and I hoped he would not refuse.[17]

Majotu eventually undertook to send a messenger to Raka on the Niger to see if the road was open, though in point of fact his hands were tied. The old road to Raka, once Oyo's principal Niger port and the ferry point on the traditional trade route linking Oyo with Nupe and the Hausa states, was in rebel hands. The port itself was closed.

Scenting prevarication, Clapperton feared for the viability of his plans. The River Niger was so close; according to the people of Katunga it entered the sea either at Benin or Ijebu (not far from Lagos). When he heard that an Oyo official had just ridden to Raka and back in a single day, and that the river itself was but two hours' easy walk from the town, his frustration knew no bounds. Once in Nupe he would undoubtedly be able to settle the matter of the final course of the river; and he knew there were several reliable roads by which he could travel from Nupe to Hausaland. Aware that Houtson was anxious to return to Badagry, Clapperton was unnerved by the delay; and the return of his illness awoke old apprehensions about being pinned down by the rains.

A week after arrival in Katunga Clapperton was laid low with aching limbs, vomiting and slight delirium, which last he treated with calomel and croton (castor) oil; there followed stabbing pains in the head and eyes, for which he blistered the back of his skull, rubbed ether on his forehead and dosed himself with laudanum. When the pains were somewhat reduced he took bark three times a day as a tonic. His illness lasted only four days, but the sudden incapacitation left him more determined than ever to move on.

The following week Clapperton had it out with Majotu. He would remain in Katunga only twelve days more; if at the end of that time the Alafin had not made the necessary arrangements for his travel to Borno he would return immediately to England and tell His Majesty King George that Majotu had refused him. It was an effective ultimatum. The Alafin at last revealed that he was not able to send his visitor direct to Nupe, or even to Raka just to look upon the River Niger, because the Fulani held the road. Instead, he offered to advance the traveller and his party to Yaro, King of Kaiama in the country of Borgu, which the Alafin claimed as a tributary province (in fact he retained neither the influence of his predecessors nor good communications with the Borgu kings). The roads were safe, and King Yaro could forward the traveller northwards along the western bank of the Niger – opposite Nupe – to Bussa and Yawri. The idea appealed to Clapperton; Thomas Dickson was supposed to be heading there and Yawri he knew to be some ten days' travel from Sokoto, his undisclosed initial destination. He was therefore glad to accept the offer, and couriers were sent to Kaiama to set matters in train.

While awaiting the return of Majotu's messengers, Clapperton reorganized his affairs. He wrote to Thomas Dickson; in the event of any difficulty progressing inland from Abomey Dickson must return to the coast and go to Badagry. And he sent a message to Frederick James in Whydah to say that his good offices as agent were no longer needed, and another to Captain Willes, releasing him from his commitment to remain on the coast in support of the mission. Richard Lander and William Pasco were given written instructions to be followed in the event of Clapperton's death, depending on which side of the River Niger it occurred; his orders to them were in part based on the premise, or at least the hope, that John Tyrwhitt remained alive and well in Kukawa.

He squared up his accounts with Houtson, who witnessed the legal paperwork and agreed to deliver all the letters and journals to Captain Willes. And together they drew up a list (for the trader to take back to Badagry) of items Majotu wanted from England: a brass crown, some fine cloth, large coral, an English drum and brightly coloured carpeting as well as about half a ton of cowries. Clapperton would miss Houtson; he had proved a shrewd adviser and a resolute companion.

Finally, he summarized his decisions and the reasoning behind them in a long dispatch to Hay at the Colonial Department; all future communication, he informed the Under-Secretary, would be through Tripoli. Clapperton had burnt his bridges. He would be out of contact for some considerable time. It could well take him two months to reach Hausaland and from there, even under the most favourable circumstances, ten months were needed for an exchange of correspondence with England. He penned a short letter to Fraser at Cape Coast Castle,

> You will no doubt have heard, long ere this reaches you, of the death of my companions and no doubt would expect to hear of mine by the next arrival. I had a very strong attack of fever but had to stand my own doctor and of course recovered. I now enjoy as good health as a man can expect in Africa who is not actually a native. Houtson has been here with me has also been sick as also every Man and Boy Black or White belonging to my party owing to the bad roads swamps cold caught in the Harmattan [&] a superabundance of Goat's Flesh and Yams ~ I have often wished myself under your Hospitable roof or that I possessed the lamp of Aladin to have you and your house conveyed here or that I could have been conveyed there[18]

His letters and other paperwork completed, he settled down to wait for permission to leave. They were very well looked after, receiving daily supplies from the palace and regular visits from Majotu himself who brought little gifts each time (an ebony box carved in the shape of a tortoise, for gora nuts, and presents of food – a duck or perhaps a bowl of rice). And the enforced delay was spent agreeably enough. With Houtson, Clapperton took short walks through the shady parkland around the compounds of the Alafin and his court, whom he entertained with occasional demonstrations of the mission's equipment, firing off several signal rockets to the alarm and delight of the crowds. It was the time of the traditional yam festival, the greatest of the annual celebrations in Yoruba country, and chiefs and tributaries came from all over Oyo and neighbouring lands to pay their respects to the Alafin. Clapperton called upon visiting dignitaries, and wrote lively and often lengthy accounts of the colourful proceedings.

Nor had contact with the coast yet been completely severed. In mid-February a courier arrived from Ijanna; while there was no word of Dickson, he carried letters from England put ashore by a naval brig, 'and ½ dozen porter & ½ dozen wine ~ the other dozen having been drunk or broken on the roads ~ this supply was as welcome as unexpected and shows that with very little trouble and expense the communication may be kept open'.[19]

February turned to March, and time and again Majotu declined to appoint a day for their departure, promising always that he would have news on the morrow; he was clearly taking immense pleasure in the prestige derived from the presence of the King of England's representative at his court during the festival. Although exasperated by the blatant procrastination, Clapperton was careful to keep up diplomatic courtesies. He was also keenly aware of the transportation problem, encumbered as they were by a massive amount of personal baggage and stores. Reliable transport on the scale required was not easily arranged. He had to be patient.

At last, on 6 March, the Alafin was able to report that Yaro's representatives were ready to leave; and he even produced the promised horse – not a very good one, but that was the least of the traveller's concerns. The following day, accompanied by the ceremonial troop which had brought them into Oyo's capital six weeks earlier, Clapperton, Lander, Pasco and Ali left Katunga. Houtson saw them off on the road before he too set out, to return to the coast.

Chapter 17: The River Niger 1826
a gamester throwing his last stake

*Hunters and merchants in Borgu – difficulties with caravaneers
the widow Zuma's plot – a visit to Bussa – the River Niger
Mungo Park and the Niger rapids – the ferry at Komi*

Travelling north across the savannah from Katunga, Clapperton
was disconcerted to find that Oyo's dominions reached no further
than one day's journey beyond the caravan encampment on the
capital's outskirts. The next village was under Borgu's control, and
the man he had taken for King Yaro's ambassador at the Alafin's
court was in fact the village butcher. He grew a little uneasy about
some of the other promises made to him.

They were initially held up when Lander was again taken ill,
but the young fellow managed to continue 'by a man holding him
on the bare back of the horse, for we had no saddles'.[1] They were
then able to make good time, accompanied by the butcher and his
armed crew, past deserted habitations and lonely, impoverished
settlements, and over the rock-strewn beds of the Moshi river's
tributaries into the thorn-scrub savannah of southern Borgu.

The official escort from the King of Kaiama made its appearance
three days later. Though mounted on very fine horses, Yaro's men
proved a despicable, lawless set. Brandishing spears, they would
ride full tilt through the flimsy straw-built compounds relieving
the luckless inhabitants of goats, fowls and anything else they
could lay their hands on. Contrasting his party of men on their
unsaddled and unsuitable little Yoruba mares 'with the gallant
looking troop who were guarding us'[2], Clapperton consoled himself with the thought that at least he had not ransacked those
villages; unobserved by the escort, he gave one local headman
some cloth and knives by way of compensation.

Borgu was an attractive country and its people agreeable. On
the bank of a river, among some shady trees, the party stopped at
a fetish house, the grass and weeds around it all carefully cleared
away. The messenger and his men went one after another to pray
at the door, 'appearing to be as devout as Christian or Mahometan
at their prayers ~ I asked if I might go and look in ~ they objected
to this but on asking who they prayed to they said it was the god
that gave them plenty of water & Corn'.[3] Game was plentiful:

antelope of all sizes, elephant, buffalo and lion, and hippopotami
and crocodiles in the river pools ('the poor crocodiles eggs are
eaten here and the shells stuck on the top of the house by way of
Ornament').[4] It was famous hunting country; Clapperton was in
his element, 'the village we last left & this one is inhab[d] by hunters
only ~ as we arrived at this Village we met one of the inh[bts] armed
with bow & arrows & light short spear, attended by three dogs,
half grey hound half cur, of a red color with collars round their
necks ~ It is a beautifull sight and which we seldom see but often
read of ~ he was a bold manly looking fellow'.[5] Accompanied by a
servant carrying the antelope he had killed, the hunter strode
proudly down the road with never a glance in the direction of the
British expeditionary party.

Kaiama itself was a walled town of considerable size, with a
population of around thirty thousand. It was the hub of an east-
west trade which had grown in importance as a consequence of
the wars further south in Nupe and Oyo, and Clapperton was
very pleased to come across a Hausa caravan. He immediately
made contact with its *taya* (director), one Abdullah Kalu of Kano.

Numbering over one thousand merchants and their servants
and as many baggage animals, Kalu's caravan was returning from
Gonja, in the upper Volta region to the west, where they had been
held up for twelve months or so on account of the wars in Ashanti.
They had exported natron, red glass beads (imported via Tripoli),
'and a few slaves, principally refractory ones which they cannot
manage'[6]; their cargo on the return journey consisted mainly of
kola nuts, spices and sandalwood, borne by bullocks, mules and
asses and by a number of female slaves and hired carriers. Many
members of the caravan were petty traders transporting only what
could be carried on their own heads (always high-value articles).
Among the merchants were former acquaintances and Clapperton
was considerably diverted by the enquiries they made about Rais
Abdullah, 'they not knowing me in my English dress, and without
a beard. They talk to me about having seen me in Borno and
Sudan: I do not yet tell them I am that same person'.[7]

He entered upon protracted negotiations with the *taya* for transport of the mission's voluminous baggage to Hausaland. Kalu
urged him to leave Kaiama because the people of Borgu were all
thieves and rogues – a cynical Clapperton assumed that the *taya*
had been fleeced too often for his own liking. Kalu also cautioned
him against going to Yawri since they were still at war with the
Fulani and the roads from Yawri north to Sokoto and Kano were

consequently closed. He then offered to take the baggage to Kano by way of Kulfu on the northern frontiers of Nupe, apparently the only reliable route, for a price to be agreed later. Thanking him, Clapperton declared that, representing the King of England, he still hoped to have the mission's goods transported free of charge. And there the matter rested awhile.

That evening, King Yaro of Kaiama (Sultan Mura Amali) came to call at Clapperton's house. The King was a well-built man with a handsome Roman nose and a short grizzled beard; he wore a tall red Moorish cap, and sat well to horse, mounted on a fine dark bay bedecked with bells and charms. He was attended by a train of fifty horsemen and rather unusual personal spear-bearers, '6 naked young girls from 15 to 17 years of age ~ the only earthly thing they had on was a white bandau around the head of woven cloth ~ about 6 inches of the ends flying behind ~ and a string of beads round their waists ~ in their right hands they carried 3 light spears each – their light forms & the vivacity of their eyes and the ease with which they flew over the ground made them appear some thing more than human'.[8] The girls put a blue cloth about their waists before entering the house; and on departure they undressed again.

Yaro sent over provisions of milk, eggs, bananas, fried cheese, *fu fu* (pounded yam) and curds. And Clapperton presented his gifts: a large blue silk umbrella, one of Tatham's African swords, several fathoms of cloth, beads and coral, an imitation gold chain, knives and scissors, two phosphorous boxes and prints of famous men and events in British history; he had had to make a special effort with his presents to Yaro since there were more European goods available in Kaiama (brass and pewter dishes, earthenware, pieces of woollen and cotton cloth and even a Toby jug) than there were in Katunga or indeed anywhere else in the interior.

It became Yaro's custom to call round to drink tea in the afternoons, after which they went to watch 'some not bad horse racing'[9] in the square. On one occasion at the palace, Yaro's principal wife and a daughter came in to receive cloth and beads. When the King offered Clapperton another daughter for a wife, he duly called on her, bearing gifts of beads; she reciprocated his call, receiving yet more beads, but that appears to have concluded the affair. All in all it proved rather an expensive interlude. The womenfolk of the town's other notables also visited him, bringing small gifts and departing with red beads, scissors and needles, considerably depleting the mission's stocks. Clapperton decided to turn his medical consultations to good account, charging fees (some yams, or perhaps a fowl or a sheep, in order to replenish their supplies), 'without that I should never have a moment's peace for patients'.[10]

He clearly took a liking to 'stout Yaro'; to the traveller, stout signified reliability and openness, qualities he particularly valued; and the approval was no doubt reciprocated, for Clapperton was in the best of spirits. As Lander later observed, his master's hearty handshake and smiling manner, with plenty of flattery, made a very favourable impression on his African interlocutors. When he heard that the *taya* had offered, for a price, to carry the mission's goods to Hausaland and was ready to depart forthwith, King Yaro was bluntly dismissive, 'You must not believe these stories. He would take you for a day or two on the road and then leave you; where is he to get the means to carry your things? And besides he has not paid his customs yet, and until that is paid he cannot go'.[11] Yaro also affirmed that no representative of a foreign king need pay dues at toll points on the road; if he were being forwarded from one king to another gifts were naturally expected, but no financial payment. (It was a familiar system but practices varied from one part of the interior to another, and the value of gifts depended as much on the status of the chief or headman as on the size of the party and the duration of stay.)

To Clapperton's considerable satisfaction, the King offered to forward him under a personal escort to Wawa, and from there to Bussa, the capital of eastern Borgu on the River Niger, where he must pay his respects to the Sultan or he would be held to be travelling through the Kingdom of Borgu like a thief and not as an ambassador of the King of England; the escort could be ready in a day or two. Concerned about the mission's slow rate of progress and prepared to take a chance 'like a gamester throwing his last stake'[12], Clapperton decided to take up Yaro's offer of help for the first leg of the next stage. Once over the Niger, and on established trade routes, he would arrange transportation of the baggage with a large and reliable merchant caravan, and pay the fee in Kano by raising cash on a bill drawn on the Consulate-general in Tripoli.

Yaro was as good as his word. One week later, accompanied by the promised escort, Clapperton left Kaiama to travel some forty miles to the northwest and over the River Oli to Wawa in north-eastern Borgu. On arrival there, having been kept waiting an unconscionable time outside the palace gates (King Mohamed was dressing), he was received in friendly fashion, although the King declined to shake his hand 'for fear my touch would infect him'.[13]

Mohamed said they should talk the following day, and appointed the weary traveller to a very good house in a compound owned by the widow of one of his late viziers; and in the evening, he sent round a goat, ass's milk, honey and eggs.

Wawa was an active trading town, and Clapperton received an early visit from a group of travellers who were announced to him as an embassy from the King of Dahomey. Struck by the alarming possibility that the cities of Borgu might be under Dahomey's control and that a deputation had come to take him back to King Gezo, Clapperton experienced a rare moment of panic, 'I thought that all my hopes were blasted and that they had been sent to stop my further progress – I kept an unruffled face & in a moment formed my resolutions ~ but the cloud was soon dispelled'.[14] They turned out to be Dahomeyan slave-merchants on the way back to their own country. Having arrived in Yawri a year earlier to trade, they had found themselves caught up in the Emir's war against the rebels; they had offered their mercenary services and modern guns in exchange for being able to take some slaves, and they were currently awaiting King Mohamed's permission to return home.

They warned Clapperton that the war in Yawri was bitter and uncertain of issue; he should certainly avoid going anywhere near it. They also confirmed that Nikki, the capital of Borgu, was five days' journey east from Kaiama and Abomey only another ten days' travel beyond Nikki. The apparent ease of travel between Dahomey and Borgu underlined Clapperton's growing fears that Dickson had not after all got through, and he redoubled his efforts to arrange the next stage of his journey. The weather turned sultry, heralding the onset of the rains (the noon temperature varying from 102°F to 105°F); and the River Niger was so close, three days away, with merchants regularly coming and going via the Komi ferry to Kulfu, a major trading centre three days' journey further east. As soon as Kalu's caravan appeared in Wawa, therefore, Clapperton sounded him out once more about transportation of the baggage from Kulfu to Kano.

The *taya* would not name a price without an agreement which should stipulate a sum, payable immediately, for the purchase of bullocks and supplies for the journey. Declaring that he would pay nothing in advance, but would settle the account on arrival in Kano, Clapperton turned to King Mohamed for help in getting to Kulfu, and asked to leave as soon as possible, 'if I travled as Slow as I had done of late I would be caught by the rains in Haussa and

I might as well have a sword in my breast'.[15] Mohamed agreed to arrange an escort as far as Kulfu but, as Yaro had done, insisted that Clapperton should first pay a courtesy call on the Sultan of Bussa, his superior and the second most important person in Borgu after the King of Nikki. Clapperton was content to go to Bussa; it was only two days' travel away and he did not wish to miss an opportunity to unearth further details about the fate of Mungo Park and his companions. Messengers were accordingly dispatched and the mission settled down once again to wait.

Clapperton hoped for a change of luck; and while awaiting news occupied himself in writing up an account of Wawa. He was taken to see a *kwankwani* tree, the source of their arrow-poison, and was shown how the deadly substance was prepared[16]; and he searched for musical instruments for his collection of curios. The town's affairs, he noted, revolved around the constant presence of trading caravans; and religion was lightly observed – some were loosely Moslem, the majority not, 'and what they worship it is hard to tell; everyman choosing his own God, which they pray to that he may intercede with the Supreme Being for them'.[17]

But there were some decidedly less attractive sides to Wawa, which functioned as an entrepôt for the slave trade. Clapperton noted that the captives, many of them taken during the civil war in Nupe, were seldom seen in the town, remaining closely confined and guarded; on the march they were fastened neck to neck with thongs or chains, and often bore heavy loads, and the refractory slaves were clapped in irons at night. They went in constant fear of being sold to the coast, since it was universally held that 'all those who are sold to the whites are eaten; retorting back on us the accusation of cannibalism of which they have perhaps the greatest right to blame us'.[18] The inhabitants were much given to drink; Clapperton had already had some trouble with Ali, his Shuwa servant, who despite his master's vigilance was frequently discovered to be the worse for wear for rum, palm wine or country beer. All in all, Ali had proved most unsatisfactory, thoroughly lazy, 'a confirmed liar and thief, and I have often regretted that I gave him his freedom, as I cannot well get rid of him here'.[19]

For the British travellers kicking their heels in Wawa, however, life was unexpectedly cheered by a light-hearted passage with the wealthy widow Zuma, daughter of an Arab and niece by marriage to Yaro, King of Kaiama, 'a widow very fair & wants a white husband and is the richest person in the place having a good house ~ the best in the town ~ and a 1000 slaves ~ she showed a great regard for my servant Richard who is younger and better looking than I am – but she was past her 20th ~ fat and a perfect turkish beauty just as large as a walking water but[t] and all her arts were unavailing ~ Richard could not be induced by her to visit her though he had my permission'.[20]

Lander described the encounter as a game they embarked upon 'to enliven ourselves', Clapperton standing to one side observing the proceedings, delighted but impenetrably grave, 'his arms folded on his breast, while thick volumes of tobacco-smoke rolled from his pipe'.[21] Concluding that Richard Lander was not a likely prospect, Zuma then made a play for the master. She gave Pasco a handsome female slave to encourage him to bring matters about, but Clapperton himself had no qualms about visiting the widow, and wanted to see the interior of her house; he found her sitting cross-legged on a small Turkish rug,

> under her left knee her goro pot which was an English pewter mug [and] a calabash of water to wash her mouth out as she kept alternatly chewing snuff or Goro nuts which [is] the custom with all ranks male & female who can procure them… the lady her self was dressed in a white coarse muslin turban ~ her neck profusely decorated with neck laces of coral & gold chains amongst which was a necklace of rubies and gold beads alternatly ~ she had one of the finest country cloths wrapped round her which come up as high as her tremendous breasts… she told me her husband had been dead these last 10 years ~ that she had only one son who was darker than her self ~ She loved white men and she would go to Boussa with me ~ that she would send for a Malem (or man of learning) and read the Fatha with me ~ this I thought was carrying the joke too far and I began to look very serious ~ on which she sent for the looking glass and first looking at herself and then offering it to me said to be sure she was rather older than me but very little & what of that ~ this was too much & I made my retreat as soon as I could determined never to come to such close quarters with her again[22]

Though Clapperton made good his escape from the merry widow's toils, he had by no means heard the last of her.

Pasco did rather well out of the whole affair, getting himself a new wife, at least for a short while. Five foot tall, with a broad, rubbery face and Hausa scarifications, Pasco had dark, restless eyes and a sly grin; he was quite a man for the ladies, 'enforcing his pretensions with commanding eloquence'.[23] In Badagry one of King Adele's wives had fallen for him, or so he claimed. And in Ijanna he had found a girl whom he married according to local custom and took to Katunga; on the eve of their departure from the capital, however, she decamped with the coral beads and other trinkets which he had been given by Belzoni's widow. If Pasco was in need of consolation, he evidently found it in Wawa.

When the King's messengers returned, Clapperton set out for Bussa, accompanied by his servant Ali and escorted by one of Mohamed's sons. Lander and Pasco remained in Wawa to oversee transfer of the expedition's baggage to the ferry at Komi. Aware that he would be the next European after Park to reach the River Niger, Clapperton was filled with patriotic fervour, and on the journey named a prominent granite inselberg near the road Mount George after His Majesty the King. On arrival at a low-lying promontory opposite the walled town of Bussa, however, he could not yet see the River Niger, only a small western tributary. He eagerly crossed over to the town, where he was received by the Sultan, a fine-looking young man apparently in his mid-twenties, and the Midaki, the official queen mother (in fact, the senior wife of his predecessor), about whom the widow Zuma had forewarned him, 'She they [say] is every thing in Boussa ~ or as they say in Scotland the Gray Mare is the better horse... the Midaki has been his nurse I think as she is old enough to be so'.[24]

Clapperton was very taken with the amiable couple who ruled over a small but ancient kingdom, successfully remaining aloof from local wars and neighbouring disturbances, and who, with no ulterior motive, appeared genuinely willing to help him. Word of his arrival had preceded him, even reaching Yawri, and the young Sultan informed him that the Emir of Yawri was expecting him; indeed, the Emir's representative, with seven boats, had been in Bussa for a week waiting to collect the traveller. Clapperton explained that because of the war he did not actually wish to make a detour to Yawri (even so he would have to send presents, they said) and strongly urged his case for proceeding to Kulfu as soon as possible because of the rains; the Sultan promised to help in any way he could. However, on the subject of Mungo Park, he and the Midaki appeared embarrassed and rather less forthcoming; some books and papers had apparently been saved from the wreck, but they had been taken away by a Fulani imam who had since left the town.

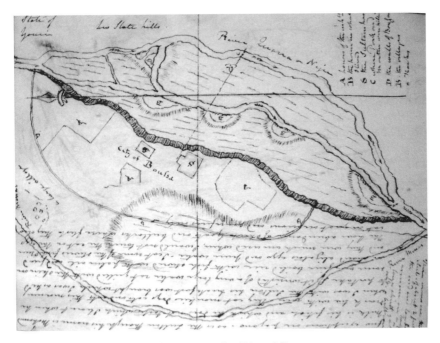

Sketch plan of the town of Bussa on the River Niger

The following day Clapperton walked out to view the famous river and to visit the spot where Mungo Park had died, 'The place pointed out to me where the boat and crew were lost is in the East^m channel ~ the river being divided into three branches at this place not one of which is above a good pistol shot across ~ a low flat Isl^d of about ¼ of a mile in breadth lies between the town of Boussa ~ and the spot is in a line with a double trunked tree with white bark standing singly on the low flat Isl^d and with the North end of the Sultans houses'.[25] He sketched a map of the town, the river and the islands. From the main island he could clearly make out the tops of the hills near Yawri, his former goal and only ten days' march from Sokoto; but he intended to stick to his latest plan.

On 2 April he turned south for the ferry at Komi, riding a fine young horse presented to him by the Midaki and escorted by the Sultan's brother and his men. Passing through the Kambari settlements, on a track seldom far from the Niger, he was brought to a halt by a thunderous roar of water. Scrambling up a high bank he gazed down upon the River Niger, whose turbulent stream swirled round islets and rocks and crashed against a fifty-foot cliff below,

'It occurred to me that even if Park and Martin had passed Bussa in safety they would have been in imminent danger of perishing here, most likely unheard of and unseen'.[26] Contemplating and sketching the scene (the figure in a wide-brimmed hat), he sat still for too long and when he got up he passed out momentarily from sunstroke – the only time he recorded such an incident.

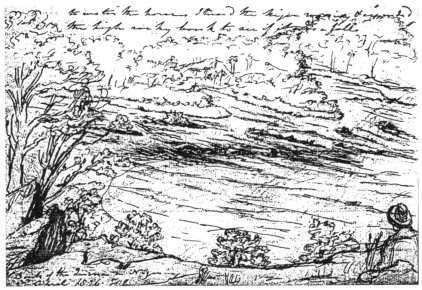

Banks of the Quarra or Niger 2nd April 1826

At Komi, merchant caravans spread out in huge encampments on both shores; the well-organized markets were crowded with travellers, men and horses in their gayest trappings, and the long evenings saw dancing, drumming, drinking and riotous merry-making. And awaiting Clapperton at the ferry crossing was his old friend the widow Zuma; she sent him food and a pressing invitation to her camp, which latter he declined. Lander, Pasco and the baggage not having put in an appearance, he sent King Mohamed's son back to Wawa to investigate. The young man duly returned with word from the King who had ordered that nothing should leave until Zuma returned to the town; if he wanted his belongings, Clapperton must fetch her back – Richard Lander had apparently already set out for Bussa to let him know.

Clapperton had had no inkling that the widow Zuma had been dabbling in local politics. She had apparently instigated a plot to overthrow the government of Wawa and so install herself as its governor, a lucrative prospect given the town's enormous revenues deriving from its key position on the trade route. Already in touch with dissidents at court, she liked the idea of having Clapperton at her side, if not as her consort at least as a powerful collaborator and she had come to Komi to intercept him.

Insisting to the King's son that he had nothing whatever to do with Zuma's machinations – he had no intention even of calling on her – Clapperton travelled swiftly back to Wawa where he 'was glad to find all my things safe; and was more amused than vexed to think that I had been so oddly let into the politics of Wawa... I certainly would not have thought that the widow Zuma would have been at the head of the malcontents in Wawa... It would have been a fine end to my journey indeed, if I had deposed old Mohamed, and set up for myself, with a walking tun-butt for a queen'.[27] When he called on the King to assure him that he knew nothing of the widow's schemes, it became clear that the traveller himself had never been under suspicion, 'the old governor meant me no harm, but just to let me see his consequence before I left Wawa'.[28] King Mohamed had also been vexed because Pasco had accepted one of Zuma's slaves for a wife; Clapperton stood his ground, protesting that he had neither interest nor influence in Pasco's relationships.

All was eventually resolved. Pasco gave up his wife, mournfully protesting that she had fallen in love with him at first sight. And the next morning Zuma returned to Wawa, divested of her customary finery, to make her obeisance to the King. She was clearly far from contrite, however. When she stepped outside the palace after receiving Mohamed's rebuke, she shook the dust from her clothes with the greatest possible contempt, 'That,' said the King, 'is a bad woman'.[29] Clapperton was just a little intrigued, 'Had she been somewhat younger and less corpulent, there might have been great temptation to head her party, for she has certainly been a very handsome woman, and such as would have been thought a beauty in any country in Europe'.[30]

Having rescued his baggage, Clapperton returned to Komi only to face further domestic problems. The escort officer whom the Sultan of Bussa's brother had appointed to see him safely over the river to Kulfu was a reliable sort; but the four Hausa slaves sent by the King to assist him had proved dishonest and insubordinate, stealing from others along the road and at the ferry, and causing a great disturbance in the house. He had supplied them with one of his goats, 'but they not content with this went & seized one of the best I had ~ I could not stand this & instead of taking the gun I took the Whip & put them out of my house'.[31] Clapperton was again unwell and having trouble sleeping; he put up with King Mohamed's slaves for a while longer, but when they offered to take his horse across the river ahead of him, he detected a ruse to relieve him of the animal and dismissed them. (They outwitted the traveller, however, and the following day made good their escape with a horse and a saddle.) He was also a little put out when an ambassador arrived from the Sultan of Yawri begging presents for his master, supplies which Clapperton could ill afford to spare; he handed over a modest token and the Sultan's messengers went away, apparently well pleased. It was high time to move on.

Chapter 18: Return to Hausaland 1826
all my cares were over

*Nupe and the rebel Majiya – more manœuvrings of caravaneers
the widow Ladi and the topers of Kulfu – journey to Gwari
return to Hausaland – Borno and Sokoto at war*

Monday 10th Cloudy – prepared every thing for crossing the
river – at 9 AM the things began to move from the house to
the water side – Islands above & below the ferry ~ can hear
people conversing on the other side ~ at 10 the things crossed
– current 2 Knots ~ fired rifle by request ~ very sick ~ the slaves
of Wawa take away one horse & saddle ~ at Noon crossed
the Niger ~ 12-15 PM St[d] Course N.E by E – gravel & clay ~
at 2 halted [by] a beautifull stream[1]

On 10th April 1826 Hugh Clapperton finally went afloat on the
River Niger. In a succession of crossings in twenty-foot canoes the
mission and its baggage were ferried over to the encampment on
the opposing woody banks; the horses and cattle were made to
swim. The Niger at that spot, he observed, was 'not above ¾ as
broad as the Thames at Waterloo bridge at high water ~ nearly of
the same color being a dirty red ~ and from 2½ to 3 fms in depth as
I sounded all the way as I crossed ~ the current about 2 or 3 knots
~ I have seen it now for upwards of thirty miles of its course and
no where for above half a mile is it clear of Islds or rocks'.[2] And he
marked the occasion by firing a ball into a tree on the opposite
bank, which impressed not a few around him.

He had good reason to celebrate the river crossing after all the
alarms and disappointments of the previous four months. Even
though he was a long way from being able to follow the Niger's
final path to the sea, he had a very clear picture of its course – his
landlord at Komi, a former senior official in Nupe, was another
who had confirmed that the river entered the sea at Funda, and he
reported that the Funda people came to southern Nupe by canoe
to trade, while the people of Benin arrived by ferry after travelling
overland. Despite the uncertainties ahead there was at least some
consolation in having achieved his first goal ahead of Gordon
Laing, of whose whereabouts there had been no word anywhere
on the river. There remained, however, much to do to meet his

other objectives, and in all probability he would be acting on his own since there was still no news of Thomas Dickson[†].

'Having crossed this wonderful river'[3] Clapperton turned east into Nupe on the caravan road to Kulfu. With the assistance of the Bussa messenger he hired new carriers and headed out of the broad Niger valley into an undulating countryside on a track winding among towering ant-hills and past a number of small settlements occupied by blacksmiths and iron ore smelters. The following day they descended to the River Maingyara which they crossed by a small bridge, 'the first I have seen in Africa'[4], constructed of palm trunks covered with packed earth and fronds.

At the first village in the valley they were confronted by a large group of its Kambari inhabitants, bows and arrows at the ready. The carriers dropped their loads and fled. Since the Bussa escort officer was travelling some distance behind the main party and Pasco and the other servants had no language in common with the armed men, it appeared to be a stand-off. Clapperton climbed slowly off his horse and sat on his own belongings, ordering the servants to follow suit. To everyone's surprise, the villagers then shouldered their bows, rushed forward, seized the baggage and set off up the valley at a tremendous pace. Clapperton and his men followed them to the next village, from which the voluntary

---

[†] Armed with £500 worth of gifts for King Gezo and trade goods for the journey, and accompanied by Frederick James, Francisco de Souza and 45 men from the British forts at Whydah, Thomas Dickson had reached Abomey, the capital of Dahomey, in mid-December 1825. From there he was forwarded to Itsa on the northern border of the territory controlled by Gezo (150 miles from the coast). The doctor's last letters, written on 28 January 1826 and received in Whydah the following month, reported his safe arrival at Itsa and the promise of its ruler to forward him with an escort to Borgu, en route for Yawri. Dickson intended sending back the men from the forts with the exception of three, but would still retain Bambo, a boy assigned to him by Gezo as personal servant and interpreter.
At the end of March de Souza informed Commodore Bullen at Cape Coast that Dickson was said to be advancing, but 'such is the irritability of his temper, that he very often offends the Natives most seriously' – there had already been one regrettable incident, for which the traveller had had to make amends with expensive presents. Conflicting rumours continued to reach the coast, and in July 1826 Fraser had acquainted London of reports in circulation that Dickson had been murdered in the interior. No further information was received until 1845, when King Gezo himself told Lieutenant Forbes, member of an official British mission to Abomey, that Dickson had reached Nikki, the capital of Borgu, but that he had not been heard of thereafter. The irascible doctor may have met his end as the result of an attack, or possibly a quarrel; or, like many of his peers, he may simply have succumbed to tropical disease or fever.

bearers set off again. In due course they all arrived at a small town where everything was unceremoniously dumped in front of the chief's house. Though the headman spoke Hausa (so Pasco was able to interpret), Clapperton did not know where they were or with whom he had to deal; he therefore responded extremely cautiously to questions concerning his destination and the reasons behind his journey. The chiefly personage particularly wanted to know whether the traveller intended to visit his king. Fortunately, Abdullah Kalu's caravan was encamped nearby, having arrived some days earlier, and the *taya* was able to throw light on the situation. They had arrived at Tabria, the capital of Mohamed Jiya (known as Majiya), Moslem contender for the Nupe throne and leader of the Sokoto-backed rebellion in Nupe and northern Oyo. Majiya himself was away at his war camp two days' journey south.

On the evening of his arrival Clapperton also learnt that there was a small Fulani force in Kulfu, one hour's ride away, readying itself to return to Sokoto after campaigning with Majiya's army. He composed a note to Sultan Bello and early the next morning sent Ali to deliver it to the Fulani commander. But Ali arrived too late; the troop had left at first light. Clapperton was aghast. He had missed by a matter of hours the prospect on which he had pinned his hopes – the opportunity to travel with an armed Fulani escort straight to Sokoto. He at once arranged for his letter to be forwarded to Bello by a courier who was directed to catch up with the Fulani force with all possible speed.

On making a courtesy visit to the queen, a dignified elderly woman who turned out to be King Majiya's mother rather than his wife, Clapperton was put out to discover that he was expected to call on the King at his war camp. The queen-mother promised that her son would forward him wherever he wanted to go; but he was loath to leave Tabria, suspecting that attendance on Majiya would entail further delay and lose him the chance to travel with Kalu's caravan. The queen brooked no argument, however; she offered to arrange an escort to Majiya and undertook to detain the *taya* in Tabria against the traveller's return.

The senior resident Arab merchant, Mohamed ben Ahmed of Murzuq, provided Clapperton with sensible advice and a good deal of information about Nupe's history and Sokoto's interest in the civil war. Majiya was Sokoto's man, and one of his viziers was travelling to Bello's capital with the Fulani troop which had just left. Pending the arrival of a viceroy (already appointed), Sultan Bello had also attached a personal representative to Majiya's court, one Omar Zurmi. Clapperton had to reach Sokoto as soon as possible and it seemed that the well-connected Nupe contender might be the very person to assist him. Easier in his mind about the obligatory visit, therefore, he set off for Majiya's camp, taking ben Ahmed as his interpreter and with Omar Zurmi in company, leaving Lander and Pasco in Tabria with the baggage.

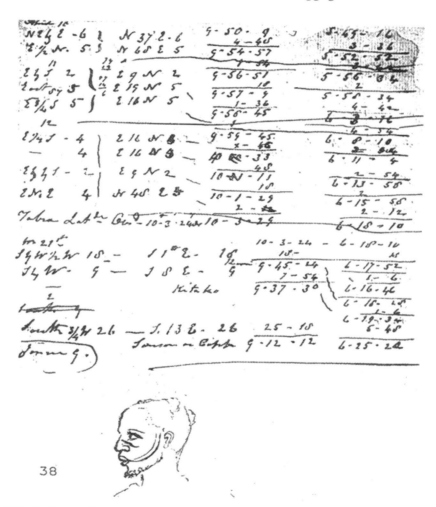

Calculations of latitudes at Tabria and Sansan

The two-day journey to the King's *sansan* (war camp) took them through a country quite empty of settlements, a dusty landscape of grey thorn trees and pale high grasses intersected by occasional small river valleys in narrow, steep-sided ravines. Clapperton once more fell ill and had to halt several times. On the third morning they passed through more open land, ruined villages on all sides, to the *sansan* where Majiya was discovered, 'attended by a great rabble, armed with pickaxes, hoes and hatchets'.[5] The so-called war appeared to be little more than a series of haphazard raids on un-defended villages – taking slaves, seizing crops and burning huts.

A tall man with a vacuous expression, Majiya wore a ragged black velvet cap (partly trimmed with red silk) and tattered boots; he was accompanied by slaves carrying a coast umbrella and his sword. Unimpressed by the aspiring King of Nupe, Clapperton nevertheless paid him 'every decent respect & courtesy as I was master of & put as many smiles in my face as possible as I know that ragged & dirty usurpers expect more attention than a real King or great man'.[6]

Led by one of the King's eunuchs to a small makeshift straw hut, he closed it up tight, hoping to sweat out his fever, 'a good steem bath and fasting is a good cure for most disorders'.[7] But he had little rest over the next twenty-four hours, Majiya continually pestering him for conversation and gifts; though he had already been given presents, including an umbrella, the King begged for more. He asked for the traveller's sword, or his pistol, or his camp knife and fork; and he wanted a silver-topped cane, he was sure Clapperton would have one. Fending off the persistent requests as diplomatically as he could, Clapperton turned the conversation to his own onward travel. Majiya said he would arrange to send him to Kano in five or six days' time, and, as the traveller was leaving, made him a gift of a small Nupe horse (which Clapperton thought would do well enough for Lander or Pasco).

Once back in Tabria, Clapperton re-examined his options. He was doubtful that much would come of Majiya's offer to organize travel and transport for him. His best hope was a positive response to the letter he had dispatched to Sokoto; if there was no word from the Sultan, it would be necessary to make arrangements with a merchant caravan in Kulfu. One week later he moved there.

Partly as a result of civil war in both Yawri and Nupe, Kulfu had become an important centre for east-west commerce; it was the terminus to which Hausa merchants came to trade with their counterparts from Oyo, Borgu and Dahomey in the west. Goods were exchanged at the markets at Komi and Wawa, but only the largest long-distance caravans from Hausaland actually crossed over the Niger. In Kulfu a caravaneer's every need could be met and traders came there from as far away as Fezzan, Ghadamis and Tripoli as well as from the central Sudan.

Clapperton made enquiries of those merchants who operated on a promisingly large scale (lesser traders were unlikely to have sufficient working capital to finance the transport of the mission's goods to Kano). The costs involved in a thirty-day journey were sizeable: extra bullocks, bullock-drivers and other helpers had to be hired, ropes and hides had to be purchased to secure and cover the baggage, and a fair investment had to be made in kola nuts to exchange for provisions on the road. Mohamed, a Borno merchant trading on behalf of Sheikh Al-Kanemi, offered to take the baggage for two hundred thousand cowries, payable half in advance and half on arrival in Kano, assuring Clapperton he would be ready to leave as soon as he had sold his natron at the Niger markets. He also maintained that the previous February, when he himself had left Kukawa, John Tyrwhitt had been in good health; if true, that was cheering news. And Abdullah Kalu was still around, forever stalling and holding out for improved terms.

In Kulfu Clapperton was lodged in the compound of a wealthy widow. Very fat and deaf, with an only child (a spoilt five-year-old daughter), the widow Ladi was an extremely successful merchant, but what she was most famed for was her *bouza* (corn liquor) and her *ruwan bomi* (palm wine), '& every night the outer hut is filled with the Topers of Koulfu who are provided with music as well as drink & keep it up until the dawn of morning separates them'.[8] The *bouza* consumed in widow Ladi's hospitable tavern was a mixture of guinea corn, honey, chilli peppers and the root of a coarse grass crop used as cattle fodder; the ingredients were left to ferment in water in large open earthenware jars beside a slow fire for seven or eight days and sold for ten cowries a quart, 'It is very fiery & intoxicating & Mohamedan & infidell all drink and agree very well in their cups... I could get no sleep either me or my servants the first two nights for their noise and was thinking of giving them a few small shot or watering them with a syringe but I soon got used to it ~ & far better I did not for there would have been surely a riot in Koolfu & I would have got the Worst of it'.[9]

Caravan traffic was in abeyance for the month of Ramadan. The waiting grew increasingly tedious and uncomfortable, and at the end of the growing season supplies of fresh food were running out. Clapperton and his men once again found themselves being fleeced left and right, but there was little he could do about it –

except shoot pigeons for the pot. And word had evidently got about of the presents given on the mission's travels in Oyo, Borgu and Bussa, and each one wanted his or her share. The chief of Ingaski, the principal ferry south of Yawri, was most disappointed to have missed out; he sent a messenger with small gifts, hoping to receive better in return but Clapperton ignored the ploy.

To add to their troubles, it came on to rain and first Clapperton and then Lander fell ill, rendering them incapable of travel even had the opportunity presented itself. On the evening of the feast celebrating the end of Ramadan there was an apocalyptic storm. Fearing an outbreak of panic, Clapperton had the firearms loaded, secured the doors and took command of his compound, 'one old slave woman was with the greatest unconcern roasting cashew nuts over a spreading fire which on ordering it out she made as much noise or more as if the house had been in flames ~ at last the rain fell... & we escaped with the loss of the roof of one hut & the sheds blown down – all was now quiet & I went to rest with that satisfaction I believe every man feels on his neighbours suffring a great misfortune that might have happened to himself & thanks god that it has not come to his turn yet'.[10]

Incarcerated in Kulfu, Clapperton grew weary and depressed and for the next four weeks he made very few journal entries. He remained in daily expectation of a reply from Bello, but no word came from Sokoto. One day, however, a messenger arrived from the Sultan and Midaki of Bussa, bringing a beautiful little mare as a present. They also sent Clapperton a gift of money to have a goat killed and the flesh distributed when he left Kulfu; it would bring him luck. On another occasion the Midaki sent a female slave with a supply of rice and butter, and a warning that Clapperton should be wary of accepting any food from Majiya's relations because she had heard that they wanted to poison him. And a messenger from the Emir of Yawri told him that his master had in his possession a number of hand-written journals and printed books belonging to Mungo Park which he was prepared to sell for one hundred and seventy *mitqals* of gold[11]; Clapperton was sceptical but felt duty-bound to investigate. He sent ben Ahmed to Yawri; and he paid a *shereef* to go to Rabba to look for a former imam of Bussa who allegedly also held some of Park's papers.

In early June the rains slackened. Mohamed, the merchant of Borno, reappeared, his trading complete; but he raised his price by thirty dollars and Clapperton turned him down. And the ever hopeful Abdullah Kalu popped up again. Clapperton fended him off too; he would continue to wait and see. Another message came from the Sultan of Bussa, proposing to put them up for the rainy season or until he could organize an escort and carriers to forward them to Kano. But Clapperton was in a hurry, and if the Sultan's generous offer did not meet his needs it did at least cause Kalu to lower his own asking price; Clapperton feigned indifference.

Then two caravans arrived from Hausaland bringing disturbing news. It was said that Borno and Sokoto had joined hostilities. Al-Kanemi had declared war. He had attacked Bello's eastern emirate of Hadejia and was advancing on Kano; and the Emir of Kano was apparently preparing to give battle. Clapperton was unsure how to interpret the intelligence, 'Whither true or false time only will prove ~ I rather think it is an idle report to please the people of Nyffe [Nupe] who cannot bear the Fellatahs'.[12]

Increasingly uneasy, and in the continuing absence of word from Sokoto, the traveller turned his attention to the offer from a new arrival, Musa Dalik, a Tripolitan merchant who might prove more reliable and better placed to organize transport of the goods. But Dalik's terms were no lower than any others. Everyone in the town was running out of local currency. Abdullah Kalu's latest proposal involved taking Clapperton and his belongings as far as the borders of Hausaland for sixty-eight dollars. But that offer was withdrawn three days later when the caravaneer reported that he could not get anything like a fair rate of exchange for his dollars in Kulfu – only seventeen hundred cowries for a dollar, compared with the usual three thousand.

Desperate, the traveller went back to Musa Dalik, who asked for an even larger advance, to help fund the necessary preparatory purchases. Clapperton agreed the new terms and paid him one hundred Spanish dollars – there had been no one else to turn to. Dalik equipped himself and made ready to leave (and Mohamed of Borno also signed up to join the caravan).

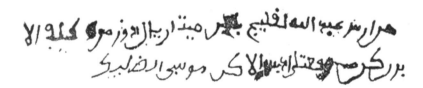

Receipt given by Musa Dalik: *From the Ra'is 'Abd Allah Laaqlij* [Englishman] *one hundred riyal duru from Kulfu to Birni Kanu by Musa Dalik*

Lander was still very pulled down, so Clapperton, determined to travel hard and fast, took on an additional servant before his departure. For twenty-five thousand, seven hundred cowries (the equivalent of some fourteen silver dollars or about four pounds sterling), he bought from a visiting Fulani merchant the freedom of one Mohamed Allah bar Sarki (Madi) of Borno origin. A former slave of Bu Khulum, Madi it was who had brought off Tripoli's flag when the Arab force was defeated on the battlefield in Mandara and who had rescued Denham's horse. When Clapperton first saw him, the man had been clad only in a leather waist-band; he was at once provided with the same clothes as the mission's other servants and paid a proper wage. It was a good decision; Madi proved to be an enterprising, tough and reliable addition to their party.

Though impatient to leave Kulfu, Clapperton clearly held the townspeople in some affection; they led an opportunistic life, catering for the multifarious wants of countless passing caravans, but he had always found them kind and generous. And he held his landlady in particular esteem – she had given away a number of her female slaves to freemen for wives, but continued to treat them and their new families as her own children, attending them when sick and arranging feasts for them on special occasions. The market people openly cheated him, 'but they had an idea that I was possessed of inexhaustible riches; and besides I differed with them in colour, in dress, in religion, and in my manner of living. I was considered therefore as a pigeon for them to pluck. Had they been rogues, indeed, they might have taken all I had; but, on the contrary, I never had an article stolen, and was treated with the most perfect respect and civility they were masters of'.[13]

'The long looked for day came at last'[14]; on 20 June Clapperton rode out of Kulfu to join the caravans gathering three miles to the east where he set up camp – with three horses, five bullocks, an ass and a camel – and discovered that the widow Ladi had also come along, 'I thought it had been out of a great regard for me; but I was soon let into the secret, by five of her slaves arriving with booza and bum, which she began selling in my court-yard to the different merchants, bullock-drivers and slaves assembled here'.[15] The next day they set out for Hausaland, Lander mounted on the Yoruba mare, Pasco on the Borno horse and Clapperton riding the horse presented by the Sultan and Midaki of Bussa.

Thankful to be independent of unreliable chiefs and warring kings, and with growing confidence in Musa Dalik, Clapperton now set out in a much more hopeful mood. They headed north-east across the dusty savannah into the remote, thinly populated and backward country lying between the provinces of Nupe to the south, Yawri and Zamfara to the north and Gwari to the east. Nominally at least, the towns were under the dominion of Yawri, but they had seen better days, their earthworks collapsed, ditches choked up and the walls in a state of ruinous decay. Petty wars and highway robbery were rife. When they encountered a larger Hausa caravan, Musa joined forces for a safer passage through the dangerously unsettled region ahead.

Clapperton was glad of any support, particularly since the rains had started again in earnest and Richard Lander was not yet fully recovered – he could ride only at a very gentle pace and even that so weakened the young fellow that Clapperton had to carry him on his back over streams. At camp, they subsisted on whatever meagre fare was available from the village; if meat was on offer it was given to Lander, Clapperton himself dining on the usual mess of potage, 'raw flour, water and an onion'[16], and at night he gave up his bed and slept on Lander's mat, 'I had to sit up all night in my wet cloths having got twice wet to the skin in saving the tent from being blown down on the top of my sick servant who has been unable to do any thing these last 6 weeks ~ however by the assistance of Pascoe I kept the tent up and the night was one of those severe nights of suffering that a man remembers the whole of his remaining life'.[17]

Clapperton felt for the plight of the simple folk he met along the road, 'a good looking, active set of people'[18], more frightened than frightening, tilling their fields or grinding corn beside the track and scrambling hurriedly to defensive positions on rocky outcrops on catching sight of the large caravan (every two or three women working in the fields had an armed man in attendance). As non-Moslems, they were ill-used by their rulers and by the freebooters who came to steal their wives and children and sell them as slaves. In one valley the inhabitants, who appeared parti-cularly belligerent, began to take aim with their bows. Believing that they were in for trouble, Clapperton loaded his gun; but it turned out that the people had mistaken the travellers for a party of armed Fulani come to attack their villages, and they soon fell in with the caravan, offering basic foodstuffs and bean cakes for sale.

At the end of June they reached Womba, formerly part of the Hausa state of Katsina, where Clapperton, satisfied with their progress, halted to allow Lander and Pasco to rest. He obviously

took to Womba's jovial headman, readily forgiving him for inter-
rupting an evening he had planned to devote to writing up his
journals. A heavily built man of middle age, the chief padded his
chest with clothes to make himself appear even larger, a fashion
followed by his people. His mannered, repetitious style of speech
was also practised by his courtiers so Clapperton followed suit, 'I
became a perfect great man'.[19] At the next halt, the twin towns of
Galama, the two communities were at odds over rights to control
the caravan road, take tolls, and sell their produce; one lived on
the mountain to the south, the other in the valley below and they
fought each other regularly on the ground in between.[20]

Once ferried over the swollen Mariga river (in canoes and on
makeshift reed rafts) the caravan began a series of long treks over
higher ground into the forests of western Gwari. The winding trail
through muddy ravines made for difficult going; and when they
stopped for the night at Gubir 'n Duche they found the village
deserted, its inhabitants all away in temporary huts in the distant
fields, busy with the harvest. There was thus neither food nor
anything else to be had for their comfort and at night the thunder
and lightning, wind and rain continued unabated.

The last day's march into the large and shady town of Birni
Gwari was exhausting, but Sultan Abu Bakr made them very
welcome. He provided Clapperton with excellent quarters, and
sent over a sheep, stewed capon and a fine pudding of flour, suet
and eggs, together with millet for the horses. And in exchange,
Clapperton presented him with a silk umbrella, a gold chain, a
phosphorous box, knives and scissors, and various prints – one
picture, of the Duke of York on horseback (the horse with a fine
bridle and bit, the saddle with a tiger skin), was passed around
from hand to hand and much admired.

In better health and correspondingly good spirits, Clapperton
relaxed and set himself to explore the town (remarking on the
many partridge and guinea fowl inside its extensive walls). The
Sultan was facing difficult times. Gwari had followed Zamfara in
the rebellion against Sokoto in 1818, taking the opportunity to
declare itself independent of Katsina. There was fighting along
most of its frontiers and Abu Bakr's men were all out on campaign;
meanwhile at home harvests had failed. Rumours of war between
Borno and Sokoto persisted but, notwithstanding Clapperton's
declared intention of proceeding to Sokoto, Abu Bakr generously
offered to produce an armed escort to protect him against Fulani
marauders on the journey into Zaria province.

At Gwari, Musa Dalik had to quit the caravan to return to Kulfu where he had left his sick wife and all his personal belongings; and for one hundred dollars Clapperton bought from him his bullocks and servants, thereby acquiring a novel and satisfactory degree of independence. A reflection of the explorer's renewed confidence on nearing familiar territory, the deal was also a snub to Abdullah Kalu, whose caravan had just appeared in the town.

Clapperton took stock. He had arrived in Hausaland one year later than he had originally hoped. Since crossing over the River Niger he had had a run of bad luck but, nothing daunted, he reviewed his instructions from London to see what might yet be salvaged. Contemplating his prospective meeting with Sultan Bello and reflecting upon the agreement they had reached in 1824, Clapperton was aware that the scales were weighted heavily on the minus side. He had neither consul nor doctor to offer; he had been unable to identify the water passage from the sea to Bello's ports; and he had left on board ship the main military materiel he had promised to bring. But he could deliver King George's letter and handsome gifts, and promise an early return mission. With respect to the slave trade, however, Clapperton was primed and eager to argue his case. Throughout the journey he had recorded his observations on divers practices of domestic and commercial slavery and the volume and character of the trade on the margins of the Caliphate. Determined to ensure that British officers coming after him received appropriate treatment and full diplomatic privileges, he had prepared a short speaking note for his presentation to Sultan Bello. The approach was soundly based,

1st In the event of the King of Great Britain sending a consul to regulate the trade to reside in any of the Sultan of Haussa's – towns under in his dominions that he shall be allowed the same priviliges that are allowed to the Consuls of Great Britain in other Mohamedan countries – that is he shall be allowed to hoist a flag of great Britain on his residence – & that his house shall be a refuge to criminals &c- & he shall regulate all affairs between the Subjects of Great Britain and those of the Sultan Bello
2nd That the Sultan Bello will use all his influence in putting a stop to the selling of slaves to the agents of Slave dealers who frequent Koolfu and the other towns on the Eastn bank of the Niger and in his towns of Rabba, Rakah and Affaga or Elora in Youriba – and that he will cause this article to be published

by the Gov[rs] of Kano, Zeg zeg and Raba and to order them to put it [in] force ~ that no merchants will be allowed to carry slaves to the Westd- for sale but only such as are necessary for carrying their goods. That he will also write to the Magaia Mohamed the present Sultan of Nyffe to induce him to do the same & to the King of Boussa and all the other powers whom he is on terms of Friendship to follow his example[21]

Clapperton left Gwari in company with Abu Bakr's twenty-man armed escort, and arrived at the border of Hausaland one week later. At the great gathering place of caravans outside Fatika he found several merchants whose acquaintance he had made on his first visit to the Sudan; they sent over puddings and meat for him and his servants, and corn for the animals. Surrounded by friendly people and familiar languages, in a country where travel was uncomplicated and the social order agreeable, Clapperton felt comfortable, even light-hearted, 'All my cares were over; not even thinking of my sick servant, or the chance of my having perhaps tomorrow as much anxiety as ever I had before'.[22]

When he arrived in Zaria the Emir was away from the capital, but the Waziri, Sai Abdulkerim, 'a very good fellow … as decent a Fellatah as I ever met with'[23], provided every assistance. The news from Kano, however, was bad. Borno and Sokoto were indeed at war; and the townspeople in Zaria were particularly concerned because they traditionally enjoyed good personal and commercial connections with Borno. Refugees from the region of conflict were flooding into the city, and the eastern emirates were planning to go on the attack. Clapperton was uncertain how best to proceed. He was committed to travelling to Sokoto first, but carrying out the Colonial Department's instructions to deliver the presents in Borno and develop relations with Sheikh Al-Kanemi, now Sultan Bello's enemy, was likely to be fraught with difficulty. He was also puzzled by the rumour, carried by Kano merchants on their way through Zaria to Kulfu, of the arrival of another British officer in Kukawa. Was the alleged newcomer an additional officer or (if in fact John Tyrwhitt had not survived) a replacement?[24]

On 16 July Clapperton set out for Kano, accompanied for a short distance by Abdulkerim who obviously had something on his mind. After much embarrassed hemming and hawing, the Waziri admitted to a personal problem. He had three wives, one the daughter of the Emir, but he was impotent; he received some sympathy and a supply of Seidlitz powders. But as they continued along the road, they had an unfortunate falling out. Abdulkerim confessed himself surprised to learn that two years previously a British force had been defeated in Mandara and thirty Englishmen killed. Clapperton was exasperated by this misrepresentation of Denham's participation in the abortive raid. He explained that the defeated force was in fact an Arab army; had it been English the Fulani troops would not have stood a chance. His interlocutor was not quite persuaded, however. In his determination to quash a rumour tarring the British with an anti-Sokoto brush Clapperton waxed increasingly heated and ended up by declaring that Abdulkerim lied like a thief. The Waziri hurriedly backed down, maintaining that he known all along that the tale was an invention of the Arabs to save face; not surprisingly, 'we parted not quite such good friends as we had been'.[25]

On the road to Kano, while Richard Lander slumped wearily in the saddle of a hired horse (the Yoruba mare had fallen sick in Zaria), Clapperton strode ahead and shot good bags of game. But the rains continued in full force and the going was very slow. He therefore decided to rest for a day at the old Hausa town of Bebeji, where he watched the weaver birds at their nests in the spreading trees, made a drawing of the headman's elegant palace[26] and, with the enthusiastic help of village lads, shot pigeons for supper.

Bebeji mosque and tower

Since Richard Lander continued unwell, Clapperton decided to leave him in Bebeji to rest a while longer and follow on later with Pasco and all the baggage. Leaving his own horse for Lander to ride, he borrowed one from the headman and with two of the latter's officers in company he set off, riding hard. Having forded the River Challawa on horseback, and rested under a tree to dry out, Hugh Clapperton entered Kano by the city's south gate at five o'clock in the evening of 20th July 1826 and went directly to the house of Hadje Hat Salah, his agent in the city during the previous mission.

Chapter 19: Sokoto 1826–1827
I do not know how this matter will end

Sokoto and Borno at war – an abortive journey in the rain
a military raid on Gobir – the travellers under suspicion
possessions seized – hunting in Makariya – death in Sokoto

That Clapperton's mission had not travelled to the city by way of Borno clearly discomfited Hat Salah, 'He gave me a very warm reception but I saw he and those that were present would rather I had come by the East – but they are all in low spirits about the war with Bornou which has shut them up for this some time past from all communication with Tripoli and Fezzan'.[1] The rupture in trans-Saharan contact was the worst possible news, since Clapperton had counted on dispatching couriers to Warrington immediately on arrival; not only was the Borno road to Fezzan inaccessible, but the more westerly route to the Mediterranean coast through Aïr had fallen into the hands of Tuareg tribesmen.

Kano's defences were being strengthened against attack; its citizens were nervous and prices in the markets had more than doubled. The city itself was crowded with refugees, some from the eastern frontier states, others fleeing the civil war in Nupe, and the Emir's officials looked upon all resident non-Fulani peoples, slaves and free-men alike, with suspicion. The Arab merchants in Kano were particularly apprehensive since it was believed (with some justification) that they favoured Al-Kanemi; demonstrations against the Arabs had already been held on the streets and a wider revolt against the community could not be ruled out. When Hat Salah interrogated him about his journey and repeated his concern that the British would take vital business away from the Arabs, Clapperton lost his temper, declaring that there was little trade worth coming for and anyway no Englishman would trade with merchants in the Sudan 'when he found them to be such lying cheating rogues as they are'.[2] And on his friend enquiring whether the mission had brought the guns for Al-Kanemi and if not could he, Hat Salah, send for them, Clapperton told him that the guns had been left on the ship, and warded off further questioning.

Lack of communication with Tripoli reinforced the traveller's determination to continue to Sokoto without delay, taking with him only the minimum of baggage and the presents for Mohamed

Bello; and once Lander and Pasco had arrived in Kano he made ready to depart. Hat Salah agreed to look after Lander and store the remainder of the mission's goods; he would also provide cash for the journey. And he strongly counselled against making any reference to plans for visiting Borno when Clapperton paid his call on Emir Ibrahim Dabo. Another bilious attack led to the audience being postponed, however; and when he was sufficiently recovered to wait on Dabo, Clapperton was given rather a cool reception though the Emir agreed to forward him to Sokoto whenever he wished to go; he asked to leave as soon as the rains had slackened and then retreated to his house.

The ailing explorer kept his bed for the next two weeks. The only entries in his day-book covering the period were regular but increasingly faint jottings of barometer readings, a litany from which he derived some comfort; and even those records ceased when he became too weak to hold a pen (although Lander made a couple of notes for him in an ill-formed scribble). By 20 August, however, Clapperton felt recovered enough to attempt the journey. To his consternation, he learnt that a caravan had left for Sokoto only two days before he himself reached Kano; there could be no question of waiting for another one, however. He called again on Dabo, whose troops had just returned from a military campaign in the north and were apparently very much knocked about; and the Emir suggested that Clapperton wait until both the weather and the condition of the roads improved or at least until the arrival of Gidado dan Laima, who was expected at any moment. Dabo's counsel fell on deaf ears.

Clapperton's mind was made up. Though still in poor health, he was concerned that if he did not carry out the remaining viable tasks entrusted to the mission they might not be completed by anyone for a long time to come. He had to reach Sokoto as soon as possible. From Sokoto, he could proceed to Borno after the rains, thence continuing on a journey of exploration. Communications between the caliphates were unlikely to remain closed indefinitely, and he had no real doubt but that permissions for his diplomatic passage would be forthcoming ere long. He set about organizing transport and supplies for the journey, encashing with a merchant from Misurata a bill drawn on the Consulate-general in Tripoli for five hundred dollars[3], much of which he had to spend on a horse to replace the little Bussa mare which had died a few days before. Entrusting Lander, Pasco and Ali to Hat Salah's care, he left for Sokoto on 24 August, accompanied by Madi.

The journey began well enough, through cultivated lands with fields of indigo and picturesque herds of long-horned cattle; in the evenings he was usually allocated comfortable accommodation by the local headman, and dined contentedly on the ubiquitous boiled corn pudding. When they reached the marshy low-lying lands on the border of Kano and Katsina provinces, however, travelling conditions deteriorated rapidly. Stumbling along beside the camels, Clapperton and his hired men were soon exhausted, 'the roads were the worst I have ever seen, or rather, in fact, there were no roads at all'.[4] Animals frequently became bogged down and the baggage had to be off-loaded and then painstakingly re-loaded; his men were very patient, 'up to their middles in water for ½ an hour at a time ~ the path leading through fields of millet & dourra ~ such the road continued untill 5-30 when it came on to rain th[r] & light[g] ~ My servants stripped to the buff and put their shirts under the hides that covred the baggage to have them dry when they halted – I got wet to the skin yet had a burning thirst at times hardly able to sit on horse back ~ relieved by occasionally vomiting ~ I would gladly have lain down any where but there was not a spot clear of water'.[5]

At Gyaza, the first town in Katsina province, Clapperton had to be helped off his horse and taken to lie down by a fire in the outer hut of the headman's compound. When the chief made difficulties, the traveller 'gave it to him in all the Hausa I had... At no time am I possessed of a sweet and passive temper and when the Ague is on me it is a little worse'.[6] He was left in possession and supplied with food and fodder. At night he shut himself inside the hut to try to sweat out the fever; the attacks were severely debilitating and long lasting. Two days later, however, he received the very welcome news that Gidado was expected shortly in Gyaza; and when the Waziri arrived, trumpets, pipes and drums going before him, Clapperton stumbled out from his hut to greet his old friend and they walked hand in hand to Gidado's house.

The Waziri was on his way to oversee the Caliphate's eastern defences and raise more troops. They had received Clapperton's message from Kulfu, and had been expecting his further news; but the letters sent from Katagum and Kukawa in the June of 1824, appointing the date for his return to the coast and requesting an escort from Bello's seaport to Sokoto, had apparently never arrived. Surprised but too ill to pursue the matter, Clapperton said that he wished to continue immediately to Sokoto. But Gidado urged him to return with him to Kano and, unable to summon strength enough to demur, at the turn of September he accompanied the Waziri to the city and withdrew once more to his quarters to rest.

Meanwhile, on the eastern war front, Al-Kanemi's forces had retreated in the rains, and an early resumption of armed hostilities was not expected. Gidado resolved to send the armies raised in Kano to the western front to quell a rebellion by the Gobirawa; by massing the combined might of the Caliphate against a militarily weak enemy, he hoped for a swift outcome and to have the men back in the city before the dry months returned and with them the likelihood of renewed aggression by Borno. Orders were issued accordingly and on 24 September Clapperton set off for Sokoto in the train of Gidado's assembled armies. Confident of an early return, he again left Lander and Pasco in Kano to look after the heavy stores – which included the gifts for Al-Kanemi. He took the resourceful Madi with him, and a handful of hired men and a camel, with a bullock to carry the presents for Sultan Bello. Two weeks later the army halted in the town of Zurmi to await the arrival of reinforcements from other emirates before advancing towards the border with Gobir – and in Zurmi, on 10 October, all the journals he had kept since 27 August (with the exception of one pocket book he happened to have on him) were stolen from his saddle bag. Suspicion fell on a man who had been permitted to stay in the mission's enclosure, or possibly that man's servants, but they had all disappeared the moment the theft was reported. The journals were never recovered.

Shortly after leaving Zurmi, Clapperton's camel gave up, and he had to hire five Zamfara foot-soldiers to carry its load. When their bullock became stuck shoulder-high in the mud he bribed a nearby party of infantry to haul it out; thereafter, aided by his servants, he contrived to urge the scabbed and exhausted beast on at a reasonable pace, 'with constant beating, which, in a humane country like ours would have appeared great cruelty – but a man will do a great many things here that his humanity would revolt from in such a happy country as ours'.[7] The uncertainties began to get him down again; he did not know how long the campaign might last, and it would be difficult to absent himself from it, 'I have no prospect before me but to subsist on water and boiled Indian corn. I cannot but feel a disposition to despond, but I trust things are now at their worst'.[8] His chief consolation was that Sultan Bello was not far away.

Evening halts in the inundated valleys provided some relief, 'All the acacia trees were in blossom some with white flowers others with yellow ~ forming a contrast with the small dark green leaves like gold and silver tassels on a screen or cloak of dark green velvet… the lake was smooth as glass, its surface like sheets of burnished gold and silver; some soldiers were bathing, others watering their animals; everywhere the sound of voices calling, Mohamed, Abdo, Mustafa, and in the distance drums and trumpets; and with rude huts of grass rising as if by magic beside the smoking fires on the bank, it all appeared… as if the Mohametans had actually broke into paradise'.[9] And an unexpected abundance of game naturally raised his spirits. A wild pig was sighted, and although he briefly considered setting off in chase of it, 'I could not but pity the poor animal ~ every ignorant vagabond in the camp went to have a blow at the Kaffir as they called ~~him~~ it ~ at any other place or country but in that of a Mohamed[an] I might have gone and joined the hunt but here I considered the poor pig as a sort of Martyr'.[10]

On arrival at the Sultan's encampment on 15 October he went directly with Gidado to pay his respects, a little concerned about appearing in his rough travelling clothes (Gidado assured him that it would not matter). As to Bello himself, Clapperton observed that he appeared unchanged 'except that he has got a little fatter and dresses better'.[11] Though somewhat aloof and preoccupied, the Sultan seemed pleased to welcome back his British visitor, questioning him in a kindly manner and expressing surprise that Clapperton had not been able to find time to visit friends and family at home in Scotland. And he also confirmed that he had received neither the letters sent from Borno nor the message from Tripoli; but Clapperton, though again owning himself at a loss, no longer considered the reasons for their non-arrival to be of any moment. The lengthy audience took place in the pouring rain 'but as he and the old Gidado remained I of course could not think of starting and we looked like three persons trying for a wager who could stand a shower ~ but it never interrupted in the least our conversation'.[12]

Clapperton judged that the time was not ripe for discussing previous arrangements or his present plans and, desiring only to get to Sokoto and rest, returned to his quarters near Gidado's tents (easy enough to find since the camps of the different armies were pitched in a pattern corresponding to the geographical position of the various provinces).

In the event the campaign was short-lived. Clapperton followed the combined forces eastwards up the Maradi river valley towards the town of Konya, and two days later witnessed their assault on the Gobirawa stronghold. Though the four-hour battle was in itself rather a ragged affair, the fighting was fierce and not without danger to both sides. The attackers shot flaming arrows over the ramparts and the defenders responded with a hail of poisoned arrows, divers other missiles and the firing of a musket (which last did considerable damage). The Caliphate's troops reassembled under the walls, retreating and rallying again and again, amid a good deal of shouting and bluster. In the skirmishing outside the town, men on both sides were killed; but there was neither a sustained siege nor any attempt to break through the Gobirawa defences.

To an impartial observer the outcome of the battle appeared inconclusive – the rebel army and their capital had not been obviously reduced – and the engagement indeed ended in a truce rather than capitulation. But Bello counted the attack a success and Clapperton himself was thankful when the following evening the Sultan ordered a withdrawal; the armies marched back to the Rima valley where the provincial forces went their separate ways. At Bello's headquarters that night, however, rumour of a counter-attack by the Gobirawa spread like wildfire. The Zurmi forces turned and fled from the valley and the other commanders clearly went in fear that their troops might follow suit. Deciding he had seen enough, and having looked to his own guns, Clapperton ordered Madi and the other servants out onto the road where they found themselves caught up in an undignified scramble. In a headlong rush down the length of the Rima valley, on its marshy floor and along its stony ridges, half-walking, half-running, the Sokoto troops retreated in complete disarray. They marched and they ran for a full twenty hours; and by the time they arrived on the wide river plain some twenty miles east of Sokoto, all were in a state of near collapse. Hugh Clapperton followed exhaustedly in their wake.

After wading across the River Rima he could barely manage another step and, sinking down under a tree, he had to rest a while before staggering the remaining five miles to Makariya, a new *ribat* on the rim of the valley. The next day, without waiting for his hosts to catch up with him, he rode on to Sokoto where he found his old friend Mohamed ben Ghamzu, the senior resident Arab, standing watch at the south gate. Back in the comfort of Gidado's palace Clapperton rejoiced in the familiar and secure surroundings but he was not at all well. The fever was still upon him and his spleen was painfully enlarged.

Summoned to Makariya a few days later by Bello, Clapperton feared he might be in for a long stay and took rice, bread, meat and flour with him (prices in the war camp were vastly inflated). The journey further drained his strength and he was again obliged to halt overnight. The following day, attired in full naval uniform, he paid a formal call on the Sultan, and presented him with the many articles chosen so carefully the previous summer in London – among them were swords, fowling pieces and pistols, classical texts in Arabic, paper, umbrellas, watches and clocks, trinkets and medicines. Bello was delighted with the gifts, but noncommittal about any further travel arrangements, though a quietly relieved Clapperton obtained permission to return to Sokoto, 'Indeed I had met with nothing but losses and difficulties since I had joined the Fellata army'.[13]

Sokoto appeared virtually unchanged since Clapperton's first visit. Travellers and traders from all across the Sudan thronged the streets. There had been two successful harvests; supplies were plentiful and living conditions good. But everyone was concerned about the progress of the wars near Sokoto and to the east, and went increasingly in fear of further local uprisings. Regarding his own situation, Clapperton found himself faced with suspicion and mistrust on all sides on account of his previous connection with Al-Kanemi. Furthermore, without Pasco to interpret, his sources of information were limited; only the educated class at Bello's court spoke Arabic (in which language he was now fluent) and he could not always obtain sufficient collateral to reassure himself that he was getting a true perspective. But he did have a good working knowledge of Hausa, and the Kanuri he had learnt in Borno was of about the same standard, and so, with a few words of Fulfulde (the language of the Fulani) he got by with a pidgin mix of all the languages of the Sudan.

While awaiting Bello's return, Clapperton received a disturbing visit from the Sultan's secretary, Sidi Sheikh, who informed him that while he was of course free to go wheresoever he wished inside the Caliphate, or to make for home by whichever route he chose, the British traveller should be aware that at the time of his last visit to Sokoto a letter had been received from Al-Kanemi advising that he be put to death. A dumbfounded Clapperton immediately requested sight of the letter and insisted that he be allowed to take a copy of it. Sidi Sheikh replied that Sultan Bello had forwarded it to his uncle Abdullahi, the Emir of Gwandu and ruler of the western provinces.

Hugh Clapperton's initial reaction was to take the matter up with the Gidado, who assured him that there was no question of Sheikh Al-Kanemi or anyone else calling for his execution – it had been wrong of Sidi Sheikh to tell such a story. Clapperton had perforce to be satisfied. His inclination was to attribute the whole thing to war hysteria, but the allegation's very existence was worrying; he would need to play his hand extremely carefully to salvage anything from a most unpromising situation.

Upon Bello's return at the end of the month, Clapperton called on him at the palace where he found the Sultan reading a copy of Euclid in Arabic (one of the presents from England). Bello at once brought up the matter of the warning letter. He explained that a communication had come from Tripoli (signed not by Yusuf Pasha himself but by Hadje Butabli, one of his advisers), counselling the Sultan to be wary of the British coming first in small numbers but who might, when they were strong enough, take over the Sudan as they had India. And Al-Kanemi had written in similar terms. Bello also made it quite clear that his own people 'would have informed me when I was there – but that I was then a stranger & they thought if they told me I would never come back'.[14]

For his part, Clapperton told Bello about his goals and received a characteristically straightforward response. The Sultan was quite prepared to forward his visitor wherever he wanted within the Caliphate, or westwards to Masina, but while he had no objection in principle to the journey to Borno, he could not authorize any such departure until the war was over. The traveller accepted that he would have to continue to possess his soul in patience.

Thankful to have re-established relations with Sultan Bello, the primary objective of his mission, and encouraged by the thought that he might soon be able to travel freely, Clapperton replenished his stores, bought camels from the Tuaregs and whiled away the time collecting further information on Sokoto and its surrounds and paying regular visits to Bello's and Gidado's relations and advisers. Without Lander or Pasco to assist him, he had also to keep a close eye on the mission's servants. Micama from Zinder had already had to be disciplined for his addiction to *cha cha*, a betting game played with stones (an inveterate gambler, he had literally lost his shirt; however, on receipt of the man's under-taking never to play again, Clapperton gave him money to buy a new one).

He wrote to Lander in Kano to keep him abreast of events, urging him to maintain his good spirits and to keep himself fit,

I feel now and then a little feverish and unwell. I sincerely wish it may not increase upon me... it would be disheartening indeed if I should be laid up at this particular time. Let me hope your health is improved since I saw you. It would grieve me exceedingly to hear an unfavourable account of it... By right you should have no idle moments. I hope you ride out every day, and amuse yourself with shooting and stuffing birds; this will tend to keep you in good health and spirits. Apply your mind strictly to the duties of religion; rely firmly on the mercy and assistance of Heaven; for in all your difficulties and distress, this alone will bear you up like a man, and render you superior to misfortune.

I pray God to bless you; and believe me to be

Your sincere friend and master, Hugh Clapperton[15]

Ten days later Clapperton was again laid low by severe pains in his side; calomel brought some slight relief but for three weeks he could neither sleep nor rest. He was to have been branded with a red hot iron, a local remedy for common internal complaints, but his doctor, Sidi Sheikh, was himself too ill with asthma to comply with the traveller's request.

The weeks passed slowly. In early December Clapperton made a short trip with Gidado to a river valley ten miles south of the capital, where the Waziri planned to build a new fortified town. Once again Madi went with him, 'my freedman Mohamed Ali Sarki, who accompanies me on all enterprises of danger'[16]; with Lander on duty in Kano, Madi was fast becoming a trusted lieutenant. The excursion was cut short by rumour of an impending attack by the Gobirawa on Rima valley settlements and Clapperton accompanied Gidado on an urgent moonlit ride to Makariya. It turned out to be a false alarm – the so-called rebels were merely thieves bent on stealing cattle – but it was again brought home to the frustrated explorer that he could not hope to advance his plans with Bello while the minds of all in Sokoto were fixed on threats of war and insurgency. Increasingly unhappy about his prospects, on 13 December he again wrote to Lander,

I am still here, contrary to my expectations, and heaven knows when I shall be permitted to leave. This cursed Bornou war has overturned all my plans and intentions, and set the minds of the people generally against me, as it is pretty well understood by both rich and poor, that I have presents for their enemy the Sheikh. I wish, with all my heart, it was ended; no matter whether the Felatahs or Bornouese be victorious, so I could conveniently pursue my journey. The Sultan has told me that I may return by way of Bornou, if I insist upon it, but raises so many obstacles, that it amounts to a prohibition. I do not know how this matter will end; I must acknowledge I do not like the appearance of things just now; God grant my fears may be groundless[17]

There was good reason to be apprehensive. Sultan Bello had begun to take a closer interest in Hugh Clapperton and his affairs. No doubt prompted by his counsellors, the Sultan had come to wonder what arrangements, military or other, the British might have made with Al-Kanemi following his visitor's return to Borno in mid-1824; he had therefore caused enquiries to be set in train in Kano.

On 18 December a messenger arrived at Clapperton's house with the news that his servants and baggage, together with his agent Hat Salah, were now at the *sansan* on the Zamfara side of the Gundumi wilderness, having been sent for on Bello's orders. Clapperton was rather taken aback, but assumed that the Sultan was bringing them to Sokoto for reasons of safety. When he later discussed the matter with Gidado and Sidi Sheikh, however, he was informed that his servants and all his effects had been brought up from Kano since, while he was quite free to leave Sokoto, he would not be permitted to travel to or through Borno. Those were the Sultan's personal instructions. Clapperton made no attempt to conceal his anger and resentment. The seizure of his men and the mission's baggage was a violation of his diplomatic status, an affront to his own honour and that of his country. Stalking out of the room he announced, in terms certain to be reported verbatim to Bello, that he had nothing more to say and that he considered his whole commerce with them to be at an end.

Sidi Sheikh visited him the following day and made it clear that though the mission was suspected of carrying guns and warlike stores for Borno, Clapperton could rest assured that no one would touch the baggage when it arrived; what they wanted was King George's letter to Al-Kanemi. Clapperton retorted that they might take the letter but he himself would never voluntarily relinquish it. In an attempt to pour oil on troubled waters, Gidado called round to assure him that the Sultan just wanted sight of the letter, not to read it but simply to see if it was enclosed in the same sort of box as the one which Bello had received – a demonstrably thin pretext which Clapperton dismissed out of hand.

Richard Lander appeared that same afternoon, accompanied by Hadje Hat Salah and all the baggage, and gave his master an account of his time in Kano and his journey to Sokoto, reporting that Pasco had twice attempted to abscond with money, guns and pistols from their house. Clapperton thereupon discharged the miscreant and delivered him into Gidado hands.

On 22 December the Sultan sent for his visitor. Gidado accompanied Clapperton and Lander to the audience, at which Sidi Sheikh and Ben Ghamzu were also present. Bello began by confirming the messages he had sent earlier: while travel to Borno remained out of the question, the mission was of course free to leave Sokoto and travel home through Yorubaland via Borgu, or across the Sahara either by way of Timbuktu or north through Aïr. But Clapperton's hackles were up. He flatly rejected any notion of a return home by way of Oyo, and protested that neither route to the north was safe even if he had had enough camels to attempt a desert crossing.

Sultan Bello then asked to see King George's letter to Al-Kanemi. Silently Clapperton held it up, together with a list of the medicines which the Sheikh required (which had long since been sent back to Badagry). Bello directed him to open the letter. Clapperton set it on the ground and refused point blank to obey, avowing that it was more than his life was worth to do such a thing. The Sultan abruptly dismissed his visitors; leaving the unopened letter where it lay, they made their bows and retired from his presence.

On 23 December, with Gidado's permission, Hat Salah called on Clapperton and reported with some relief that since he himself was no longer suspected of comforting the enemy he had been given permission to return to Kano in four days' time; he had also been forbidden to have further dealings with Al-Kanemi if he wished to continue in residence there. He earnestly begged his friend to hand over the gifts destined for the Sheikh and make his way home speedily by way of Aïr. But Hugh Clapperton was not to be moved, 'After their cheating or robbing me of the letter, they might take what they pleased. I was only one man, I could not fight against a nation: they could not, even by taking away my life, do worse with me than they had done'.[18]

On 24 December Gidado called on him bearing an olive-branch, the opportunity to go visiting with him out of Sokoto. The Waziri was suffering from a heavy cold and Clapperton recommended treatment with senna, but declined the invitation, repeating his decision to break with them all. Gidado suggested that the Sultan had perhaps acted somewhat hastily; he attempted to persuade Clapperton to be a little more reasonable, and accept that no other course had been open to Bello in time of war. Declaring that he did not consider such behaviour worthy of a prince, the angry traveller requested that Gidado inform the Sultan that he never wished to see him again, 'that I must for the future consider every part of his dominion as a prison, for he had broken his word in every thing'.[19]

Forty-eight hours later Clapperton was again visited by Hadje Hat Salah, accompanied by Mallam Mudi. They had been sent to say that the Sultan had read the letter and that it mentioned six guns for Al-Kanemi. The traveller expostulated angrily; the only arms he had in his possession were for his private use.[20] Gidado then joined them (to look over the gifts), repeating his assurances that Bello had no wish to remove personal belongings, just what was meant for Al-Kanemi – no one could be permitted to carry arms to the enemy.[21] But, roundly denouncing them all as thieves Clapperton told them to take everything. At that, Gidado made off in a passion; the other two also left, appropriating the presents for Al-Kanemi[†]. Hat Salah later returned, bringing an unconditional order from Bello: warlike stores destined for the Sheikh must be surrendered. Clapperton said that they had already taken everything, upon which the merchant urged him, if that were really the case, to give up his own guns as well. He received a predictably dusty answer.

Shortly thereafter Bello and Gidado left Sokoto to direct the continuing war against Gobir, and Hugh Clapperton found himself effectively under house arrest. He and Lander were cut off from all official contact, and the flow of private visitors to their house dried up completely, although Gidado and Mudi continued to

---

[†] Lander wrote an account of proceedings, 'arrived at sockatoo the 20 of December 21 onnown to my master ~ the sultan demanded the sheke of burnu Letters ~ master gave them to him ~ he desired master to oupon them ~ Then he said its more than my head is worth to oupon my King's Letters ~ he said then I will ~ he said that He had letters from severell respectable persons to say we where spyies ~ master said he must se them ~ but he cud not show them ~ he waved his hand for us to go ~ we Went home and in the afternoon of the same day the Kings head men came and demanded the shekes present and spare harms ~ master said is there no faith in you ~ you are worse than highway robbers ~ the[y] said take care or you will loose your head ~ he said if I do I loose it for the rites of my country ~ the[y] took the presents and harms and went off' [RL to HW, 27 May 1827, CO 2/16].

send round supplies of food. Except among a few acquaintances from his visit in 1824, Clapperton was no longer known by his travelling soubriquet, Abdullah, but was referred to simply as the Christian and Lander as the Little Christian. The disgraced Pasco had been sent to Ben Ghamzu to be disciplined, whereupon he had promptly recanted, promising to be a good Moslem. (Shortly thereafter he married one of Ben Ghamzu's slaves, Mattah Gewow – famous for her flour puddings – and set himself up as a petty trader in snuff.)

There were few breaks from the enforced solitude. Clapperton was unable to eat or to rest. Master and servant sat it out in their hut, hoping for news of peace with Borno. Christmas celebrations were subdued (although Clapperton gave the faithful Lander a present of one of his six remaining gold sovereigns) and for two weeks thereafter the traveller made not a single entry in his journal.

On 14 January Clapperton was summoned to Makariya where the Sultan told him that once the threat from Gobir was contained he could go home via Timbuktu or Aïr and a Fulani guide would be provided; meanwhile, if he so wished, he could visit Bauchi. Clapperton said that he would think about it, and returned that same evening to Sokoto. After two days of reflection, he resolved to take up part of Bello's offer, and dispatched Lander to Makariya with a request for permission to travel to Yakoba, the capital of Bauchi, and to other provinces south of Hausaland in order to establish where the Niger entered the sea. Any idea of proceeding to the western Sudan had been finally relinquished when the traveller learnt from a visiting Arab (who had seen Clapperton's rival) that Gordon Laing was, or had been, in the vicinity of Timbuktu and that he had been critically wounded in the desert.[22]

Two weeks later a courier arrived from Bello granting his guest immediate safe passage to Katsina from where he could begin his journey to Aïr or to the coast, as he wished. Believing the offer to be a ruse designed to smoke out his intentions, Clapperton sent a suitably non-committal reply, intimating that he would prefer to remain in Sokoto for the time being. The following day Gidado called to say farewell before leaving for Kano to resume command of his fighting forces, and the traveller was given permission to store all his belongings, save one trunk and one canteen, in the Waziri's palace. Once more there was nothing to do but wait.

Hugh Clapperton's ambitions for his mission to the Sudan had been only partially realized – and at enormous cost. (If he did raise with Bello the subject of the slave trade between the Caliphate and the coast, he made no mention of it in any remark-book.) What yet remained to him was his geographical brief. His intention, once travel was sanctioned, was to reach the country lying to the south of Zaria and Bauchi, to investigate the region's water highways and natural resources. Nupe and the port of Rabba lay in a zone of continuing civil war and so could not be visited; the sea-port at Funda was assuredly the key to the riddle of the Niger.

In the first weeks of 1827 Clapperton enjoyed tolerable health, although fever and the pains in his side returned intermittently. In the morning, whenever he felt up to it, he went out with his gun, sometimes staying away all day, walking the fields and the river-banks. Sporting a chest-length patriarchal beard, wearing a large flowing *tobe*, a red cap and white muslin turban, and with a dagger and a brace of pistols jammed into his broad belt, he appeared to Lander 'more like a mountain robber setting out on a predatory excursion, than a British naval officer'.[23]

In their quarters, Clapperton and Lander subsisted on such fare as was available from the market: milk, cornmeal, vegetables and the occasional piece of meat. Together they smoked the last of the cigars brought out from England, the only luxury left to them (the tea and sugar having been used up long since). Lander recorded that they 'spent the lingering hours in reading aloud, or chatting of our respective homes and reciting village anecdotes… and how often we laughed at jests which had been laughed at a thousand times before'.[24] They sang English and Scottish songs and Lander played tunes on his bugle. Clapperton's predestinarian creed was, as ever, a source of comfort; he always said Divine Service on Sundays and liked to read aloud from his prayer-book and the Bible, particularly the Book of Psalms.

In the hope that a change of air might do him good, Clapperton obtained permission to travel to Makariya for a few days' sport on the marshes. It was a happy interlude. The river's edge was home to numerous colourful birds and the broad valley was covered in spring greenery and growing crops. Women working in the fields brought him fresh water and food, and boys from the village acted as beaters and retrieved the downed game for him. He saw five elephants and came across the tracks of many more; and he gave chase to a party of wild hogs though in the end he did not like to kill them. He grew increasingly tired and listless, however, and was eventually forced to call a halt; on his last day, all-in and not able to walk one step further, he lay down on the marshy ground and was sound asleep by the time the boys drove the duck towards him. But though physically exhausted he was much refreshed in spirit; and when he returned to his lodgings, news of the defeat of Al-Kanemi's army galvanized him into action. He hurried back to Sokoto to request an audience of Bello.

He was escorted to one of the small inner rooms of the palace where the Sultan, as was his custom, sat reading. Just as they had in 1824, host and guest conversed amicably on all manner of topics. At one point Clapperton mentioned that he was very keen to procure two wild pigs, for food and for their hides; he could not go after them himself because the Sokoto people would regard it as a sin, but perhaps the Sultan might bring them in? Bello said he would send out hunters. He was intrigued by the thought that Europeans ate the flesh of pigs. Clapperton said it was very good, and much better than dog flesh which he had seen being eaten on the streets of Sokoto. Bello remarked that people did indeed eat odd things: the people of Bauchi, for instance, enjoyed human flesh and his visitor would see them when he went to Yakoba; he offered to provide the traveller with a cannibal or two to take home, to show people what those men were like. Clapperton hurriedly declared that the very idea would be repugnant to the English.

The Sultan also asked whether or not his British visitor had been in Dahomey. Confused reports had apparently led Bello to believe that the traveller was connected with the Dahomey slave-merchants who had been aiding the Yawri rebels, but he was re-assured by Clapperton's explanations. The two were again on the best of good terms. The storm clouds had passed; the way ahead was clear. Reinvigorated by the encounter, Clapperton pressed the Sultan at their next meetings for more information about the Sudan itself, the course of the River Niger, routes for travel from Mali to Egypt and the history of the Caliphate; Bello duly deputed the schoolmaster at the court, a scholar from Masina, to write a handful of notes in the visitor's journal.

Ten days later the Sultan forwarded to Clapperton a dispatch received from Gidado in Kano describing the manner in which the Caliphate's armies had put the Sheikh's forces to flight; he also sent round Al-Kanemi's personal drinking vessel, captured in the battle, for the visitor to admire. And that same afternoon the two pigs arrived, freshly slaughtered. Clapperton attempted to skin them out of public sight in his yard, but he was detected, 'now the pigs and I are the talk of the whole town'.[25]

Life in Sokoto appeared to be getting back to normal, and still Clapperton waited. For three weeks very little happened: he held divine service on Sundays; he paid the schoolmaster 20,000 cowries for a chart of the river from Kebbi to Masina; and for four days he was laid up with ague. And then on 12 March Emir Yakubu of Bauchi arrived, bringing the spoils of war as gifts for Bello. The whole town celebrated the event and the booty was displayed in the square before the palace. Sent for by the Sultan, who was in great good humour, Clapperton asked to be forwarded as soon as possible to Adamawa and the River Shari, and thence to Bauchi, without going through Kano; from Bauchi he proposed travelling to Zaria and then, after the rains, he would continue his journey with Bello's messenger to the sea, but 'before he could give me an answer, a number of the principal people of Soccatoo came in, and interrupted the conversation; so I took my leave, he appointing another day to give me the information I requested'.[26]

He must have hurried back to Lander, to pore over the maps and debate options for travel and the choice of roads to Funda: the Sultan would arrange escorts; since only three months remained before the start of the rains, it might be sensible to go straight to Funda or perhaps to head for one of the other towns they knew to be within easy reach of the sea, as time had also to be set aside for getting onto the coast by whatever means offered; and whatever they decided, they would need first to replenish their funds through Arab merchants by encashing bills drawn on Warrington.

But such heady planning sessions at the house in Gidado's compound remain pure conjecture. There was no further meeting with Sultan Bello and Hugh Clapperton had made his last journal entry. The following day he collapsed, wretchedly ill, and his condition deteriorated rapidly. By the end of the month, racked with fever and critically weakened by dysentery and a failing liver, he had become so frail that Lander, who had until then done his best to look after his master by himself, was forced to call for assistance. Mallam Mudi provided a female slave to help with the washing; she began energetically enough but quickly wearied of the task and ran away, never to return. The exhausted Lander then begged Clapperton to take Pasco back into his service; having entreated for forgiveness, Pasco was duly reinstated (with Mattah, his fourth wife of the journey).

Lander began to wonder whether his master might not have been secretly poisoned but Clapperton dismissed the possibility – it was his own fault for having lain too long in the wet grass when out shooting duck on the Makariya marshes. Mid-day temperatures in the coolest spot in the hut climbed to 109° F, and in his narrow cot Clapperton suffered severely. With Lander's help he sought rest on a makeshift couch outside the hut, but within a few days he had grown too weak to reach it; confined indoors once more, he attempted to take up pen and paper but was unable even to sit up.

Lander stayed at his master's bedside, fanning him and feeding him a little chicken soup or milk and water, and reading to him from the scriptures and psalms. At night, his patient's sleep was fitful and his dreams troubled; he frequently muttered curses in Arabic. The only stranger to call on Clapperton was a Fezzani Arab, one Abderachman, who wanted to recite prayers with him, but the man was summarily dismissed and told not to call again.

At the beginning of April the distressed explorer was unable to move without groaning in pain. Spells of sickness came and went and Lander was at a loss to know what to do to for the best. For three days Clapperton took eight drops of laudanum four times a day but, obtaining not the slightest benefit, he discontinued the dose. Other medicines he tried were Seidlitz powders (two papers) and four ounces of Epsom salts to ease the symptoms. And on one occasion his Shuwa servant Ali brought him twelve ounces of green bark from the shea-butter tree, a remedy recommended by an Arab merchant; despite Lander's objections, Ali prepared two bowls full and his master drank them down.

The following day he felt worse rather than better. He told Lander he thought he was dying, and for two hours he went over and over the details of what his servant should do if that proved to be the case. The road to Borno was apparently open again, and he advised the young man to make his way from Kano to Kukawa and from there, with help from Al-Kanemi and Arab merchants, across the desert to Tripoli with a trade caravan. He cautioned him against travelling back through territories where local leaders might resent the fact that the mission had been consorting with their enemy in Sokoto (he had in mind the Alafin), and pointed out how and where assistance and funds could best be sought. But the overriding consideration was to get the journals, reports and other papers safely back to Barrow and the Colonial Department.

That night Clapperton fell into a deep sleep, waking only to murmur that he had distinctly heard the tolling of a funeral bell. The following day, however, he said he felt somewhat better. He asked to be shaved, and gazing in the mirror declared that he had looked just as ill in Borno; he thought he should certainly get over it. The next day his condition appeared further improved, and he ate a little mashed guinea fowl, his first solid food for four weeks.

However, early on the morning of 13 April 1827, Lander awoke to the sound of harsh, laboured respiration and a rattling noise coming from his master's throat. In an urgent and anxious voice Clapperton called 'Richard!', suddenly sitting bolt upright and staring wildly about him. He tried to get to his feet, but collapsed back onto the bed, his heart palpitating fiercely. Lander held him and the throes gradually became less violent; a short while later Hugh Clapperton breathed his last in his faithful servant's arms.

With the help of Mallam Mudi and Pasco, Lander prepared his master's corpse for burial; it was then laid on a mat and wrapped in a sheet and blanket, with another large mat over it, and carried out of the house. The Sultan was informed, and at noon an officer from the court arrived with four slaves to conduct the burial party to the place where Bello had decreed that the British traveller be laid to rest. Covered with a Union Jack, the body was placed on the back of a camel and the small procession passed, unremarked, through the streets of the city and out across the Sokoto river valley, five miles north-east to the little village of Jangebe. When the slaves had dug the grave,

> the corpse was borne on a camel to the brink of the pit, and I planted the flag close to it; then, uncovering my head, and opening a prayer book, amidst showers of tears, I read the impressive funeral service of the Church of England over the remains of my valued master – the English flag waving slowly and mournfully over them at the same moment. Not a single soul listened to this peculiarly distressing ceremony, for the slaves were quarrelling with each other the whole of the time it lasted... Thus perished, and thus was buried, Captain Hugh Clapperton in the prime of life, and in the strength and vigour of his manhood. No one could be better qualified than he by a fearless, indomitable spirit, and utter contempt of danger and death, to undertake and carry into execution an enterprise of so great importance and difficulty, as the one with which he was entrusted.[27]

Chapter 20: Acclaim 1827–1829
the gallant Scotch captain

*Lander's return – reactions to news of the outcome of the expedition
the mission's affairs wound up – publication of Clapperton's journal
disappointments, acclaim and reflections on issues of policy*

The stalwart young Cornishman kept his promise; twelve months
later he delivered all the important papers to the Colonial Department. The press took up the story immediately, celebrating Hugh
Clapperton's courage and valour, and lamenting his miserable
end and lonely burial in a distant land. Regret over the deaths of
the mission's officers was mingled with cautious acclaim for its
achievements, renewed interest in the circumstances of Mungo
Park's demise and anticipation of news about Gordon Laing. And
Richard Lander's own remarkable return journey from Sokoto
back to the safety of a British ship naturally caught the public's
imagination.

Lander had sold to Sultan Bello everything for which there was
no further use and set off for Kano in company with a caravan of
Caliphate troops, taking Clapperton's servants with him. Bello had
wished to keep Pasco in Sokoto but Lander would have found himself completely at a loss without a reliable interpreter; he eventually obtained permission for Pasco to leave on condition that he
be sent back to the Sultan from Kano.

In Kano, Lander wrote immediately to Consul Warrington to
report his master's death, enclosing one copy of Clapperton's
journal, and with Hat Salah's help equipped himself for onward
travel. Uncertain about the length of time it might take him to
travel to Borno and worried about his own safety on the desert
road to Tripoli, he resolved to make for the coast. He paid off Madi
and the other servants but retained Pasco, assuring Hat Salah
(who knew of the undertaking to Bello) that the man would be
sent back to Kano from Kulfu. Once on the road to Zaria, however,
Lander decided that it would be safest to continue south through
the Caliphate. Confident in all the information his master had
collected he opted to head for Funda, and in Bebeji he found a
guide willing to take him there. But some five days short of his
goal he was overtaken and recalled to Zaria by messengers of the
Emir who was concerned for the young man's well-being.

The Emir sent Lander to Kulfu – on the caravan road by which master and servant had travelled north the previous year – for a passage to Oyo; before leaving, Lander engaged an additional servant, Jowdie, and the Emir provided him with a female slave, Aboudah. Clapperton's fear that Lander might encounter hostility along the way turned out to be unfounded and the little Christian was well received by the same headmen and kings; he sensibly followed his master's own travelling practices and Pasco was content to remain at his side. On reaching Wawa, Lander found that their old friend the widow Zuma had been forbidden to have any direct truck with him, but she sent him calabashes of honey, with her good wishes and commiserations over Clapperton's death. And in Katunga he was delayed for a month, before being forwarded to the coast through Ijanna.

When Lander arrived in Badagry on 21 November 1827 there was no English ship in the offing. Fortunately he was able to raise money from the commander of the Portuguese fort – his initial attempts to communicate with British merchants or officials in neighbouring Whydah and Accra had proved fruitless. But he was an unwelcome visitor, the townspeople having been convinced by local slave-traders that he had been sent by the English to spy on them. He was arrested and required to account for himself to Badagry's fetish priests, who compelled him to undergo trial by poison. Having manfully downed the bitter contents of the bowl, Lander retreated to his hut and induced violent and prolonged vomiting. Survival of the ordeal being tantamount to proof of innocence, he suffered no further molestation or inconvenience.

In mid-January 1828, the captain of a British merchantman (who had heard word in Whydah) came to Badagry and sent a note 'To the white traveller on shore at Badagry'[1], offering to take him to Cape Coast Castle. Ransomed by the payment of sixty-one pounds worth of goods delivered to King Adele, Richard Lander and his servants were duly forwarded to the fort, where Hugh Clapperton's papers were put into the hands of its commanding officer, Lieutenant-Colonel Lumley.

Undertaking to give Jowdie and Aboudah parcels of land and a small sum of money, Lumley put Lander and Pasco on board the naval sloop *Esk* for a passage home; Clapperton's papers, under the colonel's own seal, were handed to her captain, together with a dispatch to London, the first official notification of Clapperton's death and the true end of the mission. *Esk*'s first port of call was Clarence Cove on Fernando Po where Clapperton's former patron,

Captain William Owen, was in charge of works at the new shore establishment.[2] And by an extraordinary coincidence, the Superintendent of Liberated Africans from Sierra Leone had arrived at Clarence Cove on a visit of inspection three days earlier, none other than Lieutenant-Colonel Dixon Denham.[3]

Two months later Lander reached London and, accompanied by a Mr MacGougan (representing Clapperton's solicitors Evans and Eyton), called directly at the Colonial Department. Robert Hay took possession of all the documents and other material of official interest, which included samples of dyes and macadamia butter, a small amount of arrow poison, mineral specimens, a country flute, navigation equipment and the expensive silver watch which had incurred the wrath of the Second Secretary in the summer of 1825. Clapperton's personal belongings – writing equipment, a prayer-book, his commander's dress coat, spectacles and a silver pencil case – were returned to MacGougan. The journals and papers were sent on to Barrow at the Admiralty, and Lander was required to provide an account of his master's last days and of his own return journey to the coast.

Prior to Lander's arrival in England, the last unambiguous news of Clapperton's progress had come from John Houtson who on return to the Badagry in April 1826 had personally informed Captain Parsons of HMS *Dispatch* of the explorer's safe arrival in Kaiama in Borgu. Houtson had handed over all the letters and papers brought back from Katunga at Clapperton's request, and had intended to write his own account of the expedition but he too had succumbed to fever and died in Accra within the month.

Throughout 1826 reports had continued to reach the coast – some through de Souza in Dahomey – alleging Clapperton's safe arrival in, variously, Yawri, Kano and Sokoto. But officers at Cape Coast Castle and on board His Majesty's ships had afforded the hearsay little credence. Meanwhile in Tripoli, Warrington had been anxiously awaiting news of both Clapperton and Laing. In early 1827 he had received a report, from a reliable Arab source, that Clapperton had been in Kano the previous summer. After that nothing was heard and the following spring an increasingly concerned Consul-general dispatched Mohamed ben Sada, John Tyrwhitt's former servant, to Borno in search of news, at the same time commissioning an Arab merchant bound for the Sudan to make similar enquiries (Lander's letter sent from Kano twelve months earlier did not get through). Verification of Clapperton's death in Sokoto the previous year was eventually vouchsafed to

Warrington by the Bey of Fezzan in May 1828, and later that same month official word reached the Consulate-general from London through Livorno.[4]

Relatives and friends in Britain had also been waiting anxiously for news of Hugh Clapperton, and MacGougan made immediate contact with the explorer's uncle Samuel, still serving at Chatham. The two of them passed on word of Hugh's death to Margaret, then living in Portobello near Edinburgh, who had tried unsuccessfully to have letters forwarded to her brother in Africa. Duncan's guardians, the Gibsons, were also informed, as was the family of Hugh's brother Charles[5], who had died in Annandale two months previously. As far as Samuel was aware, they had thus reached the only surviving close kin, for contact had long since been lost with William (who, after long service as a naval surgeon overseas, eventually resurfaced in 1829).

Edward Irving had written a number of times to the Colonial Department for news, his last enquiry having been sent only a few days before Lander's arrival in England; the department had also received concerned letters from Thomas Dickson's brother Robert and other Dickson relatives in Annan. And in Lochmaben, and in James Kay's circle in Edinburgh, there were a good many keen followers of the expedition's progress who would sincerely mourn Hugh Clapperton's passing.

At the Admiralty, Barrow had been reviewing Clapperton's papers. Salamé had provided translations of the Arabic documents; experts had given their assessments of the various maps and geographical notes and Major Rennell, the eighty-seven year-old doyen of British geographers, had been consulted. John Barrow recommended publication, agreeing to take on the considerable task of preparing and editing the journals himself, and Murray paid Clapperton's estate four hundred guineas for the rights to the papers – the earlier mission's *Narrative of Travels* continued to sell well, running into further editions, and the publisher was hopeful.

At the same time, administrators at the Colonial Department set about winding up the expedition's affairs. Pasco was sent to Plymouth for a passage to Cape Coast. Richard Lander, having already provided Barrow with a record of his return journey from Sokoto following Clapperton's death, was planning to write up his own account of the whole expedition. He left London for Cornwall and on the way he fell in love and got married; once home, he was found employment in the Customs and Excise Department in Truro.

Finalizing the mission's several accounts took the Treasury some eighteen months. Bills drawn by John Houtson and Frederick James had already been honoured, following representations by the coastal merchants who encashed them. The total cost of the expedition was eventually reckoned at £3,207.0.3 – a modest sum which puts a rather niggardly construction on Barrow's reaction to Clapperton's expenditure on vital equipment (and, typically, the Second-Secretary had sent all the returned silver pocket-watches to the makers for a refund).

Arrears of salaries were paid to representatives of the participants in the mission, and Richard Lander successfully applied for Columbus's pay as an extra allowance. MacGougan presented the claims on behalf of Clapperton's estate: eight hundred and eighty-eight pounds, being six hundred and twenty-one days' pay at one pound per day from 1 August 1825 to the date of his death, and his subsistence allowance for the same period, less sums advanced to him before departure from England. MacGougan also sought, albeit unsuccessfully, payment of a gratuity to cover the very considerable expenses Clapperton had met out of his own pocket on the journey. (At the final count, however, with Murray's fees in prospect, the estate was in funds.)

Samuel Clapperton had his nephew's will proved in May 1828, but the amount of money available from the estate being still uncertain, appeals had been made for the government's charity. Throughout the winter of 1828–29, Hugh's sister Margaret sent the Colonial Department a series of letters requesting financial help, pleas supported by recommendations from Professor Jameson and other Edinburgh academics and civic worthies. Under-Secretary Hay followed the precedent set in the case of Dr Walter Oudney, when a small ex-gratia payment had been made to the doctor's sisters. Margaret received the sum of one hundred pounds, paid out of the Royal Bounty (as did Captain Pearce's sister, his only surviving close relative).

And in February 1829, William Gibson of Lochmaben sought further financial support for Hugh Clapperton's son Duncan since, as his guardian pointed out, the rather modest sum of five pounds per annum allowed him in the will was hardly 'sufficient for his support &c as I am giving him the best education that the country can afford in order that he may be fit for His Majesty's Service in any place where it may please His Majesty to call him'. The clerk at the Colonial Department minuted tersely, 'Pensions only for an officer's legitimate children'.[6]

In the meantime, initial public interest had gradually evolved into a cooler analysis of specific issues of science and policy. In the nine months between Lander's return and the publication of the *Journal of a Second Expedition*, details of Clapperton's achievements filtered through only to small professional circles in London and Edinburgh. And though government officials in the departments sponsoring the mission appreciated the importance of the material obtained, they were reluctant to broadcast their views too widely, embarrassed by the cost in lives and public money for so little in the way of tangible results.

In early 1829, enthusiasm both for information about the interior of Africa and for British investment on the coast was essentially on the wane. The government was retrenching in West Africa and, following the Ashanti wars, had decided to give up administration of the forts, returning them to the merchants. In a Britain at last emerging from a prolonged period of inflation and economic up-heaval, parliament was weary of war and foreign adventure and the general public was much more interested in internal issues – the Irish question, the emancipation of Catholics, a programme of social and political reform, and the sinister doings of William Burke.

On the eve of publication there were few in London concerned to promulgate the *Journal*. Barrow himself was in the main pre-occupied with the search for the fabled North-West Passage, and the editing and preparation of Clapperton's journals had proved a lengthy and laborious task – in November 1828, as a post-script to a letter to John Murray concerning the publication of the memoirs of Captain Beaver, Barrow added a heartfelt comment, 'Clapperton, thank God! is completed'[7]. And the account was to be launched at the same time as a new edition of the *Quarterly Review*, to which Barrow had earlier contributed conjecture on the progress of the mission and his personal (erroneous) speculation on the course of the River Niger, 'I am prepared for some saucy remarks on that subject'.[8] Young Richard Lander had neither access nor influence; of the naval captains who had seen the mission off on its journey inland none had yet returned to home waters; and Dixon Denham, who might have been moved to endorse his former colleague's recent achievements, had died in Sierra Leone in May 1828. It was thus hardly surprising that when the *Journal of a Second Expedition into the interior of Africa from the Bight of Benin to Soccatoo by Hugh Clapperton* was eventually published on 23 January 1829 its reception was somewhat low-key.

John Murray produced an elegant volume in quarto format. Barrow had provided an Introduction and Samuel Clapperton 'A Short Sketch of the Author's Life'; and Richard Lander's account of Clapperton's death and of his own journey back to the Guinea Coast was appended as a separate journal. Murray had folded in a chart of the route of the expedition, which was based in part on the map that Clapperton had drawn up in Katunga and partly on details published in the *Narrative* of the first mission. A portrait of Clapperton was engraved for the book by Thomas Lupton (from the publisher's copy of the Manton portrait in oils), but Murray had only one small engraving made from the sketches found among Clapperton's papers. Seven hundred and fifty copies of the book were printed but it did not run to a second edition.[9]

The muted acclaim for the *Journal* may have been in some part owing to the lacklustre tone of John Barrow's Introduction. Though praising 'a most valuable addition to the geography of Northern Africa', he observed that Clapperton had 'not contributed much to general science', and as to the final course and termination of the Niger, 'the reports continue to be contradictory and the question is still open to conjecture... [and] further investigation'. Furthermore, the Second Secretary declared, the *Journal* was 'written throughout in the most loose and careless manner; all orthography and grammar equally disregarded, and many of the proper names quite imposs- ible to be made out'.[10]

In the summer the reviews appeared (Barrow himself wrote a comprehensive assessment for the *Quarterly Review*). There was warm praise for the fortitude of the officers and the perseverance of their sponsors. Tribute was paid to Clapperton for gathering information about a 'long range of African kingdoms, scarcely known hitherto even by name'[11], and there was much renewed conjecture on the final course of the Niger. All the contributors covered Clapperton's additional information on Mungo Park's disappearance at Bussa; and most articles included extracts from the book to illustrate the exotic aspects of the expedition, the quaint discoveries and sentimental incidents. Aware of parliamentary attitudes and the constraints on the public purse, Barrow for his part suggested, 'It is by means of single travellers that we shall eventually be able to settle the geography of northern Africa'.[12] The tenor of all the assessments, however, was generally regretful and not a little disappointed.

Typical was the opinion of the *London Literary Gazette*. While in no doubt that the book would claim the public's attention with 'the strangeness of its adventure' and the 'melancholy sacrifice of its characters', and highlighting 'the perils which attended our brave countrymen', the article referred to 'guesses at, rather than approximations to, a certain knowledge of African geography... Science, it is but too true, has gained little by this attempt'.[13] The *Edinburgh Review* was of like mind, 'This volume records another expedition, and another sacrifice, made for African discovery; and still the grand mystery is not solved'.[14]

That Clapperton's aims and progress had been constrained by the complexities of local politics in the Sudan and the exigencies of war was widely accepted, and Barrow roundly criticized Sultan Bello's high-handed treatment of Clapperton *qua* official British envoy. The author of the article in the *Edinburgh Review*, however, offered a more penetrating analysis of the inherent difficulties,

> The first intercourse between men in dissimilar situations and states of Society is very generally friendly and even cordial... Insensibly this gay colouring fades; the hostile principles of man's nature begin to stir within him; grudges and jealousies arise, which the very ignorance and inexperience of each other render deep and difficult to remove. On seeing the King of Great Britain send such repeated embassies to such distant regions, on motives to them incomprehensible, there arose a very natural suspicion that they were sent as spies.[15]

The same reviewer found it entirely natural that precautions should be taken in Sokoto with respect to the mission from London given the rumour current in the Sudan that the British were coming to take their land, 'There does not, and probably never will, exist, in any quarter throughout this country, a single idea of annexing to Britain the immense regions of Central Africa. Yet much apology may be made for the opposite conclusion formed by its potentates'.[16] He found fault on both sides: Bello's confiscation of Clapperton's goods and the presents and letter for Al-Kanemi was reprehensible but Clapperton's intemperate stance was equally to be deplored.

Many assessments aired related policy issues. Barrow argued in favour of consolidating the new base on Fernando Po, so much closer to the Bights of Benin and Biafra for the purposes of anti-slavery activities than Britain's current headquarters in Sierra Leone. And he, like others, reaffirmed his conviction that continued European contact and the determined pursuit of agriculture would in due course do away with the abhorrent trade in slaves. Trade in produce and manufactures from the interior would be extended to the coast, 'and civilization go hand in hand, as it always has done, with commerce'.[17] The *Edinburgh Review* concluded that, given the great extent of land under regular culture, the availability of a few fine manufactures and the existence of a full network of caravan routes, the newly discovered regions afforded considerable scope for commercial exchange – provided that transactions were conducted with discretion and that due precautions were taken, not excluding the use of arms.

Later the same year, in Truro, Richard Lander completed his own personal account of the mission, written with the help of his journalist brother John; it was based partly on Clapperton's diaries and in part on his own notes and lively recollections. On advice contained in a scathing letter from Barrow, Murray turned down the modest but enjoyable memoirs. The Lander brothers found another publisher, however, and *Records of Captain Clapperton's Last Expedition to Africa* duly appeared, in two volumes, in 1830.

For the time being, the riddle of the River Niger remained unsolved. The competition to reach Timbuktu, however, was over although the affair had not been settled to British satisfaction. Major Gordon Laing had been the first European known to have reached the ancient city, but he was murdered on the road three days after departure, in September 1826; and before Laing's last letters could reach London, a twenty-nine year-old Breton, Réné Caillié, had not only made the journey (starting out from the west coast) but returned safely to Paris to tell the tale.

Throughout 1828 and 1829 several travellers and adventurers, military men and scientists sought British government support for expeditions into the interior of Africa, proposing to start from the Bights of Benin and Biafra or from the west coast. Barrow and the Colonial Department turned down each and every request. No further official mission on any substantial scale was presently in contemplation – 'the unhappy issue of Clapperton's last attempt chilled for a time the zeal for African discovery'.[18] But Richard Lander's modest proposal to attempt the completion of Hugh Clapperton's investigations into the final course and termination of the River Niger was something the British government did feel able to underwrite, both politically and financially.

In March 1830, armed with 'a bundle of beads and bafts and other trinkets'[19], and accompanied by his brother John (and Pasco and Jowdie, collected from Cape Coast), Richard was landed on the coast at Badagry and made his way to Bussa. From there the two brothers and their servants travelled downstream by canoe to the confluence of the Niger and Benue rivers, and thence, after several alarming incidents, made their way, in the clutches of river pirates, down the Niger's sprawling delta to the Bight of Benin. At the end of November they were duly ransomed at the mouth of the River Nun by a British merchant captain down on his luck, and in December were delivered to the naval establishment at Fernando Po, returning to England the following June.

In London, Richard Lander's achievement won him the newly-instituted Geographical Society's first Gold Medal and those laurels which, as Captain William Owen observed, 'nothing but the hand of death could have taken from his predecessor'[20]; and in Africa, Hugh Clapperton's offer to Sultan Mohamed Bello to bring trade to the central Sudan by sea could at last be realized.

Envoi

The rest is history – memorials – a grave at Jangebe

> more important, and unfortunately more rare among his colleagues… [Clapperton] portrayed the culture of the Western Sudan with sympathy and an unusual degree of modesty[1]

Over the following three decades, a highway into the heart of Africa was opened up in a series of expeditions mounted from the Bight of Benin by British philanthropists and evangelists, scientists and merchant adventurers. The early missions ended in disaster, their members victims for the most part of malaria and other tropical fevers, but by the mid-1860s, reinforced by naval missions sent in support by a government anxious about French ambitions south of the Sahara, the colonialists had established a foothold in the interior.

Travellers arriving from the Guinea Coast and from across the Sahara visited all the countries familiar to Clapperton and charted the routes he was the first to identify; and many were conscious of their indebtedness to their predecessor.[2] But, as Sheikh Al-Kanemi had shrewdly surmised, the British had not come in twos or threes. They arrived in iron ships and in greater numbers, well organized, armed and equipped to pursue and hold imperial interests. The once omnipotent local polities and their long-standing commercial co-imperium with Arab merchants in the central Sudan bowed to the inevitable, eventually melting away in the heat of European competition for colonial career in Africa.

By 1900 the British government had taken over from the men of commerce and in 1902 only the heartland of the Caliphate of Sokoto remained outside the authority of the new Protectorate of Northern Nigeria. The High Commissioner, Sir Frederick Lugard, was an impatient man and Sultan Abdur Rahman, nephew to Mohamed Bello, was very much on his guard. Their attempts at negotiation proved unsuccessful; and in January 1903 the British shelled Bebeji, the first town to offer any resistance, and marched into Kano. They then turned westwards, and on 14 March defeated the Sultan's army and captured Sokoto. Five days later Lugard arrived in the capital, to appoint a more tractable successor. If Britain's emissaries to Sokoto between 1824 and 1903 had sent conflicting signals as to their intentions, Lugard's message was clarity itself,

> The old treaties are dead; you have killed them. Now these are the words which I the High Commissioner have to say for the future. The Fulani in old times under Dan Fodio conquered this country. They took the right to rule over it, to levy taxes, to depose kings and to create kings. They in turn have lost their rule, which has come into the hands of the British. All these things, which I have said the Fulani by conquest took the right to do, now pass to the British.[3]

Six years later, the arguments over and the dust more or less settled, John Burdon, first British Resident in Sokoto (and one of those who had presumed to voice his doubts about Lugard's manner of dealing with the Caliph), ordered Hugh Clapperton's remains to be exhumed and re-interred in the newly-created Christian cemetery in Sokoto. Large stones were left to mark the site of the original grave at Jangebe, and at the head of a plot in the cemetery a metal cross was set bearing the simple inscription 'Commander Hugh Clapperton RN, Explorer, Died 13th April, 1827'.

Half-remembered, half-forgotten, Clapperton's name lives on in Sokoto. In the early twentieth century, colonial administrators were wont to use him as a role model for new recruits, 'You must start with a firm determination to make the best of everything; your unselfishness must be untiring; do not lose heart; things will be better tomorrow'.[4] And though it has since disappeared, a brass plaque commemorating Clapperton's visit and death was still to be seen on the wall of the Provincial Office in Sokoto in the 1950s, next to a tablet to the memory of John Burdon; but a road in the old government reservation area, a dusty avenue lined by acacia trees, bears the traveller's name to this day.

The buildings Hugh Clapperton described on his travels in the Sudan have for the most part vanished, but he would be glad to know that all remains well in Murmur. Some two hundred yards south of the village, well off the beaten track and rarely visited by outsiders today, a memorial marks the grave of Dr Walter Oudney. Erected in the 1930s by the administrators of Katagum District, a large rectangular stone slab, perched somewhat precariously on its eroded sandstone plinth, the monument stands in the middle of a sandy tract used by the children of Murmur as their playground.

References to Clapperton's journeys through Oyo in 1826 appear in compilations of oral history, together with mention of local hopes that the white stranger might be prevailed upon to make peace or to bring help in the form of arms and military support. And the archives in Sokoto still hold copies of Bello's correspondence relating to Hugh Clapperton's first mission. The traveller's visit and death is also recalled in a local legend recounting the arrival of,

strangers with white skins, but whose hair was dark. They were called by some, Tuaregs, but this they denied, pointing out that they wore no long dark robes but only short clothes. Some of us kept saying that they could only be devils as their eyes were green, like cats' eyes. Many years ago these strangers sent a European to Sarkin Musulmi Abdu, the unbaked pot. This person explained that he was an Arab and a member of the Sharifian sect and it was due to this that his life was spared. He spent some days in Sokoto before the Sultan granted a safe exit. He then left by the Kofar Marke (the gate of Marke tree) and crossed the main Sokoto river, to the village of Jangebe. There he fell ill, became feverish and soon died. He was buried near the village and his servants went on to Kano.[5]

There is here an understandable confusion of dates and references; and perhaps Clapperton's eyes were green (the portraits do not agree in this respect).

In Africa, the explorer's achievements are acknowledged in one or two other modest ways. The species of locust bean tree (a genus first identified by Mungo Park in western Sudan) most commonly found in northern Nigeria bears his name, *Parkia clappertoniana*; and Clapperton's francolin (*Francolinus clappertoni*) still runs wild in the savannah, as difficult to hunt as ever it was.

There are portraits in London and Edinburgh, and in Annan a plaque to his memory in the town hall and a street named after him. In Canada there is a road bearing his name in Barrie at the head of Kempenfeld Bay on Lake Simcoe (and there is of course Clapperton Island on Lake Huron). And around the world, at the turn of the twenty-first century, scholars continue to acknowledge the value of Hugh Clapperton's accounts of pre-colonial life in an important region of Africa south of the Sahara.

In April 1944, drawing up a list of sites of historical interest in the province, the Assistant District Officer of Sokoto, Howard Pedraza, identified Clapperton's grave with the help of a retired *mutowali* (headman) of Jangebe, and cleaned the surrounding area to reveal two marking stones embedded in the soil. The District Officer, however, rejected a recommendation for the erection of a more substantial memorial at the burial site on the grounds that there was already a cenotaph in Sokoto, 'The only action required is a hedge around the grave – to mark the spot distinctly and to keep out goats'.[6] Orders were issued, and in July Pedraza reported that an *aguwa* thorn hedge had been correctly planted and two concrete beacons of Public Works Department design, standing eighteen inches (half their total height) above ground, had been placed at the head and foot of the grave,

When the author and his wife were in Jangebe in March 1994, the owner of the land said that although he had been looking after the grave for many years there had been few visitors. Clapperton's first resting place lies one third of a mile north-west and uphill from the present village, on a rise affording a panoramic view over the Sokoto river valley; and at the time of our visit, silhouetted against the skyline above the grave a train of some thirty camels was passing slowly along the traditional caravan road. The thorn hedge stood about fifteen feet high and was apparently effective in keeping out the goats and stray animals; and Pedraza's concrete beacons were just visible above the sandy soil.

The elders told us that Jangebe had been selected as the site for the burial of an unbeliever because the inhabitants at that time had been backsliding in their faith and had failed to build a mosque. Shortly after Clapperton's interment, however, they had moved their settlement to another site half a mile down the hill and duly built the obligatory place of worship. But Alhaji Dr Junaidu, the distinguished historian and former Waziri of Sokoto, dismissed the story, 'Village talk,' he said.

BIBLIOGRAPHIC NOTES

PUBLISHED SOURCES
Editions of contemporary journals, in order of publication, with abbreviations used in reference notes:

NT   Denham (Major), Captain Clapperton and the late Doctor Oudney, *Narrative of travels and discoveries in northern and central Africa in the years 1822, 1823 and 1824*, John Murray, London, 1826, 1st ed., with XXIV appendices. Quotations are sourced, however, from E.W. Bovill's *Missions to the Niger* [*MN*, see below].

JSE   Clapperton, Hugh, *Journal of a second expedition into the interior of Africa from the Bight of Benin to Soccatoo, to which is added the Journal of Richard Lander from Kano to the Sea-coast*, John Murray, London, 1829, repr. Frank Cass, London, 1966

RL   Lander, Richard, *Captain Clapperton's last expedition to Africa*, 2 vols, Henry Colburn and Richard Bentley, London, 1830, repr. Frank Cass, London, 1967

MN   Bovill, E.W., *Missions to the Niger*, Vols II-IV, The Bornu Mission 1822–1825, Hakluyt Society, Cambridge, 1966

CB   Lockhart, J.R.B., ed., *Clapperton in Borno: journals of the travels in Borno of Lieutenant Hugh Clapperton RN, from January 1823 to September 1824*, Westafrikanische Studien, Bd 12, Rüdiger Köppe Verlag, Köln, 1996

DDR   Bruce-Lockhart, Jamie and John Wright, eds, *Difficult and Dangerous Roads, Hugh Clapperton's travels in Sahara and Fezzan, 1822-25*, Sickle Moon Books, with Society for Libyan Studies, London, 2000

HCA   Bruce Lockhart, Jamie and Paul E. Lovejoy, eds, *Hugh Clapperton into the Interior of Africa, Records of the Second Expedition, 1825-1827*, Brill, Leiden, 2005

DOCUMENTARY SOURCES

Unpublished journals
RBB   The author has drawn on other manuscript remark-books, covering Clapperton's travels in Fezzan in 1822 and his journey from Kano to Sokoto and back in January to June 1824, in the collection of The Brenthurst Library, Johannesburg, MS 171/1-4.

RBC   Reference is also made to Clapperton's manuscript remark-book (parts of it barely legible) held in The National Archive, Public Record Office, CO 2/16, ff. 7-170, which was compiled during the second expedition, from December 1825 to November 1826.

Documentary material
TNA   The National Archive, Public Record Office, Kew

–   Admiralty Series, ADM 55/10 and 11 (Miscellaneous Logs of Serving Personnel, Clapperton journals), ADM series 36 and 37 (Ships' Records), 51 (Captain's Logs), 53 (Ships' Logs), 107 (Muster Books), together with Station Records and Memorials of Service
–   Colonial Office Series, CO 2/13-17 (Missions to the Interior of Africa 1821-30), CO 392 (Africa Exploration), CO 267-8 (Sierra Leone)
–   Foreign Office Series, FO 8/8-12 (Barbary States 1822-25), FO 76/15-20 (Tripoli Consulate-general 1820-26)

HUR   Huronia Historical Parks, Midland, Ontario, Canada, MS collections and extracts of Public Archives of Canada 1814-17

JMA   The John Murray Archive, National Library of Scotland, correspondence 1822-32

RGS   Royal Geographical Society, London, Lib. MS, Mus. 403/3 (Clapperton letters), 408/7 (Oudney letters), AR 64 (Denham papers) and MR Nigeria, S/S 39 (Clapperton maps)

Note
Quotations from Clapperton's journals transcribed direct from the raw material – in *CB*, *DDR* and *HCA* – have been re-edited for ease of reading. Tildes marking breaks in unpunctuated text have been retained.

BACKGROUND MATERIAL

There are three important sources relating to Clapperton's Scottish youth and his early life at sea (from which other nineteenth-century accounts were for the greatest part derived):

'Short Sketch of the Life of Captain Clapperton' in Introduction to the *Journal of a Second Expedition*, pp. i – viii, written by Lieutenant-Colonel Samuel Clapperton, Hugh's uncle in the Royal Marines;

'Captain Clapperton the African traveller' in *Sketches from Nature*, Edinburgh, 1830, pp. 322-36, by John McDiarmid, editor of the *Dumfries and Galloway Courier* from 1817 to his death in 1852;

A biographical memoir of the late Dr. Walter Oudney, Captain Hugh Clapperton and Major Gordon Laing, Edinburgh, 1830, pp. 36-99, by the Reverend Thomas Nelson, a publicist and amateur botanist well acquainted with Walter Oudney and his circle of friends in Edinburgh.

With respect to Hugh Clapperton's naval career during the Napoleonic Wars, C. Northcote Parkinson's *War in the Eastern Seas 1793-1815*, London, 1954, was a valuable source of background – as was the account of the invasion of Mauritius by Captain Phillip Beaver who masterminded the operation.

Background material for Clapperton's service on the Great Lakes of Canada was drawn from numerous articles appearing in journals of historical societies in Ontario and from documents in the Huronia libraries. The diary of Lieutenant David Wingfield RN provided a particularly fresh account of naval life on Lake Huron; and George Head's memoir, *Forest Scenes and incidents in the wilds of North America*, John Murray, London, 1829, repr. Coles Publishing Co., Toronto, 1970, provided an enjoyable record of contemporary military pioneering in Upper Canada.

The author is under obligation to many scholars of nineteenth-century Africa for vital background information, and Bovill's *Missions to the Niger* makes of course an essential starting point for any study of the Borno Mission. Selections of contemporary works, secondary books and articles furnishing further material relevant to Clapperton's travels in Africa are given in the modern editions of his journals edited and co-edited by the author.

REFERENCE NOTES

Note: abbreviations used

HC	Hugh Clapperton
WO	Walter Oudney
DD	Dixon Denham
JB	John Barrow
HW	Hanmer Warrington

Chapter 1: Annandale 1788-1805

1 The Clappertons hailed from the central Border region, with branches in Galashiels, Selkirk and Langholm. Dr Robert's grandfather lived at Newlands and his father, George, at nearby Innerleithen Mill, where most of the family remained all their lives.

2 Cardonnel, Adam de, *Picturesque Antiquities of Scotland*, 2 vols, London, 1793, Preface, Vol. 2

3 In 1915 the house was occupied by a Mr Gardiner, Fish and Chip Merchant, but was demolished in the 1950s to make way for a new agricultural market.

4 Clapperton, Samuel, Lieutenant-Colonel RM, *JSE*, p. v

5 In 1790 Jean Gass bore an illegitimate son, baptized George, by an unnamed father (quite possibly George Clapperton); the child, two years older than Hugh, either did not survive until Jean's move to Butts Street or was being cared for by Jean's family.

6 McDiarmid, John, 'Captain Clapperton the African traveller' in *Sketches from Nature*, Edinburgh, 1830, p. 323

7 Miller, F., 'Bibliography of the Parish of Annan' in *Transactions of Dumfries-shire and Galloway Natural History and Antiquarian Society* [*TDGNHAS*], Series III, Vol. 10, 1922-23, p. 29

8 McDiarmid, p. 324

9 Carlyle, Thomas, (Froude, J. A., ed.), *Reminiscences*, London, 1881, p. 16

10 Ibid, pp. 5-6

11 Nelson, Rev. Thomas, *A biographical memoir of the late Dr. Walter Oudney, Captain Hugh Clapperton and Major Gordon Laing*, Edinburgh, 1830, p. 53

12 Carlyle, pp. 5-9

13 Royal Charter, 1 March 1538, in Little, James, *Annan Ancient and Modern*, Annan, 1853, pp. 47-8

14 Andrew Brown to George Chalmers, 24 March 1801, Edinburgh University Library, MS II 453/24

15 Roddick, John, 'Lieut. General Alexander Dirom (1757-1830)' in *TDGNHAS*, Vol. XXXV, 1956-7

16 Carlyle, p. 13

17 Chambers, Rev. Robert (Rev. Thomas Thomson, ed.), *A biographical dictionary of eminent Scotsmen*, Vol. III, Glasgow, 1875, p. 358

18 Dodds, James, *Eminent men of Dumfries-shire*, 1873, Edinburgh, 1865, p. 31

19 Chambers, p. 358

20 Clapperton, S., *JSE*, p. vi

Chapter 2: The Mediterranean 1806-1809

1 When Clapperton later submitted his official Record of Service he began it from entry on board HMS *Renommee*.

2 Samuel Clapperton was commissioned into the Royal Marines in 1793; promoted brevet major in 1814, he was made lieutenant-colonel in

September 1827. He died in 1830 or
1831.

3 Clowes, Sir William Laird, *The Royal
Navy: a history from the earliest times to
the present*, 6 vols, London, 1898-1903,
Vol. V, p. 403

4 Clapperton, S., *JSE*, p. vi

5 Nelson, pp. 65-7

Chapter 3: The East Indies 1810-1813

1 Annual Register 1810, p. 262

2 Francis Humberstone Mackenzie
(1755-1815) inherited the chieftaincy
of the clan Mackenzie in 1794. He
raised a regiment on the outbreak of
war with France, and was created
Baron Seaforth of Kintail in 1797,
becoming Governor of Barbados
(1800-1806) and then of Demerara –
no mean achievements for a man
born with a speech impairment and
deaf from the age of sixteen.

3 Hall, Basil, *Fragments of voyages and
travels*, 2nd ed., Edinburgh, 1840, p. 169

4 Benton, P. A. (ed. and transl.), A.
Schultze, *The Sultanate of Bornu*,
London, 1913, repr. London, 1968,
Appendix XX, pp. 385-6

5 Nelson, pp. 71-2

6 Clapperton, S., *JSE*, p. vi

7 Skene, William F., *Memorials of the
Family Skene*, Aberdeen, 1887

Chapter 4: Canada 1814-1817

1 Osborne, A.C., 'Old Penetanguishene
– sketches of its pioneer, naval and
military days' in *Simcoe County
Pioneer and Historical Society, Pioneer
Papers No. 6*, Barrie, 1917, pp. 42, 71

2 Nelson, p. 75

3 Wingfield, David, 'Diary of service on
the Great Lakes 1812-1816', National
Archives of Canada, MG 24 F18, p. 44

4 The massive anchor for the new
frigate, hauled by 18 yoke of oxen,
was left at Kempenfeld Bay as a
memorial to the declaration of peace.

5 Head, George, *Forest Scenes and
incidents in the wilds of North*

America..., London, 1829, repr.
Toronto, 1970, p. 179

6 Croft, Melba Morris, *Tall Tales and
Legends of Georgian Bay*, 2 vols, Owen
Sound, Ontario, 1967, p. 15

7 W.F. Owen to E.C.R. Owen, 20 July
1815, ADM 1/2263

8 W.F. Owen to E.C.R. Owen, 21
October 1815, CO 42/171-2

9 Wilson, S. D., 'Lieutenant Henry
Wolsey Bayfield in Canada', Inter-
pretive Research Project, 1978, HUR
MS Collection, p. 4

10 Nelson, p. 79

11 Dodds, p. 31

12 Smyth, Captain W.H., RN, *The life and
services of Captain Philip Beaver*,
London, 1829, p. viii

Chapter 5: Scotland 1817-1821

1 He accepted only some strands of
Frank Mackenzie's hair, to add to a
locket containing those of his father
and of some friends from his youth
[Nelson, pp. 84-5].

2 Of Clapperton's half-siblings the
oldest was Elizabeth (b. 1795) who
died in Annan in 1822; his other half-
sister Jean (b. 1803) died there in 1851.
Jean's oldest boy (b. 1804) was
baptized Robert (but renamed John
after his half-brother on the day of
whose death at sea he was born); he
died in Summergate near Annan in
1858. Samuel (b. 1802) died in
Demerara in 1820; the others were
Robert (II) (1806-1881), George
(b.?1801 but not further identified)
and David who died in Annan in
1816, aged three.

3 Broun, Sir Richard, *Memorabilia
curliana mabenensia*, Edinburgh, 1830,
pp. 40-2, 60

4 Ibid

5 Martha Bell was brought before the
Kirk Session the following February,
'confessing that about eight months
ago she brought forth a male child in
uncleanness with Mr. Hugh

Clapperton at that time residing in the town and desired to be admitted to make satisfaction. The Session considering that Mr. Clapperton had left the parish several months ago without any prospect of returning to give an account of his [word omitted], consented to the request: she was accordingly rebuked for the first time and desired to continue her appearance next Lord's day' [Minutes of the Kirk Sessions, 1 February 1821, Wilson, J.B., (ed.), *Records of Lochmaben Kirk Sessions*, Edinburgh, 1994].

6 Nelson, pp. 90-1
7 'An account of an insurrection of the Slaves on board the *Lord Cassils*, bound from Callabar to Barbados by Ecclefechanicus, Doctor's mate on board the said ship' in *Dumfries Weekly Magazine*, 5 July 1773 [A.E. Truckell, 'Some 18th century transatlantic trade documents' in *TDGNHAS*, III, 1996, Vol. 67, p. 86]
8 Park, M., *Travels in the interior districts of Africa, performed in the Years 1795, 1796 and 1797*, London, 1799, repr. London, 1971, journal entry 20 July 1796
9 JB to Joseph Banks, 8 October 1817, Dawson Turner Collection XX, No. 50, British Museum (Natural History)
10 Lyon, George Francis, *Narrative of travels in Northern Africa in the years 1818, 1819 & 1820*, London, 1821, repr. London, 1966, p. 148
11 Oudney was not yet concerned for his health, nor had his friends noticed anything amiss - indeed Rev. Thomas Nelson considered Oudney to be as fit as any of his companions, whether hill-walking or running up endless flights of stairs in lofty town houses [Nelson, pp. 40-1].
12 J. R. Scott to Henry Goulburn, 15 November 1820, CO 2/14
13 WO to Goulburn, 23 May 1821, CO 2/14

Chapter 6: London 1821
1 HC to Goulburn, 18 July 1821, CO 2/13
2 James M'Queen took an interest in the geography of the interior of West Africa and the River Niger as a result of information received from slaves (and from their owners) about their places of origin when he was manager of a sugar plantation in Grenada. Back in Glasgow, where he was editor and co-owner of the *Glasgow Courier,* he developed (and published in 1821) his theories about river deltas based on the hypotheses of German geographer Gottfried Reichardt.
3 Nelson, p. 39
4 WO to Goulburn, Edinburgh, 8 August 1821, CO 2/14
5 WO to James Kay, 1 September 1821, in Nelson, pp. 10-11
6 From Bathurst's instructions to Oudney, in *MN*, Vol. II, pp. 19-20
7 WO to Kay, in Nelson, p. 12

Chapter 7: Tripoli 1821-1822
1 Hanmer Warrington was Consul-general in Tripoli from 1814 to May 1846. He had served in the Dragoon Guards from 1794 to 1802. In 1810 he raised and commanded a yeomanry corps of cavalry, becoming inspecting field officer with the rank of lieutenant-colonel, and served in Andalusia under General Lord Blayney. He left the army in 1812.
2 Yusuf Qaramanli, who usurped the throne in 1795, was a son of the third Regent and great-grandson of Ahmad, a *kuloglu* (administrative or military officer of mixed Turkish-Arab descent) who founded the dynasty in 1711.
3 WO to Bathurst, 25 October 1821, CO 2/13
4 The Barbary states' lucrative piracy was brought to an end in 1816 when Sir Edward Pellew's squadron forced the capitulation of the corsair fleet off

Algiers and secured the release of captive British subjects.

5 The Pasha did not honour his undertaking and the British ignored the matter of a bonus.

6 HW to WO, 24 October 1821, FO 76/15

7 Beechey, F.W., *Proceedings of the expedition to explore the northern coast of Africa...*, London, 1828. pp. 7-11

8 One was a Scotsman, High Admiral *Rais* Murat (Peter de Lisle), former mate of a merchant vessel who in the previous decade had commanded the Pasha's navy but fell into disgrace. On occasion he had acted as English interpreter at the Castle.

9 HW to Bathurst, 12 December 1821, FO 76/15

10 WO to Bathurst, 21 January 1822, CO 2/13

11 HW to WO, 24 October 1821, FO 76/15; in practice, they wore the comfortable, all-enveloping Libyan baracan, keeping their British uniforms for formal occasions

12 WO, *MN*, Vol. II, pp. 140-1n

13 HW to Bathurst, 14 March 1822, FO 76/17

Chapter 8: Fezzan 1822

1 *DDR*, p. 55

2 HC and WO to Kay, 20 May 1822, in Nelson, pp. 92-3

3 DD to Bathurst, 26 August 1822, CO 2/13

4 DD to Charles Denham, 11 April and 17 May 1822, Royal Geographical Society [RGS], London, AR 64

5 HW to DD, 18 August 1824, FO 76/18

6 Clapperton's is the first known sketch of the small mausoleum, 'by far the most southerly monument of Roman type in Africa' [M. Wheeler, *Rome beyond the imperial frontiers*, Harmondsworth, 1954, p. 101]. The monument was restored in the 1960s and has become known as *Qasr al-Uatuat* (castle of the bats), after a

nearby derelict mud-brick castle.

7 *DDR*, p. 121

8 Ibid, pp. 82-3

9 Ibid, pp. 69-70

10 Ibid, pp. 106-7; *Al-fatiha* (Arabic), comprising the first seven verses of the Quran, repeated at all prayers and on numerous social occasions

11 WO, *MN*, Vol. II, p. 181

12 *Artemisia oudneyii*; a renowned delicacy, rolled into balls and dried in the sun

13 *DDR*, p. 123

14 'by repeated measuring with our chain, we found that, on tolerably even ground, our ordinary rate as the Tuarick travel was half an English geographical mile in thirteen minutes.' [Barth, Heinrich, *Travels and discoveries in north and central Africa in the years 1849-55*, 5 vols, London, 1857, repr. London, 3 vols, 1965, Vol. I, p. 168]

15 *DDR*, pp. 132-3

16 Ibid, p. 131

17 Later travellers were also seduced by their siren songs. In 1845, James Richardson became disorientated while attempting the ascent of Mount Jinun and wandered around the foot of the range for nearly two days, dangerously ill. In 1850, Heinrich Barth collapsed in fever and delirium below the mountain, remaining alone for twenty-seven hours.

18 WO, *MN*, Vol. II, p. 191

19 *DDR*, p. 139

20 *DDR*, p. 160

21 WO to HW, 20 May 1822, CO 2/13

22 DD to HW, 6 April 1823, in Benton, p. 369

23 WO to Robert Wilmot, 4 November 1822, CO 2/13; Wilmot succeeded Goulburn in December 1821.

24 Twenty-five years later, however, James Richardson complained that his predecessors' generosity 'had spoiled the roads as the British have spoiled the routes of the Continent of

Europe' [Richardson, James, *Travels in the Great Desert of the Sahara 1845-1846*, London, 1848, repr. 2 vols, London, 1970, Vol. I, p. 187].

25 *DDR*, p. 173
26 Ibid, p. 174
27 HC to JB, 19 September 1823, RGS, MS 403/3
28 WO to HW, 17 September 1822, FO 76/16
29 William Hillman to John Tyrwhitt, 17 September 1822, CO 2/16
30 DD to HW, 11 October 1822, FO 76/16
31 DD to Charles Denham, 20 September 1822, RGS, AR 64
32 Clapperton made two sketches of Oudney at that time, one in his journal (full face) and one on a page taken from Oudney's notebook of Arabic words (illustrated).

Chapter 9: The Sahara 1822-1823

1   *DDR* pp. 201-2
2   Ibid, p. 203
3   Ibid, p. 207
4   Ibid. p. 214
5   Ibid, p. 215
6   Ibid, pp. 216-17
7   Ibid, pp. 211-13
8   Ibid, pp. 229-30
9   Ibid, p. 220
10 HC to DD, 1 January 1823, CO 2/13
11 DD to Lord Bathurst, 20 February 1823, CO 2/13
12 A condition which afflicted many a European traveller in the desert, and puzzled the medical world until the late 20th century; it was discovered to be a form of silicone poisoning from constant sand abrasion.
13 *DDR*, p. 247
14 *CB*, p. 71
15 Ibid, p. 79
16 *DDR*, p. 232
17 *CB*, p. 79
18 Ibid, p. 83
19 Ibid, p. 86
20 Ibid, pp. 89-90

Chapter 10: Borno 1823

1   The Arabic script is that used in North Africa and Sudan; 'Hugh' is represented by the Arabic *Haq*, truth (one of the attributes of God).
2   HW to DD and WO, 3 September 1822, FO 76/16
3   *CB*, p. 103
4   Ibid, p. 99
5   Ibid, p. 106
6   *CB*, p. 107
7   DD to HC, 11 April 1823, FO 76/17
8   WO memo of 12 April 1823 in HW to Wilmot, 4 November 1823, FO 76/17
9   *CB*, p. 117
10 Ibid, p. 116
11 Ibid, p. 118
12 Ibid, p. 133
13 Ibid, p. 153
14 Ibid, p. 144
15 Ibid, p. 151
16 Ibid, p. 152
17 Ibid
18 DD, *MN*, Vol. III, p. 387
19 HC to HW, 10 December 1823, FO 76/18
20 DD to HW, 4 April 1823, in Benton, Appendix XV, p. 369
21 HC to HW, 10 December 1823, FO 76/18
22 Wilmot to HW, 12 January 1823, FO 8/8
23 WO to Wilmot, 14 July 1823, CO 2/13

Chapter 11: Hausaland 1824

1   *CB*, p. 177
2   Ibid, p. 179
3   Ibid, p. 184
4   *MN*, Vol. IV, p. 621
5   Ibid, p. 620
6   *CB*, p. 194; the palace today is a modern building where, in March 1994, the author was present at the Kaigana's reception of the King of the Hunters who was attended by a large troop of villagers armed with clubs, machetes, old shotguns and muskets. Drums and pipes were played, and the Kaigana called for proper

discipline on the day's outing, 'no fighting among yourselves and no attacking the farmers' goats'.

7 CB, p. 195; he modestly corrected his initial exaggeration of the distance.
8 Ibid
9 Ibid, p. 192
10 Ibid, p. 195
11 WO to DD, quoted in DD to HW, 20 January 1824, FO 76/18
12 CB, p. 197
13 MN, Vol. IV, p. 635
14 Ibid, pp. 635-6
15 Ibid, p. 640
16 Ibid, p. 638
17 HC to HW, 2 February 1824, FO 76/18
18 Cinchona bark had been used as a palliative for malarial fever since the 16th century, but quinine was first extracted in the 1820s. By the 1830s, quinine was in general use on the west coast of Africa as a cure, but its prophylactic use was only discovered (by experiment) in the 1840s. By 1848 it was being prescribed by the medical departments of the British armed services.
19 Now in RGS, MR Nigeria S/S 39, and described in HCA, Appendix V, pp. 485-515
20 HW to R. Wilmot Horton, 18 August 1824, FO 76/18
21 RBB, Sunday 22 February 1824
22 CB, p. 185
23 MN, Vol. IV, pp. 643-4
24 In the 1890s European travellers could still describe Kano market as 'probably the largest in the world' [Charles Robinson, 'The Hausa Territories' in Geographical Journal, No. 3, Vol. VIII, 1896].
25 MN, Vol. IV, p. 654
26 Ibid, p. 671
27 RBB, Sunday 7 March 1824
28 MN, Vol. IV, p. 670
29 Ibid, p. 671
30 RBB, Monday 15 March 1824
31 MN, Vol. IV, pp. 674-5

Chapter 12: Sokoto 1824

1 MN, Vol. IV, p. 675
2 RBB, Tuesday 16 March 1824
3 MN, Vol. IV, p. 677
4 Ibid
5 RBB, Wednesday 17 March 1824
6 MN, Vol. IV, p. 685
7 HC to Wilmot Horton, 6 June 1825, CO 2/13
8 Bello, Muhammad (1813), 'Infaq'ul Maisuri', transl. in Arnett, E. J., The Rise of the Sokoto Fulani, Kano, 1922, p. 16; like his father and other Fulani reformers, Bello promoted the amelioration of slave status through conversion to Islam, instituting or reinforcing mechanisms for the emancipation of slaves.
9 HC to Wilmot Horton, 6 June 1825, CO 2/13
10 MN, Vol. IV, p. 699
11 A reference to the principal river ports – Raka (two day's journey from the capital of Oyo), Rabba (the main town in Nupe at this period), Opanda (on a tributary of the Benue close to its confluence with the Niger), and Atagara (Idah, on the lower Niger). For the people of the Sudan, the sea included the nexus of rivers and creeks falling into the Bight of Benin which starts at the wide expanse of the confluence of the Niger and Benue rivers.
12 Sultan Mohamed Bello to King George IV, 18 April 1824 [transl. in HCA, pp. 444-5]
13 MN, Vol. IV, p. 685
14 Ibid, p. 695
15 Ibid, p. 694
16 See HCA, Appendix V, pp. 490-3
17 MN, Vol. IV, p. 70
18 RBB, Wednesday 5 May 1824
19 MN, Vol. IV, p. 705
20 Sheikh Mohamed al-Kanemi to HC, seal dated 1238 A.H., CO 2/13 [transl. in HCA, p. 459]
21 CB, p. 201
22 MN, Vol. IV, pp. 715-6

23 DD, MS journal, 1824, [RGS, R.P., pp. 209-10]

24 In September 1822, having recovered his health, John Tyrwhitt asked to be considered for employment on a mission into the interior of Africa 'if any more are to be sent out'. The offer was accepted, despite the recent appointment and dispatch of Ernest Toole, and Tyrwhitt travelled back to Tripoli later that same month. On arrival in Kukawa and finding that Toole had died, he formally volunteered under Denham [CO 2/13, ff. 361-75].

25 CB, p. 204

26 Ibid, p. 205

Chapter 13: Return to England 1824-1825

1 CB, p. 206

2 DD, MN, Vol. III, p. 473

3 DD, MS journal, in MN, Vol. IV, p. 753

4 Ibid, p. 754

5 Denham had earlier been rebuked by Al-Kanemi for attempting to recruit a protégé without permission [CB, pp. 208-9] – an incident not mentioned in Denham's published journal.

6 Tyrwhitt to John Tyrwhitt snr, 19 August 1824, CO 2/16, f. 359

7 Al-Kanemi to King George IV, 18 April 1824, CO 2/13 [HCA, pp. 444-5]

8 DDR, p. 272

9 Ibid, p. 275

10 Ibid

11 Ibid, p. 274

12 HC to HW, 27 November 1824, FO 76/18

13 DDR, p. 290

14 Ibid, pp. 296-7

15 Ibid, p. 297

16 Ibid, pp. 300-1

17 Wilmot Horton to HW, 29 February 1824, FO 8/8

18 DD to HW, 10 May 1824, FO 76/18

19 See Bovill, E.W., 'The Letters of Major Alexander Gordon Laing, 1824-1826', MN, Vol. I, pp. 123-394

20 HW to Laing, 11 October 1825, Royal Society, London [RS], 374 (La), 101

21 In October 1826 Denham sought official reimbursement of £91 for nine months' expenses for the boy (at the rate of one guinea per week for maintenance, tuition and clothing and 2s 6d per week pocket money).

22 HC to HW, 10 February 1825, FO 76/19

23 HC to John Murray, August 1825, JMA

Chapter 14: London 1825

1 JB to Murray, 30 May 1825, JMA

2 J.G. Children recorded his classification of Francolinus clappertoni, 'This species of Francolin… was met with in tolerable abundance. It frequented sand hills, covered with low shrubs; and was very difficult to be procured in consequence of the great speed with which it ran. We have named the species after Captain Clapperton, R.N., the intrepid and intelligent companion of Major Denham' [NT, First Edition, London 1826, Appendix XXI, p. 198].

3 The Nitta tree with its showy purple or white flowers and prickly fruits, common in the savannah of northern Nigeria, was named Parkia clappertoniana, after its identification as a distinct species of the genus Parkia [R.W.J. Keay, C.F.A. Onochie and D.P. Stanfield, Nigerian Trees, Ibadan, 1960].

4 Laurie Hamilton & Co., to Colonial Department, December 1826, CO 2/14

5 DD to Charles Denham, 26 November 1824, RGS, AR 64

6 Murray to Dr Julius (an associate in Hamburg), 15 December 1825, JMA

7 Gordon Laing to E. Sabine, 29 July 1825, RS, 374 (La), 90

8 Laing to HW, 3 August 1825, CO 2/20

9 Laing to Sabine, 29 July 1825, RS, 374 (La), 90

10 HC to Wilmot Horton, 14 June 1825, CO 2/16

11 Nelson, p. 95
12 'Mr. Irving of the unknown tongues, the most wonderful orator, eloquent beyond reason, but leading captive wiser heads…' [Grant of Rothiemurchus, Elizabeth, *Memoirs of a Highland Lady 1797-1827*, John Murray, 1898, repr. 2 vols, Edinburgh 1988, pp., 182-3]
13 Dr Thomas Dickson to HC, June 1825, CO 2/17
14 JB in *Quarterly Review [QR]*, Vol. XXXIX, No. LXXVII, p. 144
15 *RL*, Vol. I, p. 11
16 HC to Kay, in Nelson, pp. 95-6
17 DD to Wilmot Horton, 27 June 1825, CO 2/13
18 TNA, Ref. Probate 11/1740
19 Dickson to Wilmot Horton, 15 July 1825, CO 2/15
20 JB to R. W. Hay, 24 August 1825, CO 2/17
21 HC to Kay, undated (summer 1825), in Nelson, p. 96
22 HC to Wilmot Horton, 14 June 1825, CO 2/17
23 In Scotland a conspiracy was suspected, 'The silence which has hitherto been observed upon a subject of such national curiosity and interest and about a journey of discovery, undertaken at the national expense for the benefit of the nation, appears to be as unaccountable as it is unprecedented… From the information which he [Clapperton] obtained, he considers it certain that the mighty Niger terminates in the Atlantic, in the Bights of Benin and Biafra' [*Glasgow Courier*, Oct. 1825].
24 Lord Melville to Bathurst, 30 August 1825, CO 2/17
25 Bathurst to HC, 30 July 1825, CO 2/16
26 JB to Murray, 1825, in C. Lloyd, *Mr. Barrow of the Admiralty*, London, 1970, p. 122
27 *MN*, Vol. II, p. 131
28 The *Narrative of Travels (NT)* published in March 1826 in a single quarto volume, contained forty-one engravings from drawings, mostly by Denham but three by Clapperton. The book contained twenty-four appendices of scientific notes and two extracts from Bello's *Infaq'ul Maisuri*. A second edition was published later the same year, in two volumes (with fewer appendices and plates). A third edition, in two volumes octavo, appeared in 1828 and a fourth in 1831 in 16°.
29 HC to Murray, August 1825, JMA
30 HC to Kay, 27 August 1826, in Nelson, p. 96; the plant, *Oudneya Africana* R Br., (vernacular name 'zweetina') is to day an accepted genus. It is found in the wadis between Tripoli and Murzuq and browsed by camels and mules [see *NT*, Appendix XXII, p. 219 and Ali, S.I. and S.M.H. Jafri (Eds) Flora of Libya, Vol. 23, Brassicaceæ, Tripoli, 1977].

Chapter 15: The Guinea Coast 1825
1 *HCA*, p. 80
2 Major-General Charles Turner to HC, 23 October 1825, CO 2/16
3 *RL*, Vol. I, p. 33
4 Lord Bathurst regarded the fees promised to Houtson and James as 'needless extravagance' and pending explanations [later accepted] had the sums placed on an imprest against Clapperton's pay [Hay to HC, 25 April 1826].
5 Richard Lander, who found the former factotum of the Borno Mission to be overbearing, over-excitable and malicious, was 'by no means sorry' that he was not joining the main party [*RL*, Vol. I, pp. 43-4]. Columbus in fact suffered a relapse and died at Whydah before the month was out.
6 *HCA*, p. 93

Chapter 16: Journey inland 1825-1826
1 In 1994 the river here, covered with

floating reeds and lilies and overhung by trees, was no longer wide enough for canoe traffic – a humid, airless and oppressive spot.
2 *HCA*, p. 118
3 Ibid, p. 119
4 Ibid, p. 121
5 Ibid, p. 122
6 Ibid, p. 123
7 HC to Captain George Willes, 30 December 1825, CO 2/17
8 Richard Lander, *JSE*, p. 278
9 *HCA*, p. 125
10 Ibid, pp. 126-7
11 Ibid, p. 132
12 Central authority in Oyo began to implode at the turn of the century, a consequence of conflict between the *Oyo mese* (a parliament of elders) and the alafin and his executive. Former tributary states broke away, parts of Oyo's army defected and revenues fell. Having conquered Hausaland, Fulani jihadists exploited the unrest and the inability of successive alafins to maintain control, and won influence in the region.
13 *HCA*, p. 136
14 Ibid, p. 140
15 Ibid
16 Ibid, p. 143
17 Ibid, p. 148
18 HC to P. J. Fraser, 4 March 1826, in Fraser to Hay of 4 July [CO 2/15]
19 *HCA*, p. 157

Chapter 17: The River Niger 1826
1 *JSE*, p. 65
2 *HCA*, p. 170
3 Ibid, p. 169
4 Ibid
5 Ibid, p. 179
6 *JSE*, p. 68
7 Ibid
8 *HCA*, p. 176
9 Ibid
10 *JSE*, p. 71
11 Ibid, p. 69
12 RBC, undated, f. 110

13 *HCA*, p. 180
14 Ibid, p. 181
15 Ibid, p. 190
16 *Strophanthus hispidus* [Hausa, *kwankwani*), a species of forest liana in west and central Africa; the poison is extracted from the seeds, the most toxic elements being glucosides which, working through the blood stream, affect the muscles, particularly the heart. A single seed contains a sufficient dose to cause permanent contraction in animals and humans.
17 *HCA*, p. 185
18 *JSE*, pp. 94-5
19 Ibid, pp. 82-3; Clapperton kept him on; and he was paid off in Kano by Lander the following year.
20 *HCA*, p. 181
21 *RL*, Vol. I, pp. 154-5
22 *HCA*, pp. 183-4
23 *RL*, Vol. I, p. 208
24 RBC, 30 March 1826
25 *HCA*, p. 197
26 *JSE*, pp. 107-8
27 Ibid, p. 112
28 Ibid
29 Ibid, p. 115
30 Ibid, pp. 113-14
31 *HCA*, p. 206

Chapter 18: Return to Hausaland 1826
1 RBC, 10 April 1826
2 *HCA*, p. 207
3 Ibid
4 Ibid, p. 210; in 1987 a bridge of similar construction near the same spot carried farm traffic from the Maingyara valley to the main Kainji–Mokwa road.
5 Ibid, p. 217
6 Ibid
7 Ibid, p. 218
8 Ibid, p. 224
9 Ibid
10 Ibid, pp. 225-6
11 *Mitqal* (Arabic); 1/8th of an ounce of trade gold (worth 3s. 9d. on the Coast)

12 *HCA*, p. 227
13 *JSE*, p. 143
14 *HCA*, p. 235
15 *JSE*, p. 145
16 Ibid, p. 148
17 *HCA*, p. 238
18 Ibid, p. 237
19 Ibid, p. 243
20 Today the school playing fields
21 RBC, undated, f. 31; Elora is Ilorin, and Zeg Zeg is Zaria.
22 *JSE*, p. 156
23 *HCA*, p. 256
24 Tyrwhitt died in Kukawa in October 1824; he was not replaced. His death was first rumoured in Tripoli in June 1825 but only confirmed in a letter from Sheikh Al-Kanemi received by Warrington on 20 August 1825 – too late for Clapperton to be informed before departure.
25 *HCA*, p. 257
26 In 1994 the headman's fine house still stood (though empty and partly in ruins), and weaver-birds still nested colonially in the square's shady trees.

Chapter 19: Sokoto 1826-1827
1 *HCA*, p. 267
2 Ibid, p. 268
3 The bill was finally presented at the Consulate-general in March 1830.
4 *JSE*, p. 176
5 *HCA*, p. 276
6 Ibid
7 *HCA*, p. 281
8 *JSE*, pp. 182-3
9 *HCA*, p. 280
10 Ibid, p. 281
11 Ibid, p. 283
12 Ibid
13 Ibid, p. 289
14 Ibid, p. 296; at the time, Al-Kanemi's letter had been regarded by Bello as provocation.
15 *RL*, Vol. I, pp. 223-4
16 *JSE*, p. 227
17 *RL* Vol. I, pp. 223-4
18 *JSE*, p. 237

19 Ibid, p. 238
20 There were hand arms for Al-Kanemi and his generals, but the muskets and heavy ordnance had been left on board HMS *Brazen*. The only other arms were Clapperton's own and those of his deceased companions.
21 Clapperton was unaware of the reverberations across the Sudan caused by the modest British assistance afforded Al-Kanemi on campaign in 1824 (the construction by Hillman of gun-carriages for the Sheikh's two small brass guns, Denham's supervision of the manufacture of two cartridges, and the gift of a double-barrelled shotgun) which had been widely credited with having made the difference in battle.
22 Laing was attacked while asleep by Tuareg travelling companions in the desert south of Tuat in January 1826 and severely wounded. After three months recuperating in the care of a Kunta Arab sheikh he finally reached Timbuktu in the August of that year.
23 *RL*, Vol. II, p. 58
24 Ibid, pp. 60-3
25 *JSE*, p. 253
26 Ibid, p. 254
27 *RL*, Vol. II, p. 77

Chapter 20: Acclaim 1827-1829
1 Laing, Captain F., undated, CO 2/16, ff. 259-60
2 Also employed at the naval base was William Hillman, who had asked to return to Africa on pioneering duties.
3 No record exists of any conversation they might have had, only a passing reference, 'I have written to Mr. Barrow about poor Clapperton's death…' [DD to Hay, 11 February 1828, CO 267/94].
4 Hanmer Warrington remained Consul-general in Tripoli until his resignation, under pressure, in 1846; he died in Patras the following year.
5 Charles was Quartermaster-general at

286

Chatham for only a few months before being retired when the establishment was reduced.

6   William Gibson to Robert Peel, 11 February 1829, CO 2/17; Duncan married a decade later. He and his wife Janet had a son, John, born in 1841, and a daughter, Helen, born two years later. The fate of Duncan and Janet is unknown, but in 1851 their two children were living with William and Elizabeth Gibson, then in their 60s, in Lochmaben.

7   JB to Murray, 15 November 1828, JMA

8   JB to Murray, 21 January 1829, JMA

9   A reproduction of the chart of the course of the middle Niger (drawn for Clapperton in Sokoto) formed a frontispiece; the Appendix included nine historical notes translated from the Arabic, a number of meteoro-logical tables and short Yoruba and Fulfulde word-lists. An abridged version was published in 1831 in John Murray's Family Edition series.

10 *JSE*, pp. xviii-xix

11 *Edinburgh Review* [ER], XLIX, No. 97, March 1829, p. 127

12 *QR*, XXXIX, No 77, p. 180

13 *London Literary Gazette*, 24 January 1829, No. 627

14 *ER*, XLIX, No. 97, p. 127

15 Ibid, p. 138

16 Ibid

17 *QR*, XXXIX, No. 77, p. 183

18 Huish, Robert, *The Travels of Richard and John Lander... for the discovery of the course of the Niger*, London, 1836, p. 429

19 JB to Hay, 19 September 1829, CO 2/18

20 Owen, Captain W. F., *Narrative of voyages to explore the shores of Africa...*, *1822-1826*, London, 1833, p. 362

Envoi

1   Curtin, P.D., *The image of Africa: British ideas and action 1780-1850*, Madison, 1964, p. 207

2   Heinrich Barth, who admired many of Clapperton's achievements, observed in 1853 that the classical texts in Arabic which Clapperton had brought to Bello on his second expedition were still accessible in the libraries of Sokoto, 'I may assert, with full confidence, that those few books taken by the gallant Scotch captain into Central Africa have had a greater effect in reconciling the men of authority in Africa to the character of Europeans than the most costly present ever made to them' [Barth, Vol. III, p. 372].

3   Lugard's address at Sokoto, 21 March 1903, Cd 2238: Northern Nigeria Annual Report for 1903, pp. 163-4

4   Remarks by District Officer Larymore and his wife at Clapperton's grave [Heussler, Robert, *The British in Northern Nigeria*, Oxford, 1968, p. 42]

5   Remarks by M. Umaru Nagwatse (Sokoto schoolmaster and historian) to Margery Perham [Rhodes House, MSS Perham 302/9]

6   District Officer to Assistant District Officer, Sokoto, SKT/19/1/7 HIS/18 (Preservation of Antiquities 1935-55), 30 May 1944, and personal communication from Howard Pedraza

INDEX

Note: references to maps and illustrations are shown in bold

DATE DUE
